COLL...
BRITISH
STAMPS

A STANLEY GIBBONS CHECKLIST OF
THE STAMPS OF GREAT BRITAIN

2004 (55th) Edition

STANLEY GIBBONS LTD

By Appointment to H.M. the Queen
Stanley Gibbons Ltd, London Philatelists.

London and Ringwood

COLLECT BRITISH STAMPS

The 2004 edition

From the famous Penny Black of 1840 to the absorbing issues of today, the stamps of Great Britain are highly popular with collectors. *Collect British Stamps* has been our message since very early days – but particularly since the First Edition of this checklist in September 1967. This 55th edition includes all the recent issues. Prices have been carefully revised to reflect today's market. Total sales of *Collect British Stamps* are now over 3·8 million copies.

Collect British Stamps appears in the autumn of each year. A more detailed Great Britain catalogue, the *Concise,* is published each spring. The *Great Britain Concise* incorporates many additional listings covering watermark varieties, phosphor omitted errors, missing colour errors, stamp booklets and special commemorative First Day Cover postmarks. It is ideally suited for the collector who wishes to discover more about GB stamps.

Listings in this edition of *Collect British Stamps* include all 2003 issues which have appeared up to the publication date.

Scope. *Collect British Stamps* comprises:
- All stamps with different watermark (*wmk*) or perforation (*perf*).
- Visible plate numbers on the Victorian issues.
- Graphite-lined and phosphor issues, including variations in the numbers of phosphor bands.
- First Day Covers for Definitives from 1936, Regionals and all Special Issues.
- Presentation, Gift and Souvenir Packs.
- Post Office Yearbooks.
- Regional issues and War Occupation stamps of Guernsey and Jersey.
- Postage Due and Official Stamps.
- Post Office Picture Cards (PHQ cards).
- Commemorative gutter pairs and 'Traffic Light' gutter pairs listed as mint sets.
- Royal Mail Postage Labels priced as sets and on P.O. First Day Cover.

Stamps of the independent postal administrations of Guernsey, Isle of Man and Jersey are contained in *Collect Channel Islands and Isle of Man Stamps.*

Layout. Stamps are set out chronologically by date of issue. In the catalogue lists the first numeral is the Stanley Gibbons catalogue number; the black (boldface) numeral alongside is the type number referring to the respective illustration. A blank in this column implies that the number immediately above is repeated. The denomination and colour of the stamp are then shown. Before February 1971 British currency was:

£1 = 20s	One pound = twenty shillings *and*
1s = 12d	One shilling = twelve pence.

Upon decimalisation this became:

£1 = 100p	One pound = one hundred (new) pence.

The catalogue list then shows two price columns. The left-hand is for unused stamps and the right-hand for used. Corresponding small boxes are provided in which collectors may wish to check off the items in their collection.

Our method of indicating prices is:
Numerals for pence, e.g. 10 denotes 10p (10 pence). Numerals for pounds and pence, e.g. 4·25 denotes £4·25 (4 pounds and 25 pence). For £100 and above, prices are in whole pounds and so include the £ sign and omit the zeros for pence.

Colour illustrations. The colour illustrations of stamps are intended as a guide only; they may differ in shade from the originals.

Size of illustrations. To comply with Post Office regulations stamp illustrations are three-quarters linear side. Separate illustrations of surcharges, overprints and watermarks are actual size.

Prices. Prices quoted in this catalogue are our selling prices at the time the book went to press. They are for stamps in fine condition; in issues where condition varies we may ask more for the superb and less for the sub-standard. The unused prices for stamps of Queen Victoria to King George V are for lightly hinged examples. Unused prices for King Edward VIII to Queen Elizabeth II are for unmounted mint (though when not available unmounted, mounted stamps are often supplied at a lower price). Prices for used stamps refer to fine postally used copies. All prices are subject to change without prior notice and we give no guarantee to supply all stamps priced, since it is not possible to keep every catalogued item in stock. Individual low value stamps sold at 399, Strand are liable to an additional handling charge. Commemorative issues may only be available in complete sets.

In the price columns:

† = Does not exist.

(—) or blank = Exists, or may exist, but price cannot be quoted.

* = Not normally issued (the so-called 'Abnormals' of 1862–80).

Perforations. The 'perforation' is the number of holes in a length of 2 cm, as measured by the Gibbons *Instanta* gauge. The stamp is viewed against a dark background with the transparent gauge put on top of it. Perforations are quoted to the nearest half. Stamps without perforation are termed 'imperforate'.

From 1992 certain stamps occur with a large elliptical (oval) hole inserted in each line of vertical perforations. The £10 definitive, No. 1658, is unique in having two such holes in the horizontal perforations.

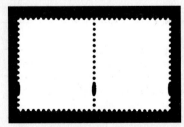

Elliptical perforations

Se-tenant combinations. *Se-tenant* means 'joined together'. Some sets include stamps of different design arranged *se-tenant* as blocks or strips and these are often collected unsevered as issued. Where such combinations exist the stamps are priced both mint and used, as singles or complete sets. The set price for mint refers to the unsevered combination plus singles of any other values in the set. The used set price is for single stamps of all values.

First day covers. Prices for first day covers are for complete sets used on plain covers (Nos. 430/8, 453/60, 462/78b, 485/90, and 503/12) or on special covers (Nos. 461, 479/84, 491/502 and 513 onwards), the stamps of which are cancelled with ordinary operational postmarks (1924–1962) or by the *standard* 'First Day of Issue' postmarks (1963 onwards). The British Post Office did not provide 'First Day' treatment for every definitive issued after 1963. Where the stamps in a set were issued on different days, prices are for a cover from each day.

Presentation Packs. Special packs comprising slip-in cards with printed information inside a protective covering, were introduced for the 1964 Shakespeare issue. Collectors packs, containing commemoratives from the preceding twelve months, were issued from 1967. Some packs with text in German from 1968–69 exist as does a Japanese version of the pack for Nos. 916/17. Yearbooks, hardbound and illustrated in colour within a slip cover, joined the product range in 1984.

PHQ cards. Since 1973 the Post Office has produced a series of picture cards, which can be sent through the post as postcards. Each card shows an enlarged colour reproduction of a current British stamp, either of one or more values from a set or of all values. Cards are priced here in fine mint condition for sets complete as issued. The Post Office gives each card a 'PHQ' serial number, hence the term. The cards are usually on sale shortly before the date of issue of the stamps, but there is no officially designated 'first day'.

Used prices are for cards franked with the stamp depicted, on the obverse or reverse; the stamp being cancelled with an official postmark for first day of issue.

For 1973–76 issues cards with stamps on the obverse are worth about 25% more than the prices quoted.

Gutter pairs. All modern Great Britain commemoratives are produced in sheets containing two panes of stamps separated by a blank horizontal or vertical margin known as a gutter. This feature first made its appearance on some supplies of the 1972 Royal Silver Wedding 3p, and marked the introduction of Harrison & Sons' new 'Jumelle' stamp-printing press. There are advantages for both the printer and the Post Office in such a layout which has now been used for almost all commemorative issues since 1974.

The term 'gutter pair' is used for a pair of stamps separated by part of the blank gutter margin.

Traffic light gutter pair

Gutter pair

Most printers include some form of colour check device on the sheet margins, in addition to the cylinder or plate numbers. Harrison & Sons used round 'dabs' or spots of colour, resembling traffic lights. For the period from the 1972 Royal Silver Wedding until the end of 1979 these colour dabs appeared in the gutter margin. Gutter pairs showing these 'traffic lights' are worth considerably more than the normal version.

Catalogue numbers used. This checklist uses the same catalogue numbers as other current Stanley Gibbons catalogues.

Latest issue date for stamps recorded in this edition is 4 November 2003.

STANLEY GIBBONS LTD

Head Office: 399 Strand, London WC2R OLX.
Auction Room and Specialist Stamp Departments–
    Open Monday–Friday 9.30 a.m. to 5 p.m.
Shop – Open Monday to Friday 9 a.m. to 5.30 p.m.
    and Saturday 9.30 a.m. to 5.30 p.m.
Telephone 0207-836 8444 for all departments
E-mail: enquiries@stanleygibbons.co.uk
Website: www.stanleygibbons.com

Stanley Gibbons Publications:

Parkside, Christchurch Road, Ringwood, Hants BH24 3SH. Telephone: 01425 472363
Publications Mail Order, FREEPHONE: 0800 611622
E-mail: info@stanleygibbons.co.uk

ISBN: 0-85259-548-4
© Stanley Gibbons Ltd 2003

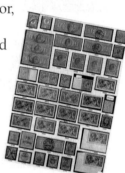

e-mail

QUEEN VICTORIA

1837 (20 June)–1901 (22 Jan.)

IDENTIFICATION. In this checklist Victorian stamps are classified firstly according to which printing method was used –line-engraving, embossing or surface-printing.

Corner letters. Numerous stamps also have letters in all four, or just the lower corners. These were an anti-forgery device and the letters differ from stamp to stamp. If present in all four corners the upper pair are the reverse of the lower. Note the importance of these corner letters in the way the checklist is arranged.

Watermarks. Further classification depends on watermarks: these are illustrated in normal position, with stamps priced accordingly.

1 Line-engraved Issues

1

1a

1b

3 White lines added above and below head

2 Small Crown watermark

4 Large Crown watermark

Letters in lower corners

1840 *Wmk Small Crown Type* **2** *Imperforate*

Cat No.	Type		Unused	Used		
2	1	1d black	£4000	£225	☐	☐
5	1a	2d blue	£9000	£500	☐	☐

1841

8	1b	1d red-brown	£250	15·00	☐	☐
14	3	2d blue	£2250	70·00	☐	☐

1854–57 (*i*) *Wmk Small Crown Type* **2** *Perf* 16

17	1b	1d red-brown	£250	18·00	☐	☐
19	3	2d blue	£2500	85·00	☐	☐

(*ii*) *Wmk Small Crown Type* **2** *Perf* 14

24	1b	1d red-brown	£400	45·00	☐	☐
23	3	2d blue	£4500	£180	☐	☐

(*iii*) *Wmk Large Crown Type* **4** *Perf* 16

26	1b	1d red	£700	80·00	☐	☐
27	3	2d blue	£5000	£250	☐	☐

(*iv*) *Wmk Large Crown Type* **4** *Perf* 14

40	1b	1d red	40·00	9·00	☐	☐
34	3	2d blue	£1750	50·00	☐	☐

7

5

8

6

9 Watermark extending over three stamps

Letters in all four corners

Plate numbers. Stamps included a 'plate number' in their design and this affects valuation. The cheapest plates are priced here; see complete list of plate numbers overleaf.

1858–70 (*i*) *Wmk Type* **9** *Perf* 14

48	7	½d red	85·00	15·00	☐	☐

(*ii*) *Wmk Large Crown Type* **4** *Perf* 14

43	5	1d red	15·00	2·00	☐	☐
52	8	1½d red	£350	45·00	☐	☐
45	6	2d blue	£275	10·00	☐	☐

PLATE NUMBERS
on stamps of 1858–70 having letters in all four corners

Positions of Plate Numbers

Shows
Plate 9 (½d)

Shows
Plate 170 (1d, 2d)

Shows
Plate 3 (1½d)

HALFPENNY VALUE (S.G. 48)

Plate	Un.	Used			Plate	Un.	Used		
1	£180	70·00	□	□	11	90·00	15·00	□	□
3	£140	35·00	□	□	12	90·00	15·00	□	□
4	£120	25·00	□	□	13	90·00	15·00	□	□
5	85·00	15·00	□	□	14	90·00	15·00	□	□
6	90·00	15·00	□	□	15	£140	35·00	□	□
8	£225	90·00	□	□	19	£160	50·00	□	□
9	£2750	£450	□	□	20	£190	70·00	□	□
10	£100	15·00	□	□					

Plates 2, 7, 16, 17 and 18 were not completed, while Plates 21 and 22 though made were not used. Plate 9 was a reserve plate, not greatly used.

PENNY VALUE (S.G. 43)

Plate	Un.	Used			Plate	Un.	Used			Plate	Un.	Used			Plate	Un.	Used		
71	35·00	3·00	□	□	112	70·00	2·25	□	□	154	50·00	2·00	□	□	190	50·00	6·00	□	□
72	40·00	4·00	□	□	113	50·00	12·00	□	□	155	50·00	2·25	□	□	191	30·00	7·00	□	□
73	40·00	3·00	□	□	114	£250	12·00	□	□	156	45·00	2·00	□	□	192	50·00	2·00	□	□
74	40·00	2·00	□	□	115	90·00	2·25	□	□	157	50·00	2·00	□	□	193	30·00	2·00	□	□
76	35·00	2·00	□	□	116	75·00	9·00	□	□	158	30·00	2·00	□	□	194	50·00	8·00	□	□
77	(—)	£120000			117	45·00	2·00	□	□	159	30·00	2·00	□	□	195	50·00	8·00	□	□
78	90·00	2·00	□	□	118	50·00	2·00	□	□	160	30·00	2·00	□	□	196	50·00	5·00	□	□
79	30·00	2·00	□	□	119	45·00	2·00	□	□	161	60·00	7·00	□	□	197	55·00	9·00	□	□
80	45·00	2·00	□	□	120	15·00	2·00	□	□	162	50·00	7·00	□	□	198	40·00	6·00	□	□
81	45·00	2·25	□	□	121	40·00	9·50	□	□	163	50·00	3·00	□	□	199	55·00	6·00	□	□
82	90·00	4·00	□	□	122	15·00	2·00	□	□	164	50·00	3·00	□	□	200	60·00	2·00	□	□
83	£110	7·00	□	□	123	40·00	2·00	□	□	165	45·00	2·00	□	□	201	30·00	5·00	□	□
84	60·00	2·25	□	□	124	28·00	2·00	□	□	166	45·00	6·00	□	□	202	60·00	8·00	□	□
85	40·00	2·25	□	□	125	40·00	2·00	□	□	167	45·00	2·00	□	□	203	30·00	16·00	□	□
86	50·00	4·00	□	□	127	55·00	2·25	□	□	168	50·00	8·00	□	□	204	55·00	2·25	□	□
87	30·00	2·00	□	□	129	40·00	8·00	□	□	169	60·00	7·00	□	□	205	55·00	3·00	□	□
88	£130	8·00	□	□	130	55·00	2·25	□	□	170	35·00	2·00	□	□	206	55·00	9·00	□	□
89	40·00	2·00	□	□	131	65·00	16·00	□	□	171	15·00	2·00	□	□	207	60·00	9·00	□	□
90	40·00	2·00	□	□	132	£130	22·00	□	□	172	30·00	2·00	□	□	208	55·00	16·00	□	□
91	55·00	6·00	□	□	133	£110	9·00	□	□	173	70·00	9·00	□	□	209	50·00	9·00	□	□
92	35·00	2·00	□	□	134	15·00	2·00	□	□	174	30·00	2·00	□	□	210	65·00	12·00	□	□
93	50·00	2·00	□	□	135	95·00	26·00	□	□	175	60·00	3·50	□	□	211	70·00	20·00	□	□
94	45·00	5·00	□	□	136	90·00	20·00	□	□	176	60·00	2·25	□	□	212	60·00	11·00	□	□
95	40·00	2·00	□	□	137	28·00	2·25	□	□	177	40·00	2·00	□	□	213	60·00	11·00	□	□
96	45·00	2·00	□	□	138	18·00	2·00	□	□	178	60·00	3·50	□	□	214	65·00	18·00	□	□
97	40·00	3·50	□	□	139	60·00	16·00	□	□	179	50·00	2·25	□	□	215	65·00	18·00	□	□
98	50·00	6·00	□	□	140	18·00	2·00	□	□	180	60·00	5·00	□	□	216	70·00	18·00	□	□
99	55·00	5·00	□	□	141	£110	9·00	□	□	181	45·00	2·00	□	□	217	70·00	7·00	□	□
100	60·00	2·25	□	□	142	70·00	24·00	□	□	182	90·00	5·00	□	□	218	65·00	8·00	□	□
101	60·00	9·00	□	□	143	60·00	15·00	□	□	183	55·00	3·00	□	□	219	90·00	70·00	□	□
102	45·00	2·00	□	□	144	95·00	20·00	□	□	184	30·00	2·25	□	□	220	40·00	7·00	□	□
103	50·00	3·50	□	□	145	30·00	2·25	□	□	185	50·00	3·00	□	□	221	70·00	16·00	□	□
104	75·00	5·00	□	□	146	40·00	6·00	□	□	186	65·00	2·25	□	□	222	80·00	40·00	□	□
105	90·00	7·00	□	□	147	50·00	3·00	□	□	187	50·00	2·00	□	□	223	90·00	60·00	□	□
106	55·00	2·00	□	□	148	40·00	3·00	□	□	188	70·00	10·00	□	□	224	£100	50·00	□	□
107	60·00	7·00	□	□	149	40·00	6·00	□	□	189	70·00	7·00	□	□	225	£1750	£650	□	□
108	80·00	2·25	□	□	150	15·00	2·00	□	□										
109	85·00	3·50	□	□	151	60·00	9·00	□	□										
110	60·00	9·00	□	□	152	60·00	5·50	□	□										
111	50·00	2·25	□	□	153	£100	9·00	□	□										

Plates 69, 70, 75, 77, 126 and 128 were prepared but rejected. No stamps therefore exist, except for a very few from Plate 77 which somehow reached the public. Plate 177 stamps, by accident or design, are sometimes passed off as the rare Plate 77.

THREE-HALFPENNY VALUE (S.G. 52)

Plate	Un.	Used			Plate	Un.	Used		
(1)	£500	65·00	□	□	3	£350	40·00	□	□

Plate 1 did *not* have the plate number in the design. Plate 2 was not completed and no stamps exist.

TWOPENNY VALUE (S.G. 45)

Plate	Un.	Used			Plate	Un.	Used		
7	£750	45·00	□	□	13	£300	20·00	□	□
8	£700	32·00	□	□	14	£375	25·00	□	□
9	£275	10·00	□	□	15	£350	25·00	□	□
12	£1350	£110	□	□					

Plates 10 and 11 were prepared but rejected.

2 Embossed Issues

Prices are for stamps cut square and with average to fine embossing. Stamps with exceptionally clear embossing are worth more.

12

11

10

13

1847–54 *Wmk* **13** *(6d), no wmk (others) Imperforate*

59	12	6d lilac	£5250	£675	☐ ☐
57	11	10d brown	£4500	£900	☐ ☐
54	10	1s green	£6000	£500	☐ ☐

3 Surface-printed Issues

IDENTIFICATION. Check first whether the design includes corner letters or not, as mentioned for 'Line-engraved Issues'. The checklist is divided up according to whether any letters are small or large, also whether they are white (uncoloured) or printed in the colour of the stamp. Further identification then depends on watermark.

PERFORATION. Except for Nos. 126/9 all the following issues of Queen Victoria are perf 14.

14

15 Small Garter   16 Medium Garter   17 Large Garter

18

19

20 Emblems

No corner letters

1855–57 (*i*) *Wmk Small Garter Type* **15**

62	14	4d red	£4000	£325	☐ ☐

(*ii*) *Wmk Medium Garter Type* **16**

64	14	4d red	£3500	£300	☐ ☐

(*iii*) *Wmk Large Garter Type* **17**

66a	14	4d red	£1000	90·00	☐ ☐

(*iv*) *Wmk Emblems Type* **20**

70	18	6d lilac	£800	85·00	☐ ☐
72	19	1s green	£1000	£250	☐ ☐

Plate numbers. Stamps Nos. 90/163 should be checked for the 'plate numbers' indicated, as this affects valuation (the cheapest plates are priced here). The mark *'Pl.'* shows that several numbers exist, priced in separate list overleaf.

Plate numbers are the small numerals appearing in duplicate in some part of the frame design or adjacent to the lower corner letters (in the 5s value a single numeral above the lower inscription).

21

22

23

24

25

Small white corner letters

1862–64 *Wmk Emblems Type* **20**, *except* 4d (*Large Garter Type* **17**)

76	21	3d red	£1400	£225	☐ ☐
80	22	4d red	£1000	80·00	☐ ☐
84	23	6d lilac	£1250	80·00	☐ ☐
87	24	9d bistre	£2500	£275	☐ ☐
90	25	1s green *Pl.*	£1500	£150	☐ ☐

| 26 | 27 | 28 | (hyphen in SIX-PENCE) | | | |

32   33 Spray of Rose   34

29   30   31

Large white corner letters

1865–67 *Wmk Emblems Type* **20** *except 4d (Large Garter Type* **17**)

92	**26**	3d red (Plate 4)	. . . . .	£1000	£100	□	□
94	**27**	4d vermilion *Pl.*	. . . . .	£425	50·00	□	□
97	**28**	6d lilac *Pl.*	. . . .	£650	75·00	□	□
98	**29**	9d straw *Pl.*	. . . . . .	£1800	£375	□	□
99	**30**	10d brown (Plate 1)	. . .	† £20000			□
101	**31**	1s green (Plate 4)	. . . .	£1200	£150	□	□

1867–80 *Wmk Spray of Rose Type* **33**

103	**26**	3d red *Pl.*	. . . .	£350	45·00	□	□
105	**28**	6d lilac (with hyphen) (Plate 6)	. . . . . .	£850	75·00	□	□
109		6d mauve (without hyphen) *Pl.*	. . . . . .	£450	75·00	□	□
110	**29**	9d straw (Plate 4)	. . . .	£1100	£200	□	□
112	**30**	10d brown *Pl.*	. . . .	£1850	£275	□	□
117	**31**	1s green *Pl.*	. . . .	£550	32·00	□	□
119	**32**	2s blue *Pl.*	. . . .	£1800	£125	□	□
121		2s brown (Plate 1)	. . .	£11000	£2000	□	□

1872–73 *Wmk Spray of Rose Type* **33**

122b	**34**	6d brown *Pl.*	. . . .	£500	45·00	□	□
125		6d grey (Plate 12)	. . . .	£1250	£200	□	□

PLATE NUMBERS
on stamps of 1862–83

Cat No.		Plate No.	Un.	Used		
Small White Corner Letters (1862–64)						
90	1s green	2	£1500	£150	□	□
		3	£17500		□	□

Plate 2 is actually numbered as '1' and Plate 3 as '2' on the stamps.

Large White Corner Letters (1865–83)						
103	3d red	4	£700	£150	□	□
		5	£350	45·00	□	□
		6	£375	45·00	□	□
		7	£450	50·00	□	□
		8	£425	45·00	□	□
		9	£425	50·00	□	□
		10	£450	90·00	□	□
94	4d verm	7	£500	80·00	□	□
		8	£450	50·00	□	□
		9	£450	50·00	□	□
		10	£500	90·00	□	□
		11	£450	50·00	□	□
		12	£425	50·00	□	□
		13	£450	50·00	□	□
		14	£500	80·00	□	□
97	6d lilac	5	£650	75·00	□	□
		6	£2000	£140	□	□
109	6d mauve	8	£450	75·00	□	□
		9	£450	75·00	□	□
		10	* £17500		□	□
122b	6d brown	11	£500	45·00	□	□
		12	£1500	£200	□	□
98	9d straw	4	£1800	£375	□	□
		5	£18000		□	□

112	10d brown	1	£1850	£275	□	□
		2	£17500	£6000	□	□
117	1s green	4	£550	32·00	□	□
		5	£600	30·00	□	□
		6	£900	30·00	□	□
		7	£900	60·00	□	□
119	2s blue	1	£1800	£125	□	□
		3	*	£6000	□	□
126	5s red	1	£4500	£550	□	□
		2	£6500	£700	□	□

Large Coloured Corner Letters (1873–83)						
139	2½d mauve	1	£450	75·00	□	□
		2	£450	75·00	□	□
		3	£700	£110	□	□
141	2½d mauve	3	£850	90·00	□	□
		4	£380	45·00	□	□
		5	£380	45·00	□	□
		6	£380	45·00	□	□
		7	£380	45·00	□	□
		8	£380	45·00	□	□
		9	£380	45·00	□	□
		10	£420	60·00	□	□
		11	£380	45·00	□	□
		12	£380	45·00	□	□
		13	£380	45·00	□	□
		14	£380	45·00	□	□
		15	£380	45·00	□	□
		16	£380	45·00	□	□
		17	£1100	£220	□	□
142	2½d blue	17	£350	50·00	□	□
		18	£375	35·00	□	□
		19	£350	30·00	□	□
		20	£350	35·00	□	□

157	2½d blue	21	£375	30·00	□	□
		22	£325	30·00	□	□
		23	£325	25·00	□	□
143	3d red	11	£325	35·00	□	□
		12	£380	35·00	□	□
		14	£400	35·00	□	□
		15	£325	35·00	□	□
		16	£325	35·00	□	□
		17	£380	35·00	□	□
		18	£380	35·00	□	□
		19	£325	35·00	□	□
		20	£380	60·00	□	□
158	3d red	20	£425	£110	□	□
		21	£375	70·00	□	□
152	4d verm	15	£1400	£325	□	□
		16	*	£17000	□	□
153	4d green	15	£800	£225	□	□
		16	£700	£200	□	□
		17	*	£10000	□	□
160	4d brown	17	£300	50·00	□	□
		18	£300	50·00	□	□
147	6d grey	13	£350	50·00	□	□
		14	£350	50·00	□	□
		15	£350	50·00	□	□
		16	£350	50·00	□	□
		17	£500	£100	□	□
161	6d grey	17	£350	55·00	□	□
		18	£350	55·00	□	□
150	1s green	8	£475	75·00	□	□
		9	£475	75·00	□	□
		10	£475	80·00	□	□
		11	£475	80·00	□	□
		12	£400	60·00	□	□
		13	£400	60·00	□	□
		14	* £20000		□	□
163	1s brown	13	£475	£110	□	□
		14	£400	£110	□	□

35

36

44

45

46

37

47   Small Anchor   **48**   Orb

38

Large coloured corner letters

1873–80 (*i*) *Wmk Small Anchor Type* **47**

139	**41**	2½d mauve *Pl.*	£450	75·00	☐	☐

(*ii*) *Wmk Orb Type* **48**

141	**41**	2½d mauve *Pl.*	£380	45·00	☐	☐
142		2½d blue *Pl.*	£350	30·00	☐	☐

(*iii*) *Wmk Spray of Rose Type* **33**

143	**42**	3d red *Pl.*	£325	35·00	☐	☐
145	**43**	6d pale buff (Plate 13) .	* £12000		☐	☐
147		6d grey *Pl.*	£350	50·00	☐	☐
150	**44**	1s green *Pl.*	£400	60·00	☐	☐
151		1s brown (Plate 13) . . .	£2850	£400	☐	☐

(*iv*) *Wmk Large Garter Type* **17**

152	**45**	4d vermilion *Pl.*	£1400	£325	☐	☐
153		4d green *Pl.*	£700	£200	☐	☐
154		4d brown (Plate 17) . . .	£1250	£325	☐	☐
156	**46**	8d orange (Plate 1) . . .	£900	£250	☐	☐

39   Maltese Cross   **40**   Large Anchor

1867–83 (*i*) *Wmk Maltese Cross Type* **39** *Perf* 15½ × 15

126	**35**	5s red *Pl.*	£4500	£550	☐	☐
128	**36**	10s grey (Plate 1)	£32000	£2000	☐	☐
129	**37**	£1 brown (Plate 1) . . .	£40000	£3000	☐	☐

(*ii*) *Wmk Large Anchor Type* **40** *Perf* 14

134	**35**	5s red (Plate 4)	£10000	£2000	☐	☐
135	**36**	10s grey (Plate 1)	£45000	£2800	☐	☐
132	**37**	£1 brown (Plate 1) . . .	£60000	£6500	☐	☐
137	**38**	£5 orange (Plate 1) . . .	£7000	£3500	☐	☐

41   42   43

49   Imperial Crown   **(50)**   Surcharges in red   **(51)**

3^d   6^d

1880–83 *Wmk Imperial Crown Type* **49**

157	**41**	2½d blue *Pl.*	£325	25·00	☐	☐
158	**42**	3d red *Pl.*	£375	70·00	☐	☐
159		3d on 3d lilac (surch Type **50**)	£375	£125	☐	☐
160	**45**	4d brown *Pl.*	£300	50·00	☐	☐
161	**43**	6d grey *Pl.*	£300	55·00	☐	☐
162		6d on 6d lilac (surch Type **51**)	£400	£125	☐	☐
163	**44**	1s brown *Pl.*	£400	£110	☐	☐

52

53

54

55

56

1880–81 *Wmk Imperial Crown Type* **49**

164	52	½d green	40·00	10·00	□	□
166	53	1d brown	20·00	10·00	□	□
167	54	1½d brown	£150	40·00	□	□
168	55	2d red	£200	80·00	□	□
169	56	5d indigo	£500	£100	□	□

57

 Die I

 Die II

1881 *Wmk Imperial Crown Type* **49**

(a) 14 dots in each corner, Die I

| 171 | 57 | 1d lilac | £125 | 25·00 | □ | □ |

(b) 16 dots in each corner, Die II

| 174 | 57 | 1d mauve | 2·50 | 1·50 | □ | □ |

58

59

60

1883–84 *Wmk Anchor Type* **40**

179	58	2s 6d deep lilac	£400	£125	□	□
181	59	5s red	£700	£180	□	□
183	60	10s blue	£1300	£450	□	□

61

1884 *Wmk 3 Imperial Crowns Type* **49**

| 185 | 61 | £1 brown | £20000 | £2000 | □ | □ |

1888 *Wmk 3 Orbs Type* **48**

| 186 | 61 | £1 brown | £45000 | £3250 | □ | □ |

1891 *Wmk 3 Imperial Crowns Type* **49**

| 212 | 61 | £1 green | £2500 | £500 | □ | □ |

62

63

64

65

66

1883–84 *Wmk Imperial Crown Type* **49** (*sideways on horiz designs*)

187	52	½d blue	20·00	7·00	□	□
188	62	1½d lilac	90·00	35·00	□	□
189	63	2d lilac	£150	65·00	□	□
190	64	2½d lilac	70·00	12·00	□	□
191	65	3d lilac	£180	85·00	□	□
192	66	4d dull green	£400	£175	□	□
193	62	5d dull green	£400	£175	□	□
194	63	6d dull green	£425	£200	□	□
195	64	9d dull green	£800	£375	□	□
196	65	1s dull green	£600	£200	□	□

The above prices are for stamps in the true dull green colour. Stamps which have been soaked, causing the colour to run are virtually worthless.

71

72

73

74

75

76

77

78

79

80

81

82

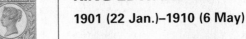

KING EDWARD VII

1901 (22 Jan.)–1910 (6 May)

83

84

85

86

87

88

89

90

91

92

93

94

95

96

'Jubilee' issue

1887–1900 *The bicoloured stamps have the value tablets, or the frames including the value tablets, in the second colour. Wmk Imperial Crown Type* **49**

197e	71	½d vermilion	1·50	1·00	☐	☐
213		½d green*	1·75	2·00	☐	☐
198	72	1½d purple and green	15·00	7·00	☐	☐
200	73	2d green and red	28·00	12·00	☐	☐
201	74	2½d purple on blue	22·00	3·00	☐	☐
203	75	3d purple on yellow	22·00	3·25	☐	☐
205	76	4d green and brown	30·00	13·00	☐	☐
206	77	4½d green and red	10·00	40·00	☐	☐
207a	78	5d purple and blue	35·00	11·00	☐	☐
208	79	6d purple on red	30·00	10·00	☐	☐
209	80	9d purple and blue	60·00	40·00	☐	☐
210	81	10d purple and red	45·00	38·00	☐	☐
211	82	1s green	£200	60·00	☐	☐
214		1s green and red	50·00	£125	☐	☐
		Set of 14	£500	£325	☐	☐

*The ½d No. 213 in blue is a colour changeling.

97

97

7

1902–13 *Wmks Imperial Crown Type* **49** (½*d to* 1*s*), *Anchor Type* **40** (2*s* 6*d to* 10*s*), *Three Crowns Type* **49** (£1) (*a*) *Perf* 14

215	83	½d blue-green	2·00	1·50	□	□
217		½d yellow-green	2·00	1·50	□	□
219		1d red	2·00	1·50	□	□
221	84	1½d purple and green . .	35·00	18·00	□	□
291	85	2d green and red	25·00	20·00	□	□
231	86	2½d blue	20·00	10·00	□	□
234	87	3d purple on yellow . .	35·00	15·00	□	□
238	88	4d green and brown . .	40·00	18·00	□	□
240		4d orange	20·00	15·00	□	□
294	89	5d purple and blue . . .	28·00	20·00	□	□
245	83	6d purple	35·00	18·00	□	□
249	90	7d grey	10·00	18·00	□	□
307	91	9d purple and blue . . .	60·00	60·00	□	□
311	92	10d purple and red	60·00	60·00	□	□
314	93	1s green and red	50·00	35·00	□	□
260	94	2s 6d purple	£200	90·00	□	□
318	95	5s red	£250	£125	□	□
265	96	10s blue	£575	£350	□	□
320	97	£1 green	£1300	£550	□	□
		Set of 15 (to 1*s*)	£325	£275	□	□

(*b*) *Perf* 15 × 14

279	83	½d green	40·00	45·00	□	□
281		1d red	15·00	15·00	□	□
283	86	2½d blue	22·00	15·00	□	□
285	87	3d purple on yellow . .	45·00	15·00	□	□
286	88	4d orange	30·00	15·00	□	□
		Set of 5	£130	90·00	□	□

KING GEORGE V

1910 (6 May)–1936 (20 Jan.)

PERFORATION. All the following issues are Perf 15 × 14 except vertical commemorative stamps which are 14 × 15, unless otherwise stated.

98 (Hair dark)   99 (Lion unshaded)   100

1911–12 *Wmk Imperial Crown Type* **49**

325	98	½d green	4·50	1·50	□	□
327	99	1d red	4·50	2·50	□	□

1912 *Wmk Royal Cypher* (*'Simple'*) *Type* **100**

335	98	½d green	40·00	40·00	□	□
336	99	1d red	30·00	30·00	□	□

101 (Hair light)   102 (Lion shaded)   103

1912 *Wmk Imperial Crown Type* **49**

339	101	½d green	8·00	4·00	□	□
341	102	1d red	5·00	2·00	□	□

1912 *Wmk Royal Cypher* (*'Simple'*) *Type* **100**

344	101	½d green	7·00	3·00	□	□
345	102	1d red	8·00	3·00	□	□

1912 *Wmk Royal Cypher* (*'Multiple'*) *Type* **103**

346	101	½d green	12·00	8·00	□	□
350	102	1d red	18·00	10·00	□	□

104   105   106

107   **108**

111

1912–24 *Wmk Royal Cypher Type* **100**

351	**105**	½d green	1·00	1·00 ☐ ☐
357	**104**	1d red	1·00	1·00 ☐ ☐
362	**105**	1½d brown	4·00	1·50 ☐ ☐
369	**106**	2d orange	5·00	3·00 ☐ ☐
371	**104**	2½d blue	12·00	4·00 ☐ ☐
377	**106**	3d violet	7·00	2·00 ☐ ☐
379		4d grey-green	15·00	2·00 ☐ ☐
381	**107**	5d brown	15·00	5·00 ☐ ☐
385		6d purple	15·00	7·00 ☐ ☐
		a. Perf 14	90·00	£110 ☐ ☐
387		7d olive-green	20·00	10·00 ☐ ☐
390		8d black on yellow . . .	32·00	11·00 ☐ ☐
392	**108**	9d black	20·00	6·00 ☐ ☐
393*a*		9d olive-green	£100	30·00 ☐ ☐
394		10d blue	22·00	20·00 ☐ ☐
395		1s brown	20·00	4·00 ☐ ☐
	Set of 15	. . . .	£260	95·00 ☐ ☐

1913 *Wmk Royal Cypher ('Multiple') Type* **103**

397	**105**	½d green	£150	£180 ☐ ☐
398	**104**	1d red	£225	£225 ☐ ☐

See also Nos. 418/29.

109

110

T 109. Background around portrait consists of horizontal lines

1913–18 *Wmk Single Cypher Type* **110**   *Perf* 11 × 12

413*a*	**109**	2s 6d brown	£100	65·00 ☐ ☐
416		5s red	£250	£110 ☐ ☐
417		10s blue	£350	£160 ☐ ☐
403		£1 green	£1400	£850 ☐ ☐
	Set of 4	. . . .	£2000	£1100 ☐ ☐

See also Nos. 450/2.

1924–26 *Wmk Block Cypher Type* **111**

418	**105**	½d green	1·00	1·00 ☐ ☐
419	**104**	1d red	1·00	1·00 ☐ ☐
420	**105**	1½d brown	1·00	1·00 ☐ ☐
421	**106**	2d orange	2·50	2·50 ☐ ☐
422	**104**	2½d blue	5·00	3·00 ☐ ☐
423	**106**	3d violet	10·00	2·50 ☐ ☐
424		4d grey-green	12·00	2·50 ☐ ☐
425	**107**	5d brown	20·00	3·00 ☐ ☐
426*a*		6d purple	3·00	1·50 ☐ ☐
427	**108**	9d olive-green	12·00	3·50 ☐ ☐
428		10d blue	35·00	40·00 ☐ ☐
429		1s brown	22·00	3·00 ☐ ☐
	Set of 12	. . . .	£110	60·00 ☐ ☐

112   **112a**

British Empire Exhibition

1924–25 *Wmk* **111** *Perf* 14 (*a*) 23.4.24. *Dated* '1924'

430	**112**	1d red	10·00	11·00 ☐ ☐
431	**112a**	1½d brown	15·00	15·00 ☐ ☐
	First Day Cover		£375	☐

(*b*) 9.5.25. *Dated* '1925'

432	**112**	1d red	15·00	30·00 ☐ ☐
433	**112a**	1½d brown	40·00	70·00 ☐ ☐
	First Day Cover		£1300	☐

113   **114**   **115**

116 St George and the Dragon

117

Ninth Universal Postal Union Congress
1929 (10 May) (a) Wmk **111**

434	**113**	½d green		2·25	2·25	☐	☐
435	**114**	1d red		2·25	2·25	☐	☐
436		1½d brown		2·25	1·75	☐	☐
437	**115**	2½d blue		10·00	10·00	☐	☐

(b) Wmk **117** Perf 12

438	**116**	£1 black		£750	£550	☐	☐
434/7	*Set of 4*			15·00	14·50	☐	☐
434/7	*First Day Cover* (4 vals.)				£500		☐
434/8	*First Day Cover* (5 vals.)				£7000		☐

118   119   120

121   122

1934–36 Wmk **111**

439	**118**	½d green		50	50	☐	☐
440	**119**	1d red		50	50	☐	☐
441	**118**	1½d brown		50	50	☐	☐
442	**120**	2d orange		75	75	☐	☐
443	**119**	2½d blue		1·50	1·25	☐	☐
444	**120**	3d violet		1·50	1·25	☐	☐
445		4d grey-green		2·00	1·25	☐	☐
446	**121**	5d brown		6·00	2·75	☐	☐
447	**122**	9d olive-green		12·00	2·25	☐	☐
448		10d blue		15·00	10·00	☐	☐
449		1s brown		15·00	1·25	☐	☐
	Set of 11			50·00	20·00	☐	☐

T 109 (re-engraved). Background around portrait consists of horizontal and diagonal lines
1934 Wmk **110** Perf 11 × 12

450	**109**	2s 6d brown		70·00	40·00	☐	☐
451		5s red		£160	85·00	☐	☐
452		10s blue		£340	80·00	☐	☐
	Set of 3			£525	£190	☐	☐

123   123a

123b   123c

Silver Jubilee
1935 (7 May) Wmk **111**

453	**123**	½d green		75	50	☐	☐
454	**123a**	1d red		1·25	1·50	☐	☐
455	**123b**	1½d brown		75	50	☐	☐
456	**123c**	2½d blue		4·50	5·50	☐	☐
	Set of 4			6·00	7·00	☐	☐
	First Day Cover				£600		☐

KING EDWARD VIII

1936 (20 Jan.–10 Dec.)

124   125

1936 *Wmk* **125**

457	**124**	½d green	30	30	☐	☐
458		1d red	60	50	☐	☐
459		1½d brown	30	30	☐	☐
460		2½d blue	30	85	☐	☐
	Set of 4	. . . .	1·25	1·75	☐	☐

First Day Covers

1 Sept. 1936	Nos. 457, 459/60	£150	☐
14 Sept. 1936	No. 458	£170	☐

KING GEORGE VI

1936 (11 Dec.)–1952 (6 Feb.)

126   King George VI   127
and Queen Elizabeth

Coronation

1937 (13 MAY) *Wmk* **127**

461	**126**	1½d brown	30	30	☐	☐
		First Day Cover		35·00		☐

128   129   130

King George VI and National Emblems

1937–47 *Wmk* **127**

462	**128**	½d green	30	25	☐	☐
463		1d scarlet	30	25	☐	☐
464		1½d brown	20	25	☐	☐
465		2d orange	75	50	☐	☐
466		2½d blue	30	25	☐	☐
467		3d violet	3·75	1·00	☐	☐
468	**129**	4d green	60	75	☐	☐
469		5d brown	2·50	85	☐	☐
470		6d purple	1·25	60	☐	☐
471	**130**	7d green	4·25	60	☐	☐
472		8d red	3·75	80	☐	☐
473		9d deep green	5·50	80	☐	☐
474		10d blue	5·75	80	☐	☐
474*a*		11d plum	2·00	2·75	☐	☐
475		1s brown	6·00	75	☐	☐
	Set of 15	. . . .	32·00	10·00	☐	☐

First Day Covers

10 May 1937	Nos. 462/3, 466	5·00	☐
30 July 1937	No. 464	5·00	☐
31 Jan. 1938	Nos. 465, 467	25·00	☐
21 Nov. 1938	Nos. 468/9	45·00	☐
30 Jan. 1939	No. 470	45·00	☐
27 Feb. 1939	Nos. 471/2	60·00	☐
1 May 1939	Nos. 473/4, 475	£425	☐
29 Dec. 1947	No. 474*a*	40·00	☐

For later printings of the lower values in apparently lighter shades and different colours, see Nos. 485/90 and 503/8.

130a King George VI **131**

132 **132a**

133

1939–48 *Wmk* **133** *Perf* 14

476	**130a**	2s 6d brown	. . . .	35·00	6·00	□	□
476a		2s 6d green	. . . .	4·50	1·50	□	□
477	**131**	5s red	. . . .	9·00	2·00	□	□
478	**132**	10s dark blue	. . . . . .	£225	20·00	□	□
478a		10s bright blue	. . . . .	20·00	5·00	□	□
478b	**132a**	£1 brown	. . . .	7·00	26·00	□	□
	Set of 6	. . . .		£275	55·00	□	□

First Day Covers

21 Aug. 1939	No. 477	. . . .	£700	□
4 Sept. 1939	No. 476	. . . .	£1250	□
30 Oct. 1939	No. 478	. . . .	£2200	□
9 Mar. 1942	No. 476a	. . . .	£1250	□
30 Nov. 1942	No. 478a	. . . .	£2750	□
1 Oct. 1948	No. 478b	. . . .	£250	□

134 Queen Victoria and King George VI

Centenary of First Adhesive Postage Stamps

1940 (6 MAY) *Wmk* **127** *Perf* 14½ × 14

479	**134**	½d green	. . . .	30	30	□	□
480		1d red	. . . .	1·00	40	□	□
481		1½d brown	. . . .	50	75	□	□
482		2d orange	. . . .	50	40	□	□
483		2½d blue	. . . .	2·25	50	□	□
484		3d violet	. . . .	3·00	3·50	□	□
	Set of 6	. . . .	6·50	5·25	□	□
	First Day Cover	. . . .		55·00		□

Head as Nos. 462–7, but with lighter background

1941–42 *Wmk* **127**

485	**128**	½d pale green	. . . . . .	30	30	□	□
486		1d pale red	. . . .	30	30	□	□
487		1½d pale brown	. . . . . .	50	80	□	□
488		2d pale orange	. . . . . .	50	50	□	□
489		2½d light blue	. . . . . .	30	30	□	□
490		3d pale violet	. . . . . .	2·00	1·00	□	□
	Set of 6	. . . .	3·50	2·75	□	□

First Day Covers

21 July 1941	No. 489	. . . .	40·00	□
11 Aug. 1941	No. 486	. . . .	18·00	□
1 Sept. 1941	No. 485	. . . .	18·00	□
6 Oct. 1941	No. 488	. . . .	55·00	□
3 Nov. 1941	No. 490	. . . .	£100	□
28 Sept. 1942	No. 487	. . . .	50·00	□

135 Symbols of Peace and Reconstruction **136** Symbols of Peace and Reconstruction

Victory

1946 (11 JUNE) *Wmk* **127**

491	**135**	2½d blue	. . . .	20	15	□	□
492	**136**	3d violet	. . . .	20	40	□	□
	First Day Cover	. . . .		65·00		□

137 King George VI and Queen Elizabeth **138** King George VI and Queen Elizabeth

Royal Silver Wedding

1948 (26 APR.) *Wmk* **127**

493	**137**	2½d blue	. . . .	35	20	□	□
494	**138**	£1 blue	. . . .	40·00	40·00	□	□
	First Day Cover	. . . .		£425		□

1948 (10 MAY)

Stamps of 1d and 2½d showing seaweed-gathering were on sale at eight Head Post Offices elsewhere in Great Britain, but were primarily for use in the Channel Islands and are listed there (see after Regional Issues).

139 Globe and Laurel Wreath

140 Speed

141 Olympic Symbol

142 Winged Victory

Olympic Games

1948 (29 JULY) *Wmk* **127**

495	**139**	2½d blue	35	10	□	□
496	**140**	3d violet	35	55	□	□
497	**141**	6d purple	75	40	□	□
498	**142**	1s brown	1·40	1·60	□	□
		Set of 4	2·50	2·40	□	□
		First Day Cover	42·00		□	

143 Two Hemispheres

144 U.P.U. Monument, Berne

145 Goddess Concordia, Globe and Points of Compass

146 Posthorn and Globe

75th Anniversary of Universal Postal Union

1949 (10 OCT.) *Wmk* **127**

499	**143**	2½d blue	15	10	□	□
500	**144**	3d violet	15	50	□	□
501	**145**	6d purple	25	50	□	□
502	**146**	1s brown	60	1·25	□	□
		Set of 4	1·00	2·10	□	□
		First Day Cover	70·00		□	

4d as No. *468 and others as Nos.* *485/9, but colours changed*

1950–51 *Wmk* **127**

503	**128**	½d pale orange	30	30	□	□
504		1d light blue	30	30	□	□
505		1½d pale green	65	60	□	□
506		2d pale brown	75	40	□	□
507		2½d pale red	60	40	□	□
508	**129**	4d light blue	2·00	1·75	□	□
		Set of 6	4·00	3·25		

First Day Covers

2 Oct. 1950	No. 508	£110	□
3 May 1951	Nos. 503/7	50·00	□

147 HMS *Victory*

148 White Cliffs of Dover

149 St George and the Dragon

150 Royal Coat of Arms

1951 (3 MAY) *Wmk* **133** *Perf* 11 × 12

509	**147**	2s 6d green	2·00	1·00	□	□
510	**148**	5s red	40·00	1·50	□	□
511	**149**	10s blue	10·00	8·50	□	□
512	**150**	£1 brown	48·00	20·00	□	□
		Set of 4	90·00	27·00	□	□
		First Day Cover	£900		□	

151 Commerce and Prosperity

152 Festival Symbol

Festival of Britain

1951 (3 MAY) *Wmk* **127**

513	**151**	2½d red	15	20	□	□
514	**152**	4d blue	30	65	□	□
		First Day Cover	30·00		□	

QUEEN ELIZABETH II
6 February, 1952

153 Tudor Crown

154

155   **156**   **157**

158   **159**   **160**

1952–54 *Wmk* 153

515	**154**	½d orange	. . . .	10	15	☐ ☐
516		1d blue	. . . .	20	20	☐ ☐
517		1½d green	. . . .	10	20	☐ ☐
518		2d brown	. . . .	20	20	☐ ☐
519	**155**	2½d red	. . . .	15	15	☐ ☐
520		3d lilac	. . . .	75	55	☐ ☐
521	**156**	4d blue	. . . .	3·25	1·25	☐ ☐
		4½d (*See Nos.* 577, 594, 609 *and* 616*b*)				
522	**157**	5d brown	. . . .	75	3·50	☐ ☐
523		6d purple	. . . .	4·00	1·00	☐ ☐
524		7d green	. . . .	9·50	5·50	☐ ☐
525	**158**	8d magenta	. . . .	75	85	☐ ☐
526		9d bronze-green	. . . . .	23·00	4·75	☐ ☐
527		10d blue	. . . .	18·00	4·75	☐ ☐
528		11d plum	. . . .	30·00	15·00	☐ ☐
529	**159**	1s bistre	. . . .	80	50	☐ ☐
530	**160**	1s 3d green	. . . .	4·50	3·25	☐ ☐
531	**159**	1s 6d indigo	. . . . . .	14·00	3·75	☐ ☐
	Set of 17	. . . .		£100	40·00	☐ ☐

First Day Covers

5 Dec. 1952	Nos. 517, 519	. . . .	15·00 ☐
6 July 1953	Nos. 522, 525, 529	. . . . .	45·00 ☐
31 Aug. 1953	Nos. 515/16, 518	. . . . .	45·00 ☐
2 Nov. 1953	Nos. 521, 530/1	. . . . . .	£170 ☐
18 Jan. 1954	Nos. 520, 523/4	. . . .	£110 ☐
8 Feb. 1954	Nos. 526/8	. . . .	£225 ☐

See also Nos. 540/56, 561/6, 570/94 and 599/618*a* and for stamps as Types **154/60** with face values in decimal currency see Nos. 2031/3, 2258/9, **MS**2326, **MS**2367 and 2378/9.

161   **162**

163   **164**

Coronation

1953 (3 JUNE) *Wmk* **153**

532	**161**	2½d red	. . . .	20	25	☐ ☐
533	**162**	4d blue	. . . .	1·10	1·90	☐ ☐
534	**163**	1s 3d green	. . . .	4·25	3·00	☐ ☐
535	**164**	1s 6d blue	. . . .	8·00	4·75	☐ ☐
	Set of 4	. . . .		12·00	9·00	☐ ☐
	First Day Cover	. . . .			75·00	☐

For £1 values as Type **163** see Nos. **MS**2147 and 2380.

165 St Edward's Crown

166 Carrickfergus Castle   **167** Caernarvon Castle

168 Edinburgh Castle   **169** Windsor Castle

1955 (1–23 SEPT.) *Wmk* **165** *Perf* 11 × 12

536	**166**	2s 6d brown	. . . .	9·00	2·00	☐ ☐
537	**167**	5s red	. . . .	35·00	4·00	☐ ☐

538	168	10s blue	85·00	14·00	☐	☐
539	169	£1 black	£130	35·00	☐	☐
		Set of 4	£225	50·00	☐	☐
		First Day Cover (Nos. 538/9)				
		(1 Sept.)		£750		☐
		First Day Cover (Nos. 536/7)				
		(23 Sept.)		£550		☐

See also Nos. 595a/8a and 759/62.

1955–58 *Wmk* **165**

540	154	½d orange	15	15	☐	☐
541		1d blue	30	15	☐	☐
542		1½d green	25	30	☐	☐
543		2d red-brown	25	35	☐	☐
543b		2d light red-brown . . .	20	20	☐	☐
544	155	2½d red	20	25	☐	☐
545		3d lilac	25	25	☐	☐
546	156	4d blue	1·25	45	☐	☐
547	157	5d brown	5·50	5·75	☐	☐
548		6d purple	4·00	1·25	☐	☐
549		7d green	42·00	9·50	☐	☐
550	158	8d magenta	7·00	1·25	☐	☐
551		9d bronze-green	20·00	2·75	☐	☐
552		10d blue	20·00	2·75	☐	☐
553		11d plum	50	1·10	☐	☐
554	159	1s bistre	22·00	65	☐	☐
555	160	1s 3d green	30·00	1·60	☐	☐
556	159	1s 6d indigo	23·00	1·60	☐	☐
		Set of 18	£160	27·00	☐	☐

170 Scout Badge and 'Rolling Hitch' **171** 'Scouts coming to Britain'

172 Globe within a Compass **173**

World Scout Jubilee Jamboree
1957 (1 Aug.) *Wmk* **165**

557	170	2½d red	15	20	☐	☐
558	171	4d blue	30	80	☐	☐
559	172	1s 3d green	3·50	3·50	☐	☐
		Set of 3	3·50	4·00	☐	☐
		First Day Cover		25·00		☐

46th Inter Parliamentary Union Conference
1957 (12 Sept.) *Wmk* **165**

560	173	4d blue	1·00	1·00	☐	☐
		First Day Cover		£110		☐

Graphite-lined and Phosphor Issues

These are used in connection with automatic sorting machinery, originally experimentally at Southampton but now also operating elsewhere. In such areas these stamps were the normal issue, but from mid 1967 *all* low-value stamps bear phosphor markings.

The graphite lines were printed in black on the back, beneath the gum; two lines per stamp except for the 2d *(see below)*.

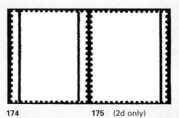

174   **175**   (2d only)
(Stamps viewed from back)

In November 1959, phosphor bands, printed on the front, replaced the graphite. They are wider than the graphite, not easy to see, but show as broad vertical bands at certain angles to the light.

Values representing the rate for printed papers (and second class mail from 1968) have one band and others have two, three or four bands according to size and format. From 1972 onwards some commemorative stamps were printed with 'all-over' phosphor.

In the small stamps the bands are on each side with the single band at left (except where otherwise stated). In the large-size commemorative stamps the single band may be at left, centre or right varying in different issues. The bands are vertical on both horizontal and vertical designs except where otherwise stated.

See also notes on page 37.

Graphite-lined issue
1957 (19 Nov.) *Two graphite lines on the back, except* 2d *value, which has one line. Wmk* **165**

561	154	½d orange	25	25	☐	☐
562		1d blue	25	30	☐	☐
563		1½d green	1·00	1·40	☐	☐
564		2d light red-brown . . .	1·40	2·25	☐	☐
565	155	2½d red	7·50	6·75	☐	☐
566		3d lilac	60	50	☐	☐
		Set of 6	10·00	10·50	☐	☐
		First Day Cover		85·00		☐

See also Nos. 587/94.

176 Welsh Dragon   **177** Flag and Games Emblem

178   Welsh Dragon

Sixth British Empire and Commonwealth Games, Cardiff
1958 (18 July) *Wmk* **165**

567	**176**	3d lilac	20	20	☐	☐
568	**177**	6d mauve	40	45	☐	☐
569	**178**	1s 3d green	2·25	2·40	☐	☐
	Set of 3		2·50	2·75	☐	☐
	First Day Cover			75·00		☐

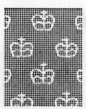

179   Multiple Crowns

WATERMARK. All the following issues to No. 755 are Watermark **179** (sideways on the vertical commemorative stamps) unless otherwise stated.

1958–65 *Wmk* **179**

570	**154**	½d orange	10	10	☐	☑
571		1d blue	10	10	☐	☑
572		1½d green	10	15	☐	☐
573		2d light red-brown	10	10	☐	☐
574	**155**	2½d red	10	20	☐	☐
575		3d lilac	10	20	☐	☐
576a	**156**	4d blue	15	15	☐	☐
577		4½d brown	10	25	☐	☐
578	**157**	5d brown	30	40	☐	☐
579		6d purple	30	25	☐	☐
580		7d green	50	45	☐	☐
581	**158**	8d magenta	60	40	☐	☐
582		9d bronze-green	60	40	☐	☐
583		10d blue	90	50	☐	☐
584	**159**	1s bistre	45	30	☐	☐
585	**160**	1s 3d green	45	30	☐	☐
586	**159**	1s 6d indigo	4·00	60	☐	☐
	Set of 17		8·00	4·25	☐	☐
	First Day Cover (No. 577)					
	(9 Feb. 1959)			£250		☐

For full information on all future British issues, collectors should write to Royal Mail, Freepost EH3647, 21 South Gyle Crescent, Edinburgh EH12 9PE.

Graphite-lined issue
1958–59 *Two graphite lines on the back, except* 2d *value, which has one line. Wmk* **179**

587	**154**	½d orange	3·25	4·00	☐	☐
588		1d blue	1·25	1·50	☐	☐
589		1½d green	38·00	35·00	☐	☐
590		2d light red-brown	7·00	3·50	☐	☐
591	**155**	2½d red	9·00	10·00	☐	☐
592		3d lilac	50	65	☐	☐
593	**156**	4d blue	4·50	5·00	☐	☐
594		4½d brown	6·50	5·00	☐	☐
	Set of 8		65·00	60·00	☐	☐

The prices quoted for Nos. 587 and 589 are for examples with inverted watermark. Stamps with upright watermark are priced at: ½d £8 *mint*, £9 *used and* 1½d £90 *mint*, £80 *used.*

1959–63 *Wmk* **179** *Perf* 11 × 12

595a	**166**	2s 6d brown	35	40	☐	☐
596a	**167**	5s red	90	50	☐	☐
597a	**168**	10s blue	4·00	4·50	☐	☐
598a	**169**	£1 black	11·00	7·00	☐	☐
	Set of 4		15·00	11·00	☐	☐

Phosphor-Graphite issue
1959 (18 Nov.) *Two phosphor bands on front and two graphite lines on back, except* 2d *value, which has one band on front and one line on back* (a) *Wmk* **165**

599	**154**	½d orange	3·25	3·50	☐	☐
600		1d blue	8·25	9·00	☐	☐
601		1½d green	3·25	3·25	☐	☐

(b) *Wmk* **179**

605	**154**	2d light red-brown (1 band)	4·25	4·25	☐	☐
606	**155**	2½d red	17·00	15·00	☐	☐
607		3d lilac	8·50	7·00	☐	☐
608	**156**	4d blue	15·00	16·00	☐	☐
609		4½d brown	24·00	20·00	☐	☐
	Set of 8		75·00	70·00	☐	☐

Phosphor issue
1960–67 *Two phosphor bands on front, except where otherwise stated. Wmk* **179**

610	**154**	½d orange	10	15	☐	☐
611		1d blue	10	10	☐	☐
612		1½d green	10	15	☐	☐
613		2d light red-brown (1 band)	16·00	18·00	☐	☐
613a		2d light red-brown (2 bands)	10	15	☐	☐
614	**155**	2½d red (2 bands)	20	30	☐	☐
614a		2½d red (1 band)	40	65	☐	☐
615		3d lilac (2 bands)	60	55	☐	☐
615c		3d lilac (1 side band)	60	55	☐	☐
615e		3d lilac (1 centre band)	40	45	☐	☐
616a	**156**	4d blue	25	25	☐	☐
616b		4½d brown	20	30	☐	☐

616c	157	5d brown	25	35	□	□
617		6d purple	30	30	□	□
617a		7d green	55	50	□	□
617b	158	8d magenta	40	45	□	□
617c		9d bronze-green	55	55	□	□
617d		10d blue	70	60	□	□
617e	159	1s bistre	35	35	□	□
618	160	1s 3d green	1·90	2·50	□	□
618a	159	1s 6d indigo	2·00	1·60	□	□
		Set of 17 (one of each value) ..	7·50	8·00	□	□

No. 615c exists with the phosphor band at the left or right of the stamp.

180 Postboy of 1660   **181** Posthorn of 1660

Tercentenary of Establishment of 'General Letter Office'
1960 (7 JULY)

619	180	3d lilac	20	20	□	□
620	181	1s 3d green	2·75	3·50	□	□
		Set of 2	2·75	3·50	□	□
		First Day Cover		40·00		□

182 Conference Emblem

First Anniversary of European Postal and Telecommunications Conference
1960 (19 SEPT.)

621	182	6d green and purple . .	50	50	□	□
622		1s 6d brown and blue . . .	6·50	5·00	□	□
		Set of 2	7·00	5·50	□	□
		First Day Cover		38·00		□

183 Thrift Plant   **184** 'Growth of Savings'

185 Thrift Plant

Centenary of Post Office Savings Bank
1961 (28 AUG.)

623A	183	2½d black and red	25	25	□	□
624A	184	3d orange-brown and violet	20	20	□	□
625A	185	1s 6d red and blue	2·25	2·25	□	□
		Set of 3	2·50	2·50	□	□
		First Day Cover		60·00		□

186 C.E.P.T. Emblem   **187** Doves and Emblem

188 Doves and Emblem

European Postal and Telecommunications (C.E.P.T.) Conference, Torquay
1961 (18 SEPT.)

626	186	2d orange, pink and brown	15	20	□	□
627	187	4d buff, mauve and ultramarine	15	25	□	□
628	188	10d turquoise, green and blue	15	80	□	□
		Set of 3	40	1·10	□	□
		First Day Cover		6·00		□

189 Hammer Beam Roof, Westminster Hall   **190** Palace of Westminster

Seventh Commonwealth Parliamentary Conference

1961 (25 SEPT.)

629	189	6d purple and gold . . .	25	25 □ □
630	190	1s 3d green and blue . . .	2·50	2·75 □ □
		Set of 2	2·75	3·00 □ □
		First Day Cover		30·00 □

191 'Units of Productivity'

192 'National Productivity'

193 'Unified Productivity'

National Productivity Year

1962 (14 Nov.) *Wmk 179* (*inverted on 2½d and 3d*)

631	191	2½d green and red	20	15 □ □
		p. Phosphor	60	50 □ □
632	192	3d blue and violet	25	15 □ □
		p. Phosphor	1·50	80 □ □
633	193	1s 3d red, blue and green .	1·50	1·75 □ □
		p. Phosphor	35·00	22·00 □ □
		Set of 3 (Ordinary)	1·75	1·90 □ □
		Set of 3 (Phosphor)	35·00	22·00 □ □
		First Day Cover (Ordinary)		48·00 □
		First Day Cover (Phosphor) . . .		£120 □

194 Campaign Emblem and Family

195 Children of Three Races

Freedom from Hunger

1963 (21 MAR.) *Wmk 179* (*inverted*)

634	194	2½d crimson and pink . .	10	10 □ □
		p. Phosphor	3·00	1·25 □ □
635	195	1s 3d brown and yellow . .	1·60	1·90 □ □
		p. Phosphor	30·00	23·00 □ □
		Set of 2 (Ordinary)	1·60	2·00 □ □
		Set of 2 (Phosphor)	32·00	24·00 □ □
		First Day Cover (Ordinary)		32·00 □
		First Day Cover (Phosphor) . . .		40·00 □

196 'Paris Conference'

Paris Postal Conference Centenary

1963 (7 MAY) *Wmk 179* (*inverted*)

636	196	6d green and mauve . .	30	40 □ □
		p. Phosphor	6·00	6·00 □ □
		First Day Cover (Ordinary)		14·00 □
		First Day Cover (Phosphor) . . .		27·00 □

197 Posy of Flowers

198 Woodland Life

National Nature Week

1963 (16 MAY)

637	197	3d multicoloured	15	15 □ □
		p. Phosphor	55	60 □ □
638	198	4½d multicoloured	20	35 □ □
		p. Phosphor	2·75	3·00 □ □
		Set of 2 (Ordinary)	35	50 □ □
		Set of 2 (Phosphor)	3·25	3·50 □ □
		First Day Cover (Ordinary)		18·00 □
		First Day Cover (Phosphor) . . .		32·00 □

199 Rescue at Sea

200 19th-century Lifeboat

201 Lifeboatmen

Ninth International Lifeboat Conference, Edinburgh

1963 (31 MAY)

639	199	2½d blue, black and red .	15	20 □ □
		p. Phosphor	50	60 □ □
640	200	4d multicoloured	40	40 □ □
		p. Phosphor	50	60 □ □

641	**201**	1s 6d sepia, yellow and blue	2·40	2·50	☐ ☐
		p. Phosphor	45·00	28·00	☐ ☐
		Set of 3 (Ordinary)	2·75	2·75	☐ ☐
		Set of 3 (Phosphor)	45·00	28·00	☐ ☐
		First Day Cover (Ordinary)		35·00	☐
		First Day Cover (Phosphor) . . .		45·00	☐

202   Red Cross

203

204

Red Cross Centenary Congress
1963 (15 Aug.)

642	**202**	3d red and lilac	15	15	☐ ☐
		p. Phosphor	1·10	85	☐ ☐
643	**203**	1s 3d red, blue and grey . .	2·50	2·50	☐ ☐
		p. Phosphor	35·00	30·00	☐ ☐
644	**204**	1s 6d red, blue and bistre .	2·50	2·50	☐ ☐
		p. Phosphor	32·00	25·00	☐ ☐
		Set of 3 (Ordinary)	4·75	4·75	☐ ☐
		Set of 3 (Phosphor)	60·00	50·00	☐ ☐
		First Day Cover (Ordinary)		40·00	☐
		First Day Cover (Phosphor) . . .		60·00	☐

205   'Commonwealth Cable'

Opening of COMPAC (Trans-Pacific Telephone Cable)
1963 (3 Dec.)

645	**205**	1s 6d blue and black	2·00	2·25	☐ ☐
		p. Phosphor	16·00	15·00	☐ ☐
		First Day Cover (Ordinary)		24·00	☐
		First Day Cover (Phosphor) . . .		30·00	☐

206   Puck and Bottom (*A Midsummer Night's Dream*)

207   Feste (*Twelfth Night*)

208   Balcony Scene (*Romeo and Juliet*)

209   'Eve of Agincourt' (*Henry V*)

210   Hamlet contemplating Yorick's skull (*Hamlet*) and Queen Elizabeth II

Shakespeare Festival
1964 (23 Apr.)   *Perf* 11 × 12 (*2s 6d*) *or* 15 × 14 (*others*)

646	**206**	3d bistre, black and violet-blue	15	15	☐ ☐
		p. Phosphor	25	30	☐ ☐
647	**207**	6d multicoloured	30	30	☐ ☐
		p. Phosphor	75	1·00	☐ ☐
648	**208**	1s 3d multicoloured	70	90	☐ ☐
		p. Phosphor	4·00	6·50	☐ ☐
649	**209**	1s 6d multicoloured	1·00	85	☐ ☐
		p. Phosphor	8·00	8·00	☐ ☐
650	**210**	2s 6d deep slate-purple . .	2·75	2·75	☐ ☐
		Set of 5 (Ordinary)	4·50	4·50	☐ ☐
		Set of 4 (Phosphor)	12·00	14·00	☐ ☐
		First Day Cover (Ordinary)		10·00	☐
		First Day Cover (Phosphor) . . .		17·00	☐
		Presentation Pack (Ordinary) . .	12·50		☐

PRESENTATION PACKS were first introduced by the G.P.O. for the Shakespeare Festival issue. The packs include one set of stamps and details of the designs, the designer and the stamp printer. They were issued for almost all later definitive and special issues.

211   Flats near Richmond Park ('Urban Development')

212   Shipbuilding Yards, Belfast ('Industrial Activity')

213   Beddgelert Forest Park, Snowdonia ('Forestry')

214   Nuclear Reactor, Dounreay ('Technological Development')

20th International Geographical Congress, London
1964 (1 JULY)

651	**211**	2½d multicoloured	. . . .	10	10 □	□
		p. Phosphor	. . . .	40	50 □	□
652	**212**	4d multicoloured	. . . .	30	30 □	□
		p. Phosphor	. . . .	1·25	1·25 □	□
653	**213**	8d multicoloured	. . . .	65	75 □	□
		p. Phosphor	. . . .	2·50	2·75 □	□
654	**214**	1s 6d multicoloured	. . . .	2·75	3·00 □	□
		p. Phosphor	. . . .	28·00	22·00 □	□
		Set of 4 (Ordinary)	. . . .	3·50	3·75 □	□
		Set of 4 (Phosphor)	. . . . . .	30·00	24·00 □	□
		First Day Cover (Ordinary)	. . . .		22·00	□
		First Day Cover (Phosphor)	. . .		35·00	□
		Presentation Pack (Ordinary)	. .	£120		□

215 Spring Gentian

216 Dog Rose

217 Honeysuckle

218 Fringed Water Lily

Tenth International Botanical Congress, Edinburgh
1964 (5 AUG.)

655	**215**	3d violet, blue and green		10	10 □	□
		p. Phosphor	. . . .	40	40 □	□
656	**216**	6d multicoloured	. . . .	30	35 □	□
		p. Phosphor	. . . .	2·50	2·75 □	□
657	**217**	9d multicoloured	. . . .	1·60	2·25 □	□
		p. Phosphor	. . . .	4·50	4·00 □	□
658	**218**	1s 3d multicoloured	. . . .	2·25	2·50 □	□
		p. Phosphor	. . . .	25·00	20·00 □	□
		Set of 4 (Ordinary)	. . . .	3·75	4·75 □	□
		Set of 4 (Phosphor)	. . . .	30·00	24·00 □	□
		First Day Cover (Ordinary)	. . . .		25·00	□
		First Day Cover (Phosphor)	. . .		35·00	□
		Presentation Pack (Ordinary)	. .	£120		□

219 Forth Road Bridge

220 Forth Road and Railway Bridges

Opening of Forth Road Bridge
1964 (4 SEPT.)

659	**219**	3d black, blue and violet	. . . .	10	10 □	□
		p. Phosphor	. . . .	50	50 □	□
660	**220**	6d blackish lilac, blue and red	. . . .	40	40 □	□
		p. Phosphor	. . . .	3·75	3·75 □	□
		Set of 2 (Ordinary)	. . . .	50	50 □	□
		Set of 2 (Phosphor)	. . . .	4·25	4·25 □	□
		First Day Cover (Ordinary)	. . . .		7·00	□
		First Day Cover (Phosphor)	. . .		18·00	□
		Presentation Pack (Ordinary)		£350		□

221 Sir Winston Churchill   **221a** Sir Winston Churchill

Churchill Commemoration
1965 (8 JULY)

661	**221**	4d black and drab	. . . .	10	10 □	□
		p. Phosphor	. . . .	25	25 □	□
662	**221a**	1s 3d black and grey	. . . .	30	40 □	□
		p. Phosphor	. . . .	2·50	3·00 □	□
		Set of 2 (Ordinary)	. . . .	40	50 □	□
		Set of 2 (Phosphor)	. . . .	2·75	3·25 □	□
		First Day Cover (Ordinary)	. . . .		8·00	□
		First Day Cover (Phosphor)	. . .		9·00	□
		Presentation Pack (Ordinary)	. .	24·00		□

700th Anniversary of Parliament

222 Simon de Montfort's Seal

223 Parliament Buildings
(after engraving by Hollar, 1647)

700th Anniversary of Simon de Montfort's Parliament
1965 (19 JULY)

663	**222**	6d green	. . . .	20	20 □	□
		p. Phosphor	. . . .	60	75 □	□
664	**223**	2s 6d black, grey and drab		80	1·00 □	□
		Set of 2 (Ordinary)	. . . .	1·00	1·10 □	□
		First Day Cover (Ordinary)	. . . .		12·00	□
		First Day Cover (Phosphor)	. . .		20·00	□
		Presentation Pack (Ordinary)	. .	45·00		□

224 Bandsmen and Banner	**225** Three Salvationists	**230** Flight of Supermarine Spitfires **231** Pilot in Hawker Hurricane Mk I

224 Bandsmen and Banner   **225** Three Salvationists

Salvation Army Centenary
1965 (9 Aug.)

665	224	3d multicoloured	....	10	15	☐	☐
		p. Phosphor	....	30	40	☐	☐
666	225	1s 6d multicoloured	....	65	1·00	☐	☐
		p. Phosphor	....	2·50	2·75	☐	☐
		Set of 2 (Ordinary)	....	75	1·10	☐	☐
		Set of 2 (Phosphor)	....	2·75	3·00	☐	☐
		First Day Cover (Ordinary)	....		22·00		☐
		First Day Cover (Phosphor)	...		30·00		☐

226 Lister's Carbolic Spray   **227** Lister and Chemical Symbols

Centenary of Joseph Lister's Discovery of Antiseptic Surgery
1965 (1 Sept.)

667	226	4d indigo, chestnut and grey		10	15	☐	☐
		p. Phosphor	....	25	25	☐	☐
668	227	1s black, purple and blue	....	70	1·10	☐	☐
		p. Phosphor	....	2·00	2·10	☐	☐
		Set of 2 (Ordinary)	....	80	1·25	☐	☐
		Set of 2 (Phosphor)	....	2·25	2·25	☐	☐
		First Day Cover (Ordinary)	....		12·00		☐
		First Day Cover (Phosphor)	...		14·00		☐

228 Trinidad Carnival Dancers   **229** Canadian Folk Dancers

Commonwealth Arts Festival
1965 (1 Sept.)

669	228	6d black and orange	..	20	20	☐	☐
		p. Phosphor	....	30	40	☐	☐
670	229	1s 6d black and violet	....	80	1·10	☐	☐
		p. Phosphor	....	2·50	2·50	☐	☐
		Set of 2 (Ordinary)	....	1·00	1·25	☐	☐
		Set of 2 (Phosphor)	....	2·75	2·75	☐	☐
		First Day Cover (Ordinary)	....		14·00		☐
		First Day Cover (Phosphor)	...		18·00		☐

230 Flight of Supermarine Spitfires   **231** Pilot in Hawker Hurricane Mk I

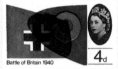 

232 Wing-tips of Supermarine Spitfire and Messerschmitt Bf 109   **233** Supermarine Spitfires attacking Heinkel HE 111H Bomber

234 Supermarine Spitfire attacking Junkers Ju 87B 'Stuka' Dive-bomber   **235** Hawker Hurricanes Mk I over Wreck of Dornier Do-17Z Bomber

The above were issued together *se-tenant* in blocks of six (3 × 2) within the sheet.

236 Anti-aircraft Artillery in Action   **237** Air Battle over St Paul's Cathedral

25th Anniversary of Battle of Britain
1965 (13 Sept.)

671	230	4d olive and black	....	50	70	☐	☐
		a. Block of 6. Nos. 671/6		6·00	10·00	☐	☐
		p. Phosphor	....	90	1·00	☐	☐
		pa. Block of 6. Nos. 671p/6p	....	10·00	15·00	☐	☐
672	231	4d olive, blackish olive and black	....	50	70	☐	☐
		p. Phosphor	....	90	1·00	☐	☐
673	232	4d multicoloured	....	50	70	☐	☐
		p. Phosphor	....	90	1·00	☐	☐
674	233	4d olive and black	....	50	70	☐	☐
		p. Phosphor	....	90	1·00	☐	☐
675	234	4d olive and black	....	50	70	☐	☐
		p. Phosphor	....	90	1·00	☐	☐

676 **235** 4d multicoloured .... 50 70 □ □
      p. Phosphor .... 90 1·00 □ □
677 **236** 9d violet, orange and
      purple .... 1·25 1·50 □ □
      p. Phosphor .... 1·25 1·50 □ □
678 **237** 1s 3d multicoloured 1·25 1·50 □ □
      p. Phosphor .... 1·25 1·50 □ □
      Set of 8 (Ordinary) 7·75 6·50 □ □
      Set of 8 (Phosphor) 11·50 8·00 □ □
      First Day Cover (Ordinary) .... 25·00 □
      First Day Cover (Phosphor) ... 28·00 □
      Presentation Pack (Ordinary) .. 45·00 □

242 Telecommunications Network
243 Radio Waves and Switchboard

I.T.U. Centenary
1965 (15 Nov.)
683 **242** 9d multicoloured .... 30 40 □ □
      p. Phosphor .... 60 75 □ □
684 **243** 1s 6d multicoloured .... 1·00 1·25 □ □
      p. Phosphor .... 4·25 5·25 □ □
      Set of 2 (Ordinary) 1·25 1·60 □ □
      Set of 2 (Phosphor) 4·75 6·00 □ □
      First Day Cover (Ordinary) .... 17·00 □
      First Day Cover (Phosphor) ... 20·00 □

238 Tower and Georgian Buildings
239 Tower and Nash Terrace, Regent's Park

Opening of Post Office Tower
1965 (8 Oct.)
679 **238** 3d yellow, blue and
      green .... 10 15 □ □
      p. Phosphor .... 15 15 □ □
680 **239** 1s 3d green and blue ... 30 45 □ □
      p. Phosphor .... 30 50 □ □
      Set of 2 (Ordinary) .... 40 60 □ □
      Set of 2 (Phosphor) .... 45 65 □ □
      First Day Cover (Ordinary) .... 6·00 □
      First Day Cover (Phosphor) ... 7·00 □
      Presentation Pack (Ordinary) .. 4·00 □
      Presentation Pack (Phosphor) .. 4·00 □

244 Robert Burns (after Skirving chalk drawing)
245 Robert Burns (after Nasmyth portrait)

Burns Commemoration
1966 (25 Jan.)
685 **244** 4d black, indigo and blue 15 15 □ □
      p. Phosphor .... 25 40 □ □
686 **245** 1s 3d black, blue and orange 40 70 □ □
      p. Phosphor .... 2·25 1·75 □ □
      Set of 2 (Ordinary) .... 55 85 □ □
      Set of 2 (Phosphor) .... 2·50 2·10 □ □
      First Day Cover (Ordinary) .... 6·00 □
      First Day Cover (Phosphor) ... 7·00 □
      Presentation Pack (Ordinary) .. 40·00 □

240 U.N. Emblem
241 I.C.Y. Emblem

20th Anniversary of UNO and International Co-operation Year
1965 (25 Oct.)
681 **240** 3d black, orange and blue 15 20 □ □
      p. Phosphor .... 25 30 □ □
682 **241** 1s 6d black, purple and blue 75 80 □ □
      p. Phosphor .... 2·75 3·00 □ □
      Set of 2 (Ordinary) .... 90 1·00 □ □
      Set of 2 (Phosphor) .... 3·00 3·25 □ □
      First Day Cover (Ordinary) .... 10·00 □
      First Day Cover (Phosphor) ... 12·00 □

246 Westminster Abbey
247 Fan Vaulting, Henry VII Chapel

900th Anniversary of Westminster Abbey
1966 (28 Feb.) *Perf* 15 × 14 (*3d*) or 11 × 12 (*2s 6d*)
687 **246** 3d black, brown and
      blue .... 15 20 □ □
      p. Phosphor .... 20 25 □ □

688	**247**	2s 6d black	55	80	☐	☐
		Set of 2	70	1·00	☐	☐
		First Day Cover (*Ordinary*)		8·00		☐
		First Day Cover (*Phosphor*) . . .		14·00		☐
		Presentation Pack (*Ordinary*) . .	20·00		☐	

248   View near Hassocks, Sussex

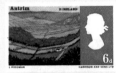

249   Antrim, Northern Ireland

250   Harlech Castle, Wales

251   Cairngorm Mountains, Scotland

Landscapes
1966 (2 MAY)

689	**248**	4d black, yellow-green and blue	10	15	☐	☐
		p. Phosphor	10	15	☐	☐
690	**249**	6d black, green and blue	15	20	☐	☐
		p. Phosphor	15	20	☐	☐
691	**250**	1s 3d black, yellow and blue	25	35	☐	☐
		p. Phosphor	25	35	☐	☐
692	**251**	1s 6d black, orange and blue	40	35	☐	☐
		p. Phosphor	40	40	☐	☐
		Set of 4 (*Ordinary*)	80	95	☐	☐
		Set of 4 (*Phosphor*)	80	1·00	☐	☐
		First Day Cover (*Ordinary*)		7·00		☐
		First Day Cover (*Phosphor*) . . .		8·00		☐

252   Players with Ball

253   Goalmouth Mêlée   254   Goalkeeper saving Goal

World Cup Football Championship
1966 (1 JUNE)

693	**252**	4d multicoloured	10	10	☐	☐
		p. Phosphor	10	10	☐	☐
694	**253**	6d multicoloured	15	25	☐	☐
		p. Phosphor	15	25	☐	☐
695	**254**	1s 3d multicoloured	50	70	☐	☐
		p. Phosphor	50	70	☐	☐
		Set of 3 (*Ordinary*)	70	95	☐	☐
		Set of 3 (*Phosphor*)	70	95	☐	☐
		First Day Cover (*Ordinary*)		15·00		☐
		First Day Cover (*Phosphor*) . . .		20·00		☐
		Presentation Pack (*Ordinary*) . .	15·00		☐	

255   Black-headed Gull   256   Blue Tit

257   European Robin   258   Blackbird

The above were issued *se-tenant* in blocks of four within the sheet.

British Birds
1966 (8 AUG.)

696	**255**	4d multicoloured	10	20	☐	☐
		a. Block of 4. *Nos.* 696/9	80	2·00	☐	☐
		p. Phosphor	10	20	☐	☐
		pa. Block of 4. *Nos.* 696*p*/9*p*	75	2·00	☐	☐
697	**256**	4d multicoloured	10	20	☐	☐
		p. Phosphor	10	20	☐	☐
698	**257**	4d multicoloured	10	20	☐	☐
		p. Phosphor	10	20	☐	☐
699	**258**	4d multicoloured	10	20	☐	☐
		p. Phosphor	10	20	☐	☐
		Set of 4 (*Ordinary*)	80	70	☐	☐
		Set of 4 (*Phosphor*)	75	70	☐	☐
		First Day Cover (*Ordinary*)		10·00		☐
		First Day Cover (*Phosphor*) . . .		10·00		☐
		Presentation Pack (*Ordinary*) . .	9·00		☐	

266

267

259 Cup Winners

268

269

England's World Cup Football Victory
1966 (18 Aug.)

700	**259**	4d multicoloured	30	30 ☐	☐
		First Day Cover		10·00	☐

The above show battle scenes, they were issued together *se-tenant* in horizontal strips of six within the sheet.

270 Norman Ship

260 Jodrell Bank Radio Telescope   261 British Motor-cars

262 SR N6 Hovercraft   263 Windscale Reactor

271 Norman Horsemen attacking Harold's Troops

British Technology
1966 (19 Sept.)

701	**260**	4d black and lemon . . .	10	10 ☐	☐
		p. Phosphor	10	10 ☐	☐
702	**261**	6d red, blue and orange	15	20 ☐	☐
		p. Phosphor	15	25 ☐	☐
703	**262**	1s 3d multicoloured	25	40 ☐	☐
		p. Phosphor	35	40 ☐	☐
704	**263**	1s 6d multicoloured	40	60 ☐	☐
		p. Phosphor	50	60 ☐	☐
		Set of 4 (Ordinary)	80	1·10 ☐	☐
		Set of 4 (Phosphor)	1·00	1·10 ☐	☐
		First Day Cover (Ordinary)		8·00	☐
		First Day Cover (Phosphor) . . .		8·00	☐
		Presentation Pack (Ordinary) . .	9·00		☐

900th Anniversary of Battle of Hastings
1966 (14 Oct.) *Designs show scenes from Bayeux Tapestry*
Wmk **179** (*sideways on* 1s 3d)

705	**264**	4d multicoloured	10	20 ☐	☐
		a. Strip of 6. Nos. 705/10	1·90	6·00 ☐	☐
		p. Phosphor	10	25 ☐	☐
		pa. Strip of 6. Nos.			
		705p/10p	1·90	6·00 ☐	☐
706	**265**	4d multicoloured . .ː. .	10	20 ☐	☐
		p. Phosphor	10	25 ☐	☐
707	**266**	4d multicoloured	10	20 ☐	☐
		p. Phosphor	10	25 ☐	☐
708	**267**	4d multicoloured	10	20 ☐	☐
		p. Phosphor	10	25 ☐	☐
709	**268**	4d multicoloured	10	20 ☐	☐
		p. Phosphor	10	25 ☐	☐
710	**269**	4d multicoloured	10	20 ☐	☐
		p. Phosphor	10	25 ☐	☐

264

265

711	**270**	6d multicoloured	10	20 ☐ ☐
		p. Phosphor	10	20 ☐ ☐
712	**271**	1s 3d multicoloured	20	40 ☐ ☐
		p. Phosphor	20	50 ☐ ☐
		Set of 8 (Ordinary)	2·00	1·60 ☐ ☐
		Set of 8 (Phosphor)	2·00	2·00 ☐ ☐
		First Day Cover (Ordinary)		8·00 ☐
		First Day Cover (Phosphor)		9·00 ☐
		Presentation Pack (Ordinary) ..	9·00	☐

272 King of the Orient

273 Snowman

Christmas
1966 (1 Dec.) *Wmk 179* (*upright on* 1s 6d)

713	**272**	3d multicoloured	10	10 ☐ ☐
		p. Phosphor	10	10 ☐ ☐
714	**273**	1s 6d multicoloured	30	30 ☐ ☐
		p. Phosphor	30	35 ☐ ☐
		Set of 2 (Ordinary)	40	40 ☐ ☐
		Set of 2 (Phosphor)	40	45 ☐ ☐
		First Day Cover (Ordinary)		4·00 ☐
		First Day Cover (Phosphor)		4·00 ☐
		Presentation Pack (Ordinary) ..	8·00	☐

274 Sea Freight

275 Air Freight

European Free Trade Association (EFTA)
1967 (20 Feb.)

715	**274**	9d multicoloured	15	20 ☐ ☐
		p. Phosphor	15	20 ☐ ☐
716	**275**	1s 6d multicoloured	30	45 ☐ ☐
		p. Phosphor	25	40 ☐ ☐
		Set of 2 (Ordinary)	45	65 ☐ ☐
		Set of 2 (Phosphor)	40	60 ☐ ☐
		First Day Cover (Ordinary)		4·00 ☐
		First Day Cover (Phosphor)		4·00 ☑
		Presentation Pack (Ordinary) ..	3·00	☐

276 Hawthorn and Bramble

277 Larger Bindweed and Viper's Bugloss

278 Ox-eye Daisy, Coltsfoot and Buttercup

279 Bluebell, Red Campion and Wood Anemone

The above sheet were issued together *se-tenant* in blocks of four within the sheet.

280 Dog Violet

281 Primroses

British Wild Flowers
1967 (24 Apr.)

717	**276**	4d multicoloured	15	15 ☐ ☐
		a. Block of 4. Nos. 717/20	80	3·00 ☐ ☐
		p. Phosphor	10	15 ☐ ☐
		pa Block of 4. Nos. 717p/ 20p	50	2·75 ☐ ☐
718	**277**	4d multicoloured	15	15 ☐ ☐
		p. Phosphor	10	15 ☐ ☐
719	**278**	4d multicoloured	15	15 ☐ ☐
		p. Phosphor	10	15 ☐ ☐
720	**279**	4d multicoloured	15	15 ☐ ☐
		p. Phosphor	10	15 ☐ ☐
721	**280**	9d multicoloured	15	20 ☐ ☐
		p. Phosphor	15	25 ☐ ☐
722	**281**	1s 9d multicoloured	20	30 ☐ ☐
		p. Phosphor	20	30 ☐ ☐
		Set of 6 (Ordinary)	1·00	1·00 ☐ ☐
		Set of 6 (Phosphor)	75	1·00 ☐ ☐
		First Day Cover (Ordinary)		5·50 ☐
		First Day Cover (Phosphor)		7·00 ☐
		Presentation Pack (Ordinary) ..	5·00	☐
		Presentation Pack (Phosphor) ..	5·00	☐

282 (value at left)   282a (value at right)

I   II

Two *types* of the 2d.
I. Value spaced away from left side of stamp.
II. Value close to left side from new multi-positive. This results in the portrait appearing in the centre, thus conforming with the other values.

1967–69 *Two phosphor bands, except where otherwise stated. No wmk.*

723	282	½d orange-brown	10	20 □ □
724		1d olive (2 bands)	10	10 □ □
725		1d olive (1 centre band)	30	35 □ □
726		2d lake-brown (Type I) (2 bands)	10	15 □ □
727		2d lake-brown (Type II) (2 bands)	15	20 □ □
728		2d lake-brown (Type II) (1 centre band) . . .	70	90 □ □
729		3d violet (1 centre band)	15	10 □ □
730		3d violet (2 bands) . . .	30	35 □ □
731		4d sepia (2 bands) . . .	10	10 □ □
732		4d olive-brown (1 centre band)	10	10 □ □
733		4d vermilion (1 centre band)	10	10 □ □
734		4d vermilion (1 side band)	1·50	1·90 □ □
735		5d blue	10	10 □ □
736		6d purple	20	25 □ □
737	282a	7d emerald	40	35 □ □
738		8d vermilion	20	45 □ □
739		8d turquoise-blue	50	60 □ □
740		9d green	40	25 □ □
741	282	10d drab	50	50 □ □
742		1s violet	45	25 □ □
743		1s 6d blue and deep blue .	50	50 □ □
		c. Phosphorised paper .	80	80 □ □
744		1s 9d orange and black . .	50	45 □ □
		Set of 16 (one of each value and colour)	4·00	4·00 □ □
		Presentation Pack (one of each value)	7·00	□
		Presentation Pack (German) . . .	45·00	□

First Day Covers

5 June 1967	Nos. 731, 742, 744	3·00 □
8 Aug. 1967	Nos. 729, 740, 743	3·00 □
5 Feb. 1968	Nos. 723/4, 726, 736	3·00 □
1 July 1968	Nos. 735, 737/8, 741	3·00 □

No. 734 exists with phosphor band at the left or right.

283 'Master Lambton' (Sir Thomas Lawrence)   284 'Mares and Foals in a Landscape' (George Stubbs)

285 'Children Coming Out of School' (L. S. Lowry)

British Paintings
1967 (10 JULY) *Two phosphor bands. No wmk*

748	283	4d multicoloured	10	10 □ □
749	284	9d multicoloured	15	15 □ □
750	285	1s 6d multicoloured . . .	25	35 □ □
		Set of 3	45	50 □ □
		First Day Cover		3·00 □
		Presentation Pack	6·00	□

286 *Gipsy Moth IV*

Sir Francis Chichester's World Voyage
1967 (24 JULY) *Three phosphor bands. No wmk*

751	286	1s 9d multicoloured	20	20 □ □
		First Day Cover		1·75 □

287 Radar Screen   288 *Penicillium notatum*

289 Vickers VC-10 Jet Engines

290 Television Equipment

British Discovery and Invention

1967 (19 SEPT.) *Two phosphor bands* (*except* 4d. *three bands*). *Wmk* 179 (*sideways on* 1s 9d)

752	287	4d yellow, black and ver-milion	10	10	☐	☐
753	288	1s multicoloured	10	20	☐	☐
754	289	1s 6d multicoloured	20	25	☐	☐
755	290	1s 9d multicoloured	20	30	☐	☐
		Set of 4	50	75	☐	☐
		First Day Cover	3·00		☐	
		Presentation Pack	2·75		☐	

NO WATERMARK. All the following issues are on unwatermarked paper unless otherwise stated.

291 'The Adoration of the Shepherds' (School of Seville)

292 'Madonna and Child' (Murillo)

293 'The Adoration of the Shepherds' (Louis Le Nain)

Christmas

1967 *Two phosphor bands* (*except* 3d, *one phosphor band*)

756	291	3d multicoloured (27 Nov.)	10	10	☐	☐
757	292	4d multicoloured (18 Oct.)	10	10	☐	☐

758	293	1s 6d multicoloured (27 Nov.)	15	30	☐	☐
		Set of 3	30	45	☐	☐
		First Day Covers (2)	3·50		☐	

Gift Pack 1967

1967 (27 Nov.) *Comprises Nos.* 715p/22p *and* 748/58

	Gift Pack	2·75		☐

1967–68 *No wmk. Perf* 11 × 12

759	166	2s 6d brown	30	45	☐	☐
760	167	5s red	70	75	☐	☐
761	168	10s blue	4·75	6·25	☐	☐
762	169	£1 black	4·50	6·00	☐	☐
		Set of 4	9·25	12·00	☐	☐

294 Tarr Steps, Exmoor

295 Aberfeldy Bridge

296 Menai Bridge

297 M4 Viaduct

British Bridges

1968 (29 APR.) *Two phosphor bands*

763	294	4d multicoloured	10	10	☐	☐
764	295	9d multicoloured	10	15	☐	☐
765	296	1s 6d multicoloured	15	25	☐	☐
766	297	1s 9d multicoloured	20	30	☐	☐
		Set of 4	50	70	☐	☐
		First Day Cover	3·00		☐	
		Presentation Pack	2·25		☐	

298 'TUC' and Trades Unionists

299 Mrs Emmeline Pankhurst (statue)

300 Sopwith Camel and English Electric Lightning Fighters

301 Captain Cook's *Endeavour* and Signature

British Anniversaries. Events described on stamps

1968 (29 MAY) *Two phosphor bands*

767	**298**	4d multicoloured	10	10 ☐	☐
768	**299**	9d violet, grey and black	10	15 ☐	☐
769	**300**	1s multicoloured	15	25 ☐	☐
770	**301**	1s 9d ochre and brown . .	35	40 ☐	☐
		Set of 4	60	80 ☐	☐
		First Day Cover		5·50	☐
		Presentation Pack	2·50		☐

302 'Queen Elizabeth I' (Unknown Artist)

303 'Pinkie' (Lawrence)

304 'Ruins of St Mary Le Port' (Piper)

305 'The Hay Wain' (Constable)

British Paintings

1968 (12 AUG.) *Two phosphor bands*

771	**302**	4d multicoloured	10	10 ☐	☐
772	**303**	1s multicoloured	10	20 ☐	☐
773	**304**	1s 6d multicoloured	20	25 ☐	☐
774	**305**	1s 9d multicoloured	25	40 ☐	☐
		Set of 4	50	85 ☐	☐
		First Day Cover		3·00	☐
		Presentation Pack	2·50		☐
		Presentation Pack (German) . . .	7·00		☐

Gift Pack 1968

1968 (16 SEPT.) *Comprises Nos. 763/74*

	Gift Pack	8·00	☐
	Gift Pack (German)	22·00	☐

Collectors Pack 1968

1968 (16 SEPT.) *Comprises Nos. 752/8 and 763/74*

	Collectors Pack	9·00	☐

306 Girl and Boy with Rocking Horse

307 Girl with Doll's House

308 Boy with Train Set

Christmas

1968 (25 NOV.) *Two phosphor bands (except 4d, one centre phosphor band)*

775	**306**	4d multicoloured	10	10 ☐	☐
776	**307**	9d multicoloured	15	15 ☐	☐
777	**308**	1s 6d multicoloured	15	30 ☐	☐
		Set of 3	35	45 ☐	☐
		First Day Cover		2·50	☐
		Presentation Pack	3·00		☐
		Presentation Pack (German) . . .	7·00		☐

RMS Queen Elizabeth 2

309 *Queen Elizabeth 2*

310 Elizabethan Galleon

311 East Indiaman

312 *Cutty Sark*

SS Great Britain

313 *Great Britain*

RMS Mauretania

314 *Mauretania I*

The 9d and 1s values were arranged in horizontal strips of three and pairs respectively throughout the sheet.

British Ships

1969 (15 Jan.) *One horiz phosphor band* (5d), *two phosphor bands* (9d) *or two vert phosphor bands at right* (1s)

778	**309**	5d multicoloured	10	15	☐	☐
779	**310**	9d multicoloured	10	25	☐	☐
		a. Strip of 3. Nos. 779/81	1·50	3·00	☐	☐
780	**311**	9d multicoloured	10	25	☐	☐
781	**312**	9d multicoloured	10	25	☐	☐
782	**313**	1s multicoloured	40	35	☐	☐
		a. Pair. Nos. 782/3 . . .	1·25	2·50	☐	☐
783	**314**	1s multicoloured	40	35	☐	☐
	Set of 6	. . . .	2·50	1·40	☐	☐
	First Day Cover	. . . .		7·00		☐
	Presentation Pack	. . . .	4·00		☐	
	Presentation Pack (German) . . .	22·00		☐	

CONCORDE

4d

9d

315 Concorde in Flight   **316** Plan and Elevation Views

1/6

317 Concorde's Nose and Tail

First Flight of Concorde

1969 (3 Mar.) *Two phosphor bands*

784	**315**	4d multicoloured	10	10	☐	☐
785	**316**	9d multicoloured	15	25	☐	☐

786	**317**	1s 6d deep blue, grey and light blue	20	30	☐	☐
	Set of 3	. . . .	40	60	☐	☐
	First Day Cover	. . . .		3·00		☐
	Presentation Pack	. . . .	3·00		☐	
	Presentation Pack (German) . . .	20·00		☐	

£1

318 (See also Type **357**)

1969 (5 Mar.) *P* 12

787	**318**	2s 6d brown	35	30	☐	☐
788		5s lake	1·75	60	☐	☐
789		10s ultramarine	6·00	7·00	☐	☐
790		£1 black	3·25	1·50	☐	☐
	Set of 4	. . . .	10·00	8·50	☐	☐
	First Day Cover	. . . .		9·50		☐
	Presentation Pack	. . . .	16·00		☐	
	Presentation Pack (German) . . .	42·00		☐	

5d

9d

319 Page from the *Daily Mail,*   **320** Europa and C.E.P.T.
and Vickers FB-27 Vimy   Emblems
Aircraft

1/-   1/6

321 I.L.O. Emblem   **322** Flags of N.A.T.O. Countries

1/9

323 Vickers FB-27 Vimy Aircraft
and Globe showing Flight

Anniversaries. Events described on stamps

1969 (2 Apr.) *Two phosphor bands*

791	**319**	5d multicoloured	10	10	☐	☐
792	**320**	9d multicoloured	15	20	☐	☐

793	**321**	1s claret, red and blue .	15	20	☐	☐
794	**322**	1s 6d multicoloured	15	25	☐	☐
795	**323**	1s 9d olive, yellow and				
		turquoise-green . . .	20	35	☐	☐
		Set of 5	65	95	☐	☐
		First Day Cover		5·00		☐
		Presentation Pack	3·50		☐	
		Presentation Pack (*German*) . . .	42·00		☐	

324 Durham Cathedral   **325** York Minster

326 St Giles' Cathedral,   **327** Canterbury Cathedral
Edinburgh

The above were issued together *se-tenant* in blocks of four within
the sheet.

328 St Paul's Cathedral   **329** Liverpool Metropolitan
Cathedral

British Architecture (Cathedrals)
1969 (28 MAY) *Two phosphor bands*

796	**324**	5d multicoloured	10	20	☐	☐
		a. *Block of* 4. *Nos.* 796/9	75	2·50	☐	☐
797	**325**	5d multicoloured	10	20	☐	☐
798	**326**	5d multicoloured	10	20	☐	☐
799	**327**	5d multicoloured	10	20	☐	☐
800	**328**	9d multicoloured	15	25	☐	☐
801	**329**	1s 6d multicoloured	15	25	☐	☐
		Set of 6	95	1·10	☐	☐
		First Day Cover		5·00		☐
		Presentation Pack	3·25		☐	
		Presentation Pack (*German*) . . .	21·00		☐	

330 The King's Gate,   **331** The Eagle Tower,
Caernarvon Castle   Caernarvon Castle

332 Queen Eleanor's Gate,   **333** Celtic Cross,
Caernarvon Castle   Margam Abbey

The 5d values were printed *se-tenant* in strips of three throughout
the sheet

334 Prince Charles

Investiture of H.R.H. The Prince of Wales
1969 (1 JULY) *Two phosphor bands*

802	**330**	5d multicoloured	10	15	☐	☐
		a. *Strip of* 3. *Nos.* 802/4	30	1·50	☐	☐
803	**331**	5d multicoloured	10	15	☐	☐
804	**332**	5d multicoloured	10	15	☐	☐
805	**333**	9d multicoloured	15	20	☐	☐
806	**334**	1s black and gold	15	20	☐	☐
		Set of 5	50	60	☐	☐
		First Day Cover		2·50		☐
		Presentation Pack	2·50		☐	
		Presentation Pack (*German*) . . .	20·00		☐	

335 Mahatma Gandhi

Gandhi Centenary Year

1969 (13 Aug.) *Two phosphor bands*

807	335	1s 6d multicoloured	20	20	☐	☐
		First Day Cover		2·00		☐

Collectors Pack 1969

1969 (15 Sept.) *Comprises Nos. 775/86 and 791/807*

	Collectors Pack	20·00	☐

336 National Giro

337 Telecommunications —
International Subscriber
Dialling

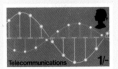

338 Telecommunications —
Pulse Code Modulation

339 Postal Mechanisation —
Automatic Sorting

British Post Office Technology

1969 (1 Oct.) *Two phosphor bands. Perf 13½ × 14*

808	336	5d multicoloured	10	10	☐	☐
809	337	9d green, blue and black	15	20	☐	☐
810	338	1s green, lavender and black	15	20	☐	☐
811	339	1s 6d multicoloured	15	35	☐	☐
		Set of 4	50	75	☐	☐
		First Day Cover		2·50		☐
		Presentation Pack	2·50		☐	

340 Herald Angel

341 The Three Shepherds

342 The Three Kings

Christmas

1969 (26 Nov.) *Two phosphor bands (5d, 1s 6d) or one centre band (4d)*

812	340	4d multicoloured	10	10	☐	☐
813	341	5d multicoloured	15	15	☐	☐
814	342	1s 6d multicoloured	20	30	☐	☐
		Set of 3	40	50	☐	☐
		First Day Cover		1·75		☐
		Presentation Pack	2·50		☐	

343 Fife Harling

344 Cotswold Limestone

345 Welsh Stucco

346 Ulster Thatch

British Rural Architecture

1970 (11 Feb.) *Two phosphor bands*

815	343	5d multicoloured	10	10	☐	☐
816	344	9d multicoloured	10	20	☐	☐
817	345	1s multicoloured	15	20	☐	☐
818	346	1s 6d multicoloured	20	30	☐	☐
		Set of 4	50	70	☐	☐
		First Day Cover		2·25		☐
		Presentation Pack	3·00		☐	

347 Signing the Declaration
of Arbroath

348 Florence Nightingale
attending Patients

349 Signing of International
Co-operative Alliance

350 Pilgrims and *Mayflower*

351 Sir William Herschel, Francis Baily, Sir John Herschel and Telescope

Anniversaries. Events described on stamps

1970 (1 Apr.) *Two phosphor bands*

819	**347**	5d multicoloured	10	10 ☐ ☐
820	**348**	9d multicoloured	15	15 ☐ ☐
821	**349**	1s multicoloured	20	25 ☐ ☐
822	**350**	1s 6d multicoloured	20	30 ☐ ☐
823	**351**	1s 9d multicoloured	25	30 ☐ ☐
		Set of 5	80	1·00 ☐ ☐
		First Day Cover		3·00 ☐
		Presentation Pack	3·00	☐

352	'Mr Pickwick and Sam' (*Pickwick Papers*)
353	'Mr and Mrs Micawber' (*David Copperfield*)
354	'David Copperfield and Betsy Trotwood' (*David Copperfield*)

355	'Oliver asking for more' (*Oliver Twist*)
356	'Grasmere' (from engraving by J. Farrington, R.A.)

The 5d values were issued together *se-tenant* in blocks of four within the sheet.

Literary Anniversaries. Events described on stamps

1970 (3 June) *Two phosphor bands*

824	**352**	5d multicoloured	10	15 ☐ ☐
		a. Block of 4. Nos. 824/7	75	2·00 ☐ ☐
825	**353**	5d multicoloured	10	15 ☐ ☐

826	**354**	5d multicoloured	10	15 ☐ ☐
827	**355**	5d multicoloured	10	15 ☐ ☐
828	**356**	1s 6d multicoloured	20	35 ☐ ☐
		Set of 5	85	85 ☐ ☐
		First Day Cover		3·75 ☐
		Presentation Pack	3·00	☐

356a

357 (Value redrawn)

Decimal Currency

1970 (17 June)–**72** *10p and some printings of the 50p were issued on phosphor paper.* Perf 12

829	**356a**	10p cerise	50	75 ☐ ☐
830		20p olive-green	60	25 ☐ ☐
831		50p ultramarine	1·25	40 ☐ ☐
831b	**357**	£1 black (6 Dec. 1972) .	3·50	80 ☐ ☐
		Set of 4	5·25	2·00 ☐ ☐
		First Day Cover (*Nos.* 829/31) . .		2·75 ☐
		First Day Cover (*No.* 831b)		3·00 ☐
		Presentation Pack (*P.O Pack No. 18*) (*Nos.* 829/31)	9·00	☐
		Presentation Pack (*P.O Pack No. 38*) (*Nos.* 830/1, 790 or 831b) . . .	10·00	☐

358	Runners
359	Swimmers

360 Cyclists

Ninth British Commonwealth Games, Edinburgh

1970 (15 July) *Two phosphor bands.* Perf 13½ × 14

832	**358**	5d pink, emerald, greenish yellow and yellow-green	10	10 ☐ ☐
833	**359**	1s 6d greenish blue, lilac, brown and Prussian blue	25	35 ☐ ☐

| 834 | 360 | 1s 9d yellow-orange, lilac, salmon and red-brown | .... | 30 | 35 □ □ |

834	360	1s 9d yellow-orange, lilac,			
		salmon and red-			
		brown		30	35 □ □
		Set of 3		60	70 □ □
		First Day Cover			1·50 □
		Presentation Pack		3·00	□

Collectors Pack 1970

1970 (14 SEPT.) *Comprises Nos.* 808/28 *and* 832/4

   Collectors Pack .... 20·00 □

361	1d Black (1840)	362	1s Green (1847)	363	4d Carmine (1855)

'Philympia 70' Stamp Exhibition

1970 (18 SEPT.) *Two phosphor bands. Perf* 14 × 14½

835	361	5d multicoloured	10	10 □ □
836	362	9d multicoloured	20	30 □ □
837	363	1s 6d multicoloured	20	45 □ □
		Set of 3	45	80 □ □
		First Day Cover		2·00 □
		Presentation Pack	2·75	□

364	Shepherds and Apparition of the Angel	365	Mary, Joseph and Christ in the Manger

366	The Wise Men bearing Gifts

Christmas

1970 (25 Nov.) *Two phosphor bands* (5d, 1s 6d) *or one centre phosphor band* (4d)

838	364	4d multicoloured	10	10 □ □
839	365	5d multicoloured	10	15 □ □
840	366	1s 6d multicoloured	20	30 □ □
		Set of 3	35	50 □ □
		First Day Cover		2·25 □
		Presentation Pack	2·75	□

PRINTING PROCESSES

There is a basic distinction between stamps printed by photogravure and those printed by lithography. Sorting the two is not as difficult as it sounds and with a little experience it should become easy to tell which method of production was employed for a particular stamp.

The tiny dots of the printing screen give uneven edges to the values on photogravure stamps (right). Litho values have clean, clear outlines (left).

All you need is a reasonably good glass giving a magnification of ×4 or more (×10 is even better!).

The image on a photogravure stamp is created from a pattern or 'screen', of minute dots which are not evident when looking at the stamp without a glass but show up quite clearly under magnification, especially in the Queen's face and around the margin of the stamp design where it meets the white background of the paper. Now look at the value; here also, what looks to the naked eye like a straight line is in fact made up of rows of tiny little dots.

'Screens' of dots are also used in the production of litho printed stamps but they are only required where the printer is attempting to produce shades and tints as is necessary in the Queen's head portion of the stamp. Where solid colour is used, as in the background of the majority of values, there is no need to resort to a screen of dots and the background is printed as a solid mass of colour. If you look at the margins or the values of stamps produced in this way you will not see any evidence of dots—just a clear clean break between the inked portion of the stamp and the uninked white of the paper.

367    **367a**

Decimal Currency
1971–96. *Type 367*

(a) Printed in photogravure by Harrison and Sons (except for some ptgs of Nos. X879 and X913 which were produced by Enschedé) with phosphor bands. Perf 15 × 14

X841	½p turquoise-blue (2 bands)	10	10	☐	☐
X842	½p turquoise-blue (1 side band)	48·00	30·00	☐	☐
X843	½p turquoise-blue (1 centre band)	40	25	☐	☐
X844	1p crimson (2 bands) . . .	10	15	☐	☐
X845	1p crimson (1 centre band)	25	20	☐	☐
X846	1p crimson ('all-over' phosphor)	15	25	☐	☐
X847	1p crimson (1 side band) .	80	1·25	☐	☐
X848	1½p black (2 bands) . . .	15	25	☐	☐
X849	2p myrtle-green (face value as in T **367**) (2 bands) .	15	20	☐	☐
X850	2p myrtle-green (face value as in T **367**) ('all-over' phosphor)	25	30	☐	☐
X851	2½p magenta (1 centre band)	20	15	☐	☐
X852	2½p magenta (1 side band) .	90	1·75	☐	☐
X853	2½p magenta (2 bands) . . .	25	50	☐	☐
X854	2½p rose-red (2 bands) . .	40	60	☐	☐
X855	3p ultramarine (2 bands) .	20	25	☐	☐
X856	3p ultramarine (1 centre band)	15	20	☐	☐
X857	3p bright magenta (2 bands)	35	35	☐	☐
X858	3½p olive-grey (2 bands) . .	25	30	☐	☐
X859	3½p olive-grey (1 centre band)	30	35	☐	☐
X860	3½p purple-brown (1 centre band)	1·10	1·25	☐	☐
X861	4p ochre-brown (2 bands)	20	25	☐	☐
X862	4p greenish blue (2 bands)	1·75	2·00	☐	☐
X863	4p greenish blue (1 centre band)	1·50	1·90	☐	☐
X864	4p greenish blue (1 side band)	1·75	1·75	☐	☐
X865	4½p grey-blue (2 bands) . .	25	30	☐	☐
X866	5p pale violet (2 bands) . .	20	20	☐	☐
X867	5p claret (1 centre band) .	1·75	2·00	☐	☐
X868	5½p violet (2 bands)	25	30	☐	☐
X869	5½p violet (1 centre band) .	25	30	☐	☐
X870	6p light emerald (2 bands)	25	20	☐	☐
X871	6½p greenish blue (2 bands)	30	35	☐	☐
X872	6½p greenish blue (1 centre band)	25	20	☐	☐
X873	6½p greenish blue (1 side band)	70	75	☐	☐
X874	7p purple-brown (2 bands)	30	35	☐	☐
X875	7p purple-brown (1 centre band)	25	30	☐	☐
X876	7p purple-brown (1 side band)	50	50	☐	☐
X877	7½p chestnut (2 bands) . . .	25	35	☐	☐
X878	8p rosine (2 bands)	25	30	☐	☐
X879	8p rosine (1 centre band) .	25	30	☐	☐
X880	8p rosine (1 side band) . .	60	75	☐	☐
X881	8½p yellowish green (2 bands)	30	25	☐	☐
X882	9p yellow-orange and black (2 bands)	45	55	☐	☐
X883	9p deep violet (2 bands) .	35	25	☐	☐
X884	9½p purple (2 bands)	35	45	☐	☐
X885	10p orange-brown and chestnut (2 bands) . . .	35	30	☐	☐
X886	10p orange-brown (2 bands)	35	25	☐	☐
X887	10p orange-brown ('all-over' phosphor)	35	45	☐	☐
X888	10p orange-brown (1 centre band)	35	25	☐	☐
X889	10p orange-brown (1 side band)	70	80	☐	☐
X890	10½p yellow (2 bands)	40	45	☐	☐
X891	10½p blue (2 bands)	45	50	☐	☐
X892	11p brown-red (2 bands) .	40	30	☐	☐
X893	11½p drab (1 centre band) . .	40	35	☐	☐
X894	11½p drab (1 side band) . . .	55	70	☐	☐
X895	12p yellowish green (2 bands)	45	45	☐	☐
X896	12p bright emerald (1 centre band)	45	45	☐	☐
X897	12p bright emerald (1 side band)	80	85	☐	☐
X898	12½p light emerald (1 centre band)	45	40	☐	☐
X899	12½p light emerald (1 side band)	70	75	☐	☐
X900	13p pale chestnut (1 centre band)	40	40	☐	☐
X901	13p pale chestnut (1 side band)	50	60	☐	☐
X902	14p grey-blue (2 bands) . .	75	80	☐	☐
X903	14p deep blue (1 centre band)	40	50	☐	☐
X904	14p deep blue (1 side band)	4·00	4·00	☐	☐
X905	15p bright blue (1 centre band)	65	65	☐	☐
X906	15p bright blue (1 side band)	3·00	3·00	☐	☐
X907	15½p pale violet (2 bands) . .	60	65	☐	☐
X908	16p olive-drab (2 bands) . .	1·25	1·40	☐	☐
X909	17p grey-blue (2 bands) . .	60	60	☐	☐
X910	17p deep blue (1 centre band)	80	85	☐	☐
X911Ea	17p deep blue (1 side band)	1·25	1·25	☐	☐
X912	18p deep olive-grey (2 bands	70	80	☐	☐
X913	18p bright green (1 centre band)	60	50	☐	☐

34

X914	19p bright orange-red (2 bands)	1·40	1·50	☐ ☐
X915	20p dull purple (2 bands) .	75	35	☐ ☐
X916	20p brownish black (2 bands)	1·40	1·60	☐ ☐
X917	22p bright orange-red (2 bands)	1·25	1·25	☐ ☐
X917a	25p rose-red (2 bands)	5·50	5·50	☐ ☐
X918	26p rosine (2 bands)	7·00	7·50	☐ ☐
X919	31p purple (2 bands)	14·00	14·00	☐ ☐
X920	34p ochre-brown (2 bands)	7·00	7·50	☐ ☐
X921	50p ochre-brown (2 bands)	2·00	60	☐ ☐
X922	50p ochre (2 bands)	4·50	4·50	☐ ☐

(b) *Printed in photogravure by Harrison and Sons on phosphorised paper. Perf 15 × 14*

X924	½p turquoise-blue	10	15	☐ ☐
X925	1p crimson	10	15	☐ ☐
X926	2p myrtle-green (face value as in T **367**)	15	20	☐ ☐
X927	2p deep green (smaller value as in T **367a**)	15	20	☐ ☐
X928	2p myrtle-green (smaller value as in T **367a**)	2·75	2·75	☐ ☐
X929	2½p rose-red	15	20	☐ ☐
X930	3p bright magenta	20	25	☐ ☐
X931	3½p purple-brown	50	60	☐ ☐
X932	4p greenish blue	25	40	☐ ☐
X933	4p new blue	20	25	☐ ☐
X934	5p pale violet	30	35	☐ ☐
X935	5p dull red-brown	25	30	☐ ☐
X936	6p yellow-olive	30	30	☐ ☐
X937	7p brownish red	1·10	1·25	☐ ☐
X938	8½p yellowish green	40	50	☐ ☐
X939	10p orange-brown	35	35	☐ ☐
X940	10p dull orange	40	35	☐ ☐
X941	11p brown-red	70	80	☐ ☐
X942	11½p ochre-brown	55	55	☐ ☐
X943	12p yellowish green	45	45	☐ ☐
X944	13p olive-grey	45	50	☐ ☐
X945	13½p purple-brown	60	60	☐ ☐
X946	14p grey-blue	50	50	☐ ☐
X947	15p ultramarine	60	60	☐ ☐
X948	15½p pale violet	60	50	☐ ☐
X949	16p olive-drab	55	55	☐ ☐
X950	16½p pale chestnut	80	75	☐ ☐
X951	17p light emerald	60	60	☐ ☐
X952	17p grey-blue	60	60	☐ ☐
X953	17½p pale chestnut	70	75	☐ ☐
X954	18p deep violet	70	70	☐ ☐
X955	18p deep olive-grey	75	60	☐ ☐
X956	19p bright orange-red	80	60	☐ ☐
X957	19½p olive-grey	1·50	1·50	☐ ☐
X958	20p dull purple	75	50	☐ ☐
X959	20p turquoise-green	75	70	☐ ☐
X960	20p brownish black	1·00	1·00	☐ ☐
X961	20½p ultramarine	1·00	1·00	☐ ☐
X962	22p blue	90	75	☐ ☐
X963	22p yellow-green	90	80	☐ ☐
X964	22p bright orange-red	90	80	☐ ☐
X965	23p brown-red	1·10	80	☐ ☐
X966	23p bright green	90	90	☐ ☐
X967	24p violet	1·40	1·50	☐ ☐
X968	24p Indian red	2·00	1·60	☐ ☐
X969	24p chestnut	70	75	☐ ☐
X970	25p purple	90	1·00	☐ ☐
X971	26p rosine	1·10	60	☐ ☐
X972	26p drab	1·50	1·25	☐ ☐
X973	27p chestnut	1·25	1·25	☐ ☐
X974	27p violet	1·50	1·25	☐ ☐
X975	28p deep violet	1·25	1·25	☐ ☐
X976	28p ochre	1·40	1·25	☐ ☐
X977	28p deep bluish grey	1·40	1·25	☐ ☐
X978	29p ochre-brown	1·75	1·75	☐ ☐
X979	29p deep mauve	1·75	1·75	☐ ☐
X980	30p deep olive-grey	1·25	1·25	☐ ☐
X981	31p purple	1·25	1·25	☐ ☐
X982	31p ultramarine	1·60	1·50	☐ ☐
X983	32p greenish blue	1·90	1·75	☐ ☐
X984	33p light emerald	1·75	1·60	☐ ☐
X985	34p ochre-brown	1·75	1·75	☐ ☐
X986	34p deep bluish grey	2·00	1·90	☐ ☐
X987	34p deep mauve	1·75	1·75	☐ ☐
X988	35p sepia	1·60	1·60	☐ ☐
X989	35p yellow	1·75	1·60	☐ ☐
X990	37p rosine	2·00	1·75	☐ ☐
X991	39p bright mauve	1·60	1·50	☐ ☐

(c) *Printed in photogravure by Harrison and Sons on ordinary paper. Perf 15 × 14*

X992	50p ochre-brown	1·60	70	☐ ☐
X993	75p grey-black (smaller values as in T **367a**)	2·50	1·50	☐ ☐

(d) *Printed in photogravure by Harrison and Sons on ordinary paper or phosphorised paper. Perf 15 × 14*

X994	50p ochre	1·75	70	☐ ☐

(e) *Printed in lithography by John Waddington. Perf 14*

X996	4p greenish blue (2 bands)	25	35	☐ ☐
X997	4p greenish blue (phosphorised paper)	35	40	☐ ☐
X998	20p dull purple (2 bands)	1·25	1·00	☐ ☐
X999	20p dull purple (phosphorised paper)	1·75	1·10	☐ ☐

(f) *Printed in lithography by Questa. Perf 14 (Nos X1000, X1003/4 and X1023) or 15 × 14 (others)*

X1000	2p emerald-green (face value as in T **367**) (phosphorised paper)	20	25	☐ ☐
	a. *Perf 15 × 14*	35	35	☐ ☐
X1001	2p bright green and deep green (smaller value as in T **367a**) (phosphorised paper)	75	70	☐ ☐
X1002	4p greenish blue (phosphorised paper)	70	75	☐ ☐

X1003	5p light violet (phosphorised paper) .	40	40	□	□
X1004	5p claret (phosphorised paper)	50	50	□	□
	a. Perf 15 × 14	65	60	□	□
X1005	13p pale chestnut (1 centre band)	70	75	□	□
X1006	13p pale chestnut (1 side band)	75	75	□	□
X1007	14p deep blue (1 centre band)	1·75	1·75	□	□
X1008	17p deep blue (1 centre band)	80	80	□	□
X1009	18p deep olive-grey (phosphorised paper) .	90	95	□	□
X1010	18p deep olive-grey (2 bands)	7·00	7·00	□	□
X1011	18p bright green (1 centre band)	75	75	□	□
X1012	18p bright green (1 side band)	1·25	1·40	□	□
X1013	19p bright orange-red (phosphorised paper) .	1·90	2·00	□	□
X1014	20p dull purple (phosphorised paper) .	1·40	1·40	□	□
X1015	22p yellow-green (2 bands)	9·00	9·00	□	□
X1016	22p bright orange-red (phosphorised paper) .	80	90	□	□
X1017	24p chestnut (phosphorised paper)	90	1·10	□	□
X1018	24p chestnut (2 bands) . . .	1·25	1·40	□	□
X1019	33p light emerald (phosphorised paper) .	2·50	2·50	□	□
X1020	33p light emerald (2 bands)	1·25	1·50	□	□
X1021	34p bistre-brown (2 bands)	7·50	7·50	□	□
X1022	39p bright mauve (2 bands)	1·50	1·60	□	□
X1023	75p black (face value as T **367**) (ordinary paper)	2·75	95	□	□
	a. Perf 15 × 14	3·25	1·60	□	□
X1024	75p brownish grey and black (smaller value as T **367a**) (ordinary paper)	9·00	8·50	□	□

(g) Printed in lithography by Walsall. Perf 14

X1050	2p deep green (phosphorised paper) .	1·00	1·10	□	□
X1051	14p deep blue (1 side band)	4·50	4·50	□	□
X1052	19p bright orange-red (2 bands)	3·00	3·00	□	□
X1053	24p chestnut (phosphorised paper)	1·10	1·25	□	□
X1054	29p deep mauve (2 bands) .	2·75	3·00	□	□
X1055	29p deep mauve (phosphorised paper) .	4·50	4·50	□	□
X1056	31p ultramarine (phosphorised paper) .	1·40	1·40	□	□
X1057	33p light emerald (phosphorised paper) .	1·25	1·25	□	□
X1058	39p bright mauve (phosphorised paper) .	1·60	1·60	□	□

Presentation Pack (P.O. Pack No. 26) (*contains* ½p (X841), 1p (X844), 1½p (X848), 2p (X849), 2½p (X851), 3p (X855), 3½p (X858), 4p (X861), 5p (X866), 6p (X870), 7½p (X877), 9p (X882)) . . . . **5·00** □

Presentation Pack ('Scandinavia 71') (contents as above) . . . . **30·00** □

Presentation Pack (P.O. Pack No. 37) (*contains* ½p (X841), 1p (X844), 1½p (X848), 2p (X849), 2½p (X851), 3p (X855 *or* X856), 3½p (X858 *or* X859), 4p (X861), 4½p (X865), 5p (X866), 5½p (X868 *or* X869), 6p (X870), 6½p (X871 *or* X872), 7p (X874), 7½p (X877), 8p (X878), 9p (X882), 10p (X885)) . . . **5·00** □

Presentation Pack (P.O. Pack No. 90) (*contains* ½p (X841), 1p (X844), 1½p (X848), 2p (X849), 2½p (X851), 3p (X856), 5p (X866), 6½p (X872), 7p (X874 *or* X875), 7½p (X877), 8p (X878), 8½p (X881), 9p (X883), 9½p (X884), 10p (X886), 10½p (X890), 11p (X892), 20p (X915), 50p (X921)) . . . **6·00** □

Presentation Pack (P.O. Pack No. 129a) (*contains* 2½p (X929), 3p (X930), 4p (X996), 10½p (X891), 11½p (X893), 11½p (X942), 12p (X943), 13p (X944), 13½p (X945), 14p (X946), 15p (X947), 15½p (X948), 17p (X951), 17½p (X953), 18p (X954), 22p (X962), 25p (X970), 75p (X1023)) . . . . **18·00** □

Presentation Pack (P.O. Pack No. 1) (*contains* ½p (X924), 1p (X925), 2p (X1000), 3p (X930), 3½p (X931), 4p (X997), 5p (X1004), 10p (X888), 12½p (X898), 16p (X949), 16½p (X950), 17p (X952), 20p (X999), 20½p (X961), 23p (X965), 26p (X971), 28p (X975), 31p (X981), 50p (X992), 75p (X1023)) . . **30·00** □

Presentation Pack (P.O. Pack No. 5) (*contains* ½p (X924), 1p (X925), 2p (X1000a), 3p (X930), 4p (X997), 5p (X1004a), 10p (X939), 13p (X900), 16p (X949), 17p (X952), 18p (X955), 20p (X999), 22p (X963), 24p (X967), 26p (X971), 28p (X975), 31p (X981), 34p (X985), 50p (X992), 75p (X1023a)) **28·00** □

Presentation Pack (P.O. Pack No. 9)
(contains 1p (X925), 2p (X1000a), 3p
(X930), 4p (X997), 5p (X1004a), 7p
(X937), 10p (X939), 12p (X896), 13p
(X900), 17p (X952), 18p (X955), 20p
(X999), 22p (X963), 24p (X967), 26p
(X971), 28p (X975), 31p (X981), 34p
(X985), 50p (X992), 75p (X1023a))   26·00   □

Presentation Pack (P.O. Pack No. 15)
(contains 14p (X903), 19p (X956),
20p (X959), 23p (X966), 27p (X973),
28p (X976), 32p (X983), 35p (X988))   11·00   □

Presentation Pack (P.O. Pack No. 19)
(contains 15p (X905), 20p (X960),
24p (X968), 29p (X979), 30p (X980),
34p (X986), 37p (X990)) . . . . . .   10·00   □

Presentation Pack (P.O. Pack No. 22)
(contains 10p (X940), 17p (X910),
22p (X964), 26p (X972), 27p (X974),
31p (X982), 33p (X984)) . . . . . .   9·00   □

Presentation Pack (P.O. Pack No. 24)
(contains 1p (X925), 2p (X927), 3p
(X930), 4p (X933), 5p (X935), 10p
(X940), 17p (X910), 20p (X959), 22p
(X964), 26p (X972), 27p (X974), 30p
(X980), 31p (X982), 32p (X983), 33p
(X984), 37p (X990), 50p (X994), 75p
(X993)) . . . .   21·00   □

Presentation Pack (P.O. Pack No. 25)
(contains 6p (X936), 18p (X913), 24p
(X969), 28p (X977), 34p (X987), 35p
(X989), 39p (X991)) . . . .   9·00   □

First Day Covers

15 Feb. 1971   ½p, 1p, 1½p, 2p, 2½p, 3p, 3½p, 4p,
5p, 6p, 7½p, 9p (Nos. X841, X844,
X848/9, X851, X855, X858, X861,
X866, X870, X877, X882) (Covers
carry 'POSTING DELAYED BY
THE POST OFFICE STRIKE
1971' cachet) . . . .   3·50   □

11 Aug. 1971   10p (No. X885) . . . .   2·25   □

24 Oct. 1973   4½p, 5½p, 8p (Nos. X865, X868,
X878) . . . .   2·00   □

4 Sept. 1974   6½p (No. X871) . . . .   3·00   □

15 Jan. 1975   7p (No. X874) . . . .   2·00   □

24 Sept. 1975   8½p (No. X881) . . . .   2·00   □

25 Feb. 1976   9p, 9½p, 10p, 10½p, 11p, 20p (Nos.
X883/4, X886, X890, X892,
X915) . . . .   3·00   □

2 Feb. 1977   50p (No. X921) . . . .   2·00   □

26 April 1978   10½p (No. X891) . . . .   2·00   □

15 Aug. 1979   11½p, 13p, 15p (Nos. X942, X944,
X947) . . . .   2·25   □

30 Jan. 1980   4p, 12p, 13½p, 17p, 17½p, 75p
(Nos. X996, X943, X945, X951,
X953, X1023) . . . .   3·25   □

22 Oct. 1980   3p, 22p (Nos. X930, X962) . . .   2·00   □

14 Jan. 1981   2½p, 11½p, 14p, 15½p, 18p, 25p
(Nos. X929, X893, X946, X948,
X954, X970) . . . .   2·25   □

27 Jan. 1982   5p, 12½p, 16½p, 19½p, 26p, 29p
(Nos. X1004, X898, X950, X957,
X971, X978) . . . .   4·00   □

30 Mar. 1983   3½p, 16p, 17p, 20½p, 23p, 28p, 31p
(Nos. X931, X949, X952, X961,
X965, X975, X981) . . . .   5·00   □

28 Aug. 1984   13p, 18p, 22p, 24p, 34p (Nos.
X900, X955, X963, X967, X985)   3·00   □

29 Oct. 1985   7p, 12p (Nos. X937, X896) . . .   7·00   □

23 Aug. 1988   14p, 19p, 20p, 23p, 27p, 28p, 32p,
35p (Nos. X903, X956, X959,
X966, X973, X976, X983, X988)   6·00   □

26 Sept. 1989   15p, 20p, 24p, 29p, 30p, 34p, 37p
(Nos. X905, X960, X968, X979/80,
X986, X990) . . . .   5·50   □

4 Sept. 1990   10p, 17p, 22p, 26p, 27p, 31p, 33p
(Nos. X940, X910, X964, X972,
X974, X982, X984) . . . .   5·50   □

10 Sept. 1991   6p, 18p, 24p, 28p, 34p, 35p, 39p
(Nos. X936, X913, X969, X977,
X987, X989, X991) . . . .   6·00   □

For similar stamps, but with elliptical perforations see Nos.
Y1667/1803 in 1993.

PHOSPHOR BANDS. See notes on page 15.
Phosphor bands are applied to the stamps, after the design has
been printed, by a separate cylinder. On issues with 'all-over'
phosphor the 'band' covers the entire stamp. Parts of the
stamp covered by phosphor bands, or the entire surface for
'all-over' phosphor versions, appear matt.

Nos. X847, X852, X864, X873, X876, X880, X889, X894, X897,
X899, X901, X906, X911, X1006 and X1012 exist with the
phosphor band at the left or right of the stamp.

PHOSPHORISED PAPER. First introduced as an experiment for
a limited printing of the 1s 6d value (No. 743c) in 1969, this
paper has the phosphor, to activate the automatic sorting
machinery, added to the paper coating before the stamps were
printed. Issues on this paper have a completely shiny surface.
Although not adopted after this first trial further experiments
on the 8½p in 1976 led to this paper being used for new
printings of current values.

368 'A Mountain Road' (T. P. Flanagan)

369 'Deer's Meadow' (Tom Carr)

370 'Slieve na brock' (Colin Middleton)

'Ulster '71' Paintings

1971 (16 JUNE) *Two phosphor bands*

881	**368**	3p multicoloured	10	10 ☐	☐
882	**369**	7½p multicoloured	35	45 ☐	☐
883	**370**	9p multicoloured	40	45 ☐	☐
		Set of 3	75	90 ☐	☐
		First Day Cover		2·50	☐
		Presentation Pack	5·00		☐

374 Servicemen and Nurse of 1921

375 Roman Centurion

376 Rugby Football, 1871

British Anniversaries. Events described on stamps

1971 (25 AUG.) *Two phosphor bands*

887	**374**	3p multicoloured	10	10 ☐	☐
888	**375**	7½p multicoloured	40	45 ☐	☐
889	**376**	9p multicoloured	40	45 ☐	☐
		Set of 3	80	90 ☐	☐
		First Day Cover		2·50	☐
		Presentation Pack	5·00		☐

371 John Keats (150th Death Anniv)

372 Thomas Gray (Death Bicentenary)

373 Sir Walter Scott (Birth Bicentenary)

Literary Anniversaries. Events described above

1971 (28 JULY) *Two phosphor bands*

884	**371**	3p black, gold and blue . .	10	10 ☐	☐
885	**372**	5p black, gold and olive .	35	40 ☐	☐
886	**373**	7½p black, gold and brown	35	45 ☐	☐
		Set of 3	70	85 ☐	☐
		First Day Cover		3·25	☐
		Presentation Pack	5·00		☐

377 Physical Sciences Building, University College of Wales, Aberystwyth

378 Faraday Building, Southampton University

379 Engineering Department, Leicester University

380 Hexagon Restaurant, Essex University

British Architecture (Modern University Buildings)

1971 (22 SEPT.) *Two phosphor bands*

890	**377**	3p multicoloured	10	10 ☐	☐
891	**378**	5p multicoloured	25	20 ☐	☐

892	379	7½p ochre, black and

892 **379** 7½p ochre, black and
purple-brown . . . . . 45 55 □ □
893 **380** 9p multicoloured . . . . 75 80 □ □
Set of 4 . . . . 1·40 1·50 □ □
First Day Cover . . . . 2·75 □
Presentation Pack . . . . 5·50 □

Collectors Pack 1971

1971 (29 SEPT.) *Comprises Nos. 835/40 and 881/93*
Collectors Pack . . . . 27·00 □

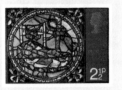

381 Dream of the Wise Men

382 Adoration of the Magi

383 Ride of the Magi

Christmas

1971 (13 OCT.) *Two phosphor bands (3p, 7½p) or one centre phosphor band (2½p)*
894 **381** 2½p multicoloured . . . . . 10 10 □ □
895 **382** 3p multicoloured . . . . . 10 10 □ □
896 **383** 7½p multicoloured . . . . . 55 75 □ □
Set of 3 . . . . 65 85 □ □
First Day Cover . . . . 2·75 □
Presentation Pack . . . . 4·50 □

384 Sir James Clark Ross

385 Sir Martin Frobisher

386 Henry Hudson   **387** Capt. Robert F. Scott

British Polar Explorers

1972 (16 FEB.) *Two phosphoured*
897 **384** 3p multicoloured . . . . . 10 10 □ □
898 **385** 5p multicoloured . . . . . 15 15 □ □
899 **386** 7½p multicoloured . . . . . 45 40 □ □
900 **387** 9p multicoloured . . . . . 70 75 □ □
Set of 4 . . . . 1·25 1·25 □ □
First Day Cover . . . . 3·50 □
Presentation Pack . . . . 4·75 □

388 Statuette of Tutankhamun   **389** 19th-century Coastguard

390 Ralph Vaughan Williams
and Score

Anniversaries. Events described on stamps

1972 (26 APR.) *Two phosphor bands*
901 **388** 3p multicoloured . . . . . 10 10 □ □
902 **389** 7½p multicoloured . . . . . 25 40 □ □
903 **390** 9p multicoloured . . . . . 35 45 □ □
Set of 3 . . . . 65 85 □ □
First Day Cover . . . . 3·00 □
Presentation Pack . . . . 4·25 □

For full information on all future British issues, collectors should write to Royal Mail, Freepost EH3647, 21 South Gyle Crescent, Edinburgh EH12 9PE.

391 St Andrew's, Greensted- juxta-Ongar, Essex

392 All Saints, Earls Barton, Northants

393 St Andrew's, Letheringsett, Norfolk

394 St Andrew's, Helpringham, Lincs

395 St Mary the Virgin, Huish Episcopi, Somerset

British Architecture (Village Churches)

1972 (21 JUNE) *Two phosphor bands*

904	391	3p multicoloured	. . . . .	10	10 ☐	☐
905	392	4p multicoloured	. . . . .	10	20 ☐	☐
906	393	5p multicoloured	. . . . .	15	20 ☐	☐
907	394	7½p multicoloured	. . . . .	60	75 ☐	☐
908	395	9p multicoloured	. . . . .	60	80 ☐	☐
		Set of 5	. . . .	1·40	1·90 ☐	☐
		First Day Cover	. . . .		3·75	☐
		Presentation Pack	. . . .	6·00		☐

'Belgica '72' Souvenir Pack

1972 (24 JUNE) *Comprises Nos. 894/6 and 904/8*

	Souvenir Pack	. . . .	12·00		☐

396 Microphones, 1924–69

397 Horn Loudspeaker

398 TV Camera, 1972

399 Oscillator and Spark Transmitter, 1897

Broadcasting Anniversaries. Events described on stamps

1972 (13 SEPT.) *Two phosphor bands*

909	396	3p multicoloured	. . . . .	10	10 ☐	☐
910	397	5p multicoloured	. . . . .	10	20 ☐	☐
911	398	7½p multicoloured	. . . . .	45	55 ☐	☐
912	399	9p multicoloured	. . . . .	50	65 ☐	☐
		Set of 4	. . . .	1·00	1·40 ☐	☐
		First Day Cover	. . . .		3·75	☐
		Presentation Pack	. . . .	3·75		☐

400 Angel holding Trumpet

401 Angel playing Lute

402 Angel playing Harp

Christmas

1972 (18 Oct.) *Two phosphor bands (3p, 7½p) or one centre phosphor band (2½p)*

913	400	2½p multicoloured	. . . .	10	10 □ □
914	401	3p multicoloured	. . . .	10	10 □ □
915	402	7½p multicoloured	. . . .	50	75 □ □
		Set of 3	. . . .	60	85 □ □
		First Day Cover			2·50 □
		Presentation Pack	. . . .	3·00	□

403 Queen Elizabeth II and Prince Philip   **404** Europe

Royal Silver Wedding

1972 (20 Nov.) *3p 'all-over' phosphor, 20p without phosphor*

916	403	3p brownish black, deep blue and silver	15	15 □ □
917		20p brownish black, reddish purple and silver	65	70 □ □
		Set of 2	80	80 □ □
		First Day Cover		2·25 □
		Presentation Pack	3·00	□
		Presentation Pack (*Japanese*) . .	7·00	□
		Souvenir Book	6·00	□
		Gutter Pair (3p)	80	□
		Traffic Light Gutter Pair (3p) . . .	14·00	□

Collectors Pack 1972

1972 (20 Nov.) *Comprises Nos. 897/918*

	Collectors Pack	27·00	□

Nos. 920/1 were issued horizontally *se-tenant* throughout the sheet.

Britain's Entry into European Communities

1973 (3 Jan.) *Two phosphor bands*

919	404	3p multicoloured	10	15 □ □
920		5p multicoloured (blue jigsaw)	25	40 □ □
		a. Pair. Nos. 920/1	80	1·40 □ □
921		5p multicoloured (green jigsaw)	25	40 □ □
		Set of 3	80	85 □ □
		First Day Cover		2·00 □
		Presentation Pack	2·50	□

405 Oak Tree

British Trees (1st Issue)

1973 (28 Feb.) *Two phosphor bands*

922	405	9p multicoloured	35	40 □ □
		First Day Cover		2·50 □
		Presentation Pack	2·25	□

See also No. 949

406 David Livingstone   **407** H. M. Stanley

The above were issued horizontally *se-tenant* throughout the sheet.

408 Sir Francis Drake   **409** Sir Walter Raleigh

410 Charles Sturt

British Explorers

1973 (18 Apr.) *'All-over' phosphor*

923	406	3p multicoloured	20	15 □ □
		a. Pair. Nos. 923/4	80	1·00 □ □

924	407	3p multicoloured	. . . .	20	15	☐ ☐
925	408	5p multicoloured	. . . .	20	35	☐ ☐
926	409	7½p multicoloured	. . . .	20	45	☐ ☐
927	410	9p multicoloured	. . . .	20	50	☐ ☐
		Set of 5		1·25	1·50	☐ ☐
		First Day Cover			3·50	☐
		Presentation Pack		3·50		☐

411

412

413

County Cricket 1873–1973

1973 (16 May) *Designs show sketches of W. G. Grace by Harry Furniss. Queen's head in gold. 'All-over' phosphor*

928	411	3p black and brown	. . . .	10	10	☐ ☐
929	412	7½p black and green	. . . .	55	75	☐ ☐
930	413	9p black and blue	. . . .	75	90	☐ ☐
		Set of 3		1·25	1·60	☐ ☐
		First Day Cover			3·50	☐
		Presentation Pack		3·50		☐
		Souvenir Book		10·00		☐
		PHQ Card (No. 928)		65·00	£225	☐ ☐

The PHQ Card did not become available until mid-July. The used price quoted is for an example used in July or August 1973.

414 'Self-portrait' (Sir Joshua Reynolds)

415 'Self-portrait' (Sir Henry Raeburn)

416 'Nelly O'Brien' (Sir Joshua Reynolds)

417 'Rev R. Walker (The Skater)' (Sir Henry Raeburn)

Artistic Anniversaries. Events described on stamps

1973 (4 July) *'All-over' phosphor*

931	414	3p multicoloured	. . . .	10	10	☐ ☐
932	415	5p multicoloured	. . . .	10	20	☐ ☐
933	416	7½p multicoloured	. . . .	40	45	☐ ☐
934	417	9p multicoloured	. . . .	50	55	☐ ☐
		Set of 4		1·00	1·25	☐ ☐
		First Day Cover			2·25	☐
		Presentation Pack		3·00		☐

418 Court Masque Costumes

419 St Paul's Church, Covent Garden

420 Prince's Lodging, Newmarket

421 Court Masque Stage Scene

The 3p and 5p values were printed horizontally *se-tenant* within the sheet.

400th Anniversary of the Birth of Inigo Jones

1973 (15 Aug.) *'All-over' phosphor*

935	418	3p deep mauve, black and gold		10	10	☐ ☐
		a. Pair. Nos. 935/6		30	40	☐ ☐
936	419	3p deep brown, black and gold		10	10	☐ ☐

937	**420**	5p blue, black and gold . .	35	40	□	□
		a. *Pair. Nos. 937/8*	1·00	1·25	□	□
938	**421**	5p grey-olive, black and gold	35	40	□	□
		Set of 4	1·25	90	□	□
		First Day Cover		2·25		□
		Presentation Pack	3·50		□	
		PHQ Card (No. 936)	£150	£150	□	□

422	Palace of Westminster seen from Whitehall	**423** Palace of Westminster seen from Millbank

19th Commonwealth Parliamentary Conference

1973 (12 SEPT.) *'All-over' phosphor*

939	**422**	8p black, grey and pale buff	45	50	□	□
940	**423**	10p gold and black	45	40	□	□
		Set of 2	90	90	□	□
		First Day Cover		2·00		□
		Presentation Pack	3·00		□	
		Souvenir Book	6·00		□	
		PHQ Card (No. 939)	40·00	£150	□	□

424	Princess Anne and Captain Mark Phillips

Royal Wedding

1973 (14 Nov.) *'All-over' phosphor*

941	**424**	3½p violet and silver	10	10	□	□
942		20p brown and silver . . .	55	75	□	□
		Set of 2	65	85	□	□
		First Day Cover		2·25		□
		Presentation Pack	2·25		□	
		PHQ Card (No. 941)	8·00	40·00	□	□
		Set of 2 Gutter Pairs	2·75		□	
		Set of 2 Traffic Light Gutter Pairs	75·00		□	

425	**426**

427	**428**

429	**430** 'Good King Wenceslas, the Page and Peasant'

The 3p values depict the carol 'Good King Wenceslas' and were printed horizontally *se-tenant* within the sheet.

Christmas

1973 (28 Nov.) *One phosphor band (3p) or 'all-over' phosphor (3½p)*

943	**425**	3p multicoloured	20	25	□	□
		a. *Strip of 5. Nos. 943/7* .	2·25	3·25	□	□
944	**426**	3p multicoloured	20	25	□	□
945	**427**	3p multicoloured	20	25	□	□
946	**428**	3p multicoloured	20	25	□	□
947	**429**	3p multicoloured	20	25	□	□
948	**430**	3½p multicoloured	20	25	□	□
		Set of 6	2·25	1·40	□	□
		First Day Cover		3·25		□
		Presentation Pack	3·75		□	

Collectors Pack 1973

1973 (28 Nov.) *Comprises Nos. 919/48*

	Collectors Pack	27·00	□

431	Horse Chestnut

British Trees (2nd issue)

1974 (27 Feb.) *'All-over' phosphor*

949	**431**	10p multicoloured	30	35	□	□
		First Day Cover		2·25		□
		Presentation Pack	2·50		□	
		PHQ Card	£110	90·00	□	□
		Gutter Pair	2·00		□	
		Traffic Light Gutter Pair	42·00		□	

432 First Motor Fire-engine, 1904

433 Prize-winning Fire-engine, 1863

434 First Steam Fire-engine, 1830

435 Fire-engine, 1766

Bicentenary of Public Fire Services

1974 (24 APR.) *'All-over' phosphor*

950	432	3½p multicoloured	10	10	☐	☐
951	433	5½p multicoloured	25	30	☐	☐
952	434	8p multicoloured	45	50	☐	☐
953	435	10p multicoloured	45	50	☐	☐
		Set of 4	1·10	1·25	☐	☐
		First Day Cover		3·50		☐
		Presentation Pack	2·75		☐	
		PHQ Card (No. 950)	£120	90·00	☐	☐
		Set of 4 Gutter Pairs	3·50		☐	
		Set of 4 Traffic Light Gutter Pairs	42·00		☐	

436 P & O Packet *Peninsular*, 1888

437 Farman H.F. III Biplane, 1911

438 Airmail-blue Van and Postbox, 1930

439 Imperial Airways Short S.21 Flying Boat *Maia*, 1937

Centenary of Universal Postal Union

1974 (12 JUNE) *'All-over' phosphor*

954	436	3½p multicoloured	10	10	☐	☐
955	437	5½p multicoloured	25	30	☐	☐
956	438	8p multicoloured	25	35	☐	☐
957	439	10p multicoloured	35	40	☐	☐
		Set of 4	85	1·00	☐	☐
		First Day Cover		3·25		☐
		Presentation Pack	2·75		☐	
		Set of 4 Gutter Pairs	2·75		☐	
		Set of 4 Traffic Light Gutter Pairs	35·00		☐	

440 Robert the Bruce

441 Owain Glyndŵr

442 Henry V

443 The Black Prince

Medieval Warriors

1974 (10 JULY) *'All-over' phosphor*

958	440	4½p multicoloured	10	10	☐	☐
959	441	5½p multicoloured	20	35	☐	☐
960	442	8p multicoloured	40	50	☐	☐
961	443	10p multicoloured	45	50	☐	☐
		Set of 4	1·00	1·25	☐	☐
		First Day Cover		3·50		☐
		Presentation Pack	3·50		☐	
		PHQ Cards (set of 4)	28·00	60·00	☐	☐
		Set of 4 Gutter Pairs	4·00		☐	
		Set of 4 Traffic Light Gutter Pairs	48·00		☐	

444 Churchill in Royal Yacht Squadron Uniform

445 Prime Minister, 1940

446 Secretary for War and Air, 1919

447 War Correspondent, South Africa, 1899

Birth Centenary of Sir Winston Churchill

1974 (9 Oct.) *Queen's head and inscription in silver. 'All-over' phosphor*

962	**444**	4½p green and blue	15	15 □ □
963	**445**	5½p grey and black	30	35 □ □
964	**446**	8p rose and lake	55	55 □ □
965	**447**	10p stone and brown . . .	55	50 □ □
		Set of 4	1·40	1·40 □ □
		First Day Cover		2·50 □
		Presentation Pack	2·50	□
		Souvenir Book (No. 963)	4·00	□
		PHQ Card (No. 963)	6·00	22·00 □ □
		Set of 4 Gutter Pairs	4·00	□
		Set of 4 Traffic Light Gutter Pairs	32·00	□

448 Adoration of the Magi (York Minster, c 1355)

449 The Nativity (St Helen's Church, Norwich, c 1480)

450 Virgin and Child (Ottery St Mary Church, c 1350)

451 Virgin and Child (Worcester Cathedral, c 1224)

Christmas

1974 (27 Nov.) *Designs show church roof bosses. One phosphor band (3½p) or 'all-over' phosphor (others)*

966	**448**	3½p multicoloured	10	10 □ □
967	**449**	4½p multicoloured	10	10 □ □
968	**450**	8p multicoloured	25	35 □ □
969	**451**	10p multicoloured	35	45 □ □
		Set of 4	70	90 □ □
		First Day Cover		3·00 □
		Presentation Pack	2·25	□
		Set of 4 Gutter Pairs	2·50	□
		Set of 4 Traffic Light Gutter Pairs	38·00	□

Collectors Pack 1974

1974 (27 Nov.) *Comprises Nos. 949/69*

	Collectors Pack	12·00	□

452 Invalid in Wheelchair

Health and Handicap Funds

1975 (22 Jan.) *'All-over' phosphor*

970	**452**	4½p + 1½p azure and blue . .	20	20 □ □
		First Day Cover		2·00 □
		Gutter Pair	60	□
		Traffic Light Gutter Pair	1·25	□

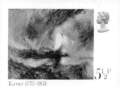

453 'Peace – Burial at Sea'

454 'Snowstorm – Steamer off a Harbour's Mouth'

455 'The Arsenal, Venice'

456 'St Laurent'

Birth Bicentenary of J. M. W. Turner

1975 (19 Feb.) *'All-over' phosphor*

971	**453**	4½p multicoloured	10	10 □ □
972	**454**	5½p multicoloured	15	20 □ □

973	**455**	8p multicoloured	. . . .	25	35	☐	☐
974	**456**	10p multicoloured	. . . .	35	40	☐	☐
		Set of 4	. . . .	75	95	☐	☐
		First Day Cover	. . . .		2·25		☐
		Presentation Pack	. . . .	2·50			☐
		PHQ Card (No. 972)	. . . .	40·00	25·00	☐	☐
		Set of 4 Gutter Pairs		2·25			☐
		Set of 4 Traffic Light Gutter Pairs		5·50			☐

457 Charlotte Square, Edinburgh

458 The Rows, Chester

The above were printed horizontally *se-tenant* throughout the sheet.

459 Royal Observatory, Greenwich

460 St George's Chapel, Windsor

461 National Theatre, London

European Architectural Heritage Year
1975 (23 APR.) *'All-over' phosphor*

975	**457**	7p multicoloured	. . . .	25	25	☐	☐
		a. *Pair. Nos. 975/6*	. . . .	80	1·00	☐	☐
976	**458**	7p multicoloured	. . . .	25	25	☐	☐
977	**459**	8p multicoloured	. . . .	25	30	☐	☐
978	**460**	10p multicoloured	. . . .	25	30	☐	☐
979	**461**	12p multicoloured	. . . .	30	35	☐	☐
		Set of 5	. . . .	1·40	1·25	☐	☐
		First Day Cover	. . . .		4·00		☐
		Presentation Pack	. . . .	3·00			☐
		PHQ Cards (Nos. 975/7)	. . . . .	10·00	27·00	☐	☐
		Set of 5 Gutter Pairs	. . . . . .	5·50			☐
		Set of 5 Traffic Light Gutter Pairs		22·00			☐

462 Sailing Dinghies

463 Racing Keel Boats

464 Cruising Yachts

465 Multihulls

Sailing
1975 (11 JUNE) *'All-over' phosphor*

980	**462**	7p multicoloured	. . . .	15	10	☐	☐
981	**463**	8p multicoloured	. . . .	25	30	☐	☐
982	**464**	10p multicoloured	. . . .	25	35	☐	☐
983	**465**	12p multicoloured	. . . .	40	50	☐	☐
		Set of 4	. . . .	95	1·10	☐	☐
		First Day Cover	. . . .		2·50		☐
		Presentation Pack	. . . .	2·50			☐
		PHQ Card (No. 981)	. . . .	6·00	20·00	☐	☐
		Set of 4 Gutter Pairs	. . . . . .	2·50			☐
		Set of 4 Traffic Light Gutter Pairs		15·00			☐

466 Stephenson's Locomotion, 1825

467 Abbotsford, 1876

468 Caerphilly Castle, 1923

469 High Speed Train, 1975

150th Anniversary of Public Railways
1975 (13 AUG.) *'All-over' phosphor*

| 984 | **466** | 7p multicoloured | . . . . | 20 | 10 | ☐ | ☐ |
| 985 | **467** | 8p multicoloured | . . . . | 30 | 35 | ☐ | ☐ |

986	468	10p multicoloured	35	35	□	□
987	469	12p multicoloured	40	40	□	□
		Set of 4	1·10	1·10	□	□
		First Day Cover		3·50		□
		Presentation Pack	3·50		□	
		Souvenir Book	6·00		□	
		PHQ Cards (set of 4)	60·00	55·00	□	□
		Set of 4 Gutter Pairs	3·00		□	
		Set of 4 Traffic Light Gutter Pairs	8·50		□	

470 Palace of Westminster

62nd Inter-Parliamentary Union Conference
1975 (3 Sept.) *'All-over' phosphor*

988	470	12p multicoloured	30	35	□	□
		First Day Cover		1·50		□
		Presentation Pack	1·60		□	
		Gutter Pair	70		□	
		Traffic Light Gutter Pair	2·00		□	

471 Emma and Mr
Woodhouse
(*Emma*)

472 Catherine Morland
(*Northanger Abbey*)

473 Mr Darcy
(*Pride and
Prejudice*)

474 Mary and Henry
Crawford (*Mansfield
Park*)

Birth Bicentenary of Jane Austen (novelist)
1975 (22 Oct.) *'All-over' phosphor*

| 989 | 471 | 8½p multicoloured . . . . . | 15 | 10 | □ | □ |
| 990 | 472 | 10p multicoloured . . . . . | 35 | 35 | □ | □ |

991	473	11p multicoloured	35	35	□	□
992	474	13p multicoloured	40	50	□	□
		Set of 4	1·10	1·10	□	□
		First Day Cover		3·50		□
		Presentation Pack	2·25		□	
		PHQ Cards (set of 4)	22·00	32·00	□	□
		Set of 4 Gutter Pairs	2·50		□	
		Set of 4 Traffic Light Gutter Pairs	7·00		□	

475 Angels with
Harp and Lute

476 Angel with Mandolin

477 Angel with Horn

478 Angel with Trumpet

Christmas
1975 (26 Nov.) *One phosphor band* (6½p). *phosphor-inked* (8½p)
(*background*) *or 'all-over' phosphor* (*others*)

993	475	6½p multicoloured	15	15	□	□
994	476	8½p multicoloured	25	30	□	□
995	477	11p multicoloured	35	35	□	□
996	478	13p multicoloured	35	35	□	□
		Set of 4	1·00	1·00	□	□
		First Day Cover		2·00		□
		Presentation Pack	2·25		□	
		Set of 4 Gutter Pairs	2·50		□	
		Set of 4 Traffic Light Gutter Pairs	7·00		□	

Collectors Pack 1975
1975 (26 Nov.) *Comprises Nos.* 970/96

| | | *Collectors Pack* . . . . | 8·00 | | □ | |

479 Housewife

480 Policeman

481 District Nurse   **482** Industrialist

Telephone Centenary
1976 (10 Mar.) *'All-over' phosphor*

997	**479**	8½p multicoloured	15	10	□	□
998	**480**	10p multicoloured	30	30	□	□
999	**481**	11p multicoloured	35	35	□	□
1000	**482**	13p multicoloured	40	40	□	□
		Set of 4	1·10	1·10	□	□
		First Day Cover		2·00		□
		Presentation Pack	2·50		□	
		Set of 4 Gutter Pairs	2·75		□	
		Set of 4 Traffic Light Gutter Pairs	6·50		□	

483 Hewing Coal (Thomas Hepburn)   **484** Machinery (Robert Owen)

485 Chimney Cleaning (Lord Shaftesbury)   **486** Hands clutching Prison Bars (Elizabeth Fry)

Social Reformers
1976 (28 Apr.) *'All-over' phosphor*

1001	**483**	8½p multicoloured	15	10	□	□
1002	**484**	10p multicoloured	30	30	□	□
1003	**485**	11p black, slate-grey and drab	35	35	□	□
1004	**486**	13p slate-grey, black and green	35	35	□	□
		Set of 4	1·00	1·00	□	□
		First Day Cover		2·00		□
		Presentation Pack	2·50		□	
		PHQ Card (No. 1001)	5·50	18·00	□	□
		Set of 4 Gutter Pairs	2·40		□	
		Set of 4 Traffic Light Gutter Pairs	6·50		□	

487 Benjamin Franklin (bust by Jean-Jacques Caffieri)

Bicentenary of American Revolution
1976 (2 June) *'All-over' phosphor*

1005	**487**	11p multicoloured	35	35	□	□
		First Day Cover		1·40		□
		Presentation Pack	1·25		□	
		PHQ Card	4·00	17·00	□	□
		Gutter Pair	75		□	
		Traffic Light Gutter Pair	1·75		□	

488 'Elizabeth of Glamis'   **489** 'Grandpa Dickson'

490 'Rosa Mundi'   **491** 'Sweet Briar'

Centenary of Royal National Rose Society
1976 (30 June) *'All-over' phosphor*

1006	**488**	8½p multicoloured	15	10	□	□
1007	**489**	10p multicoloured	25	30	□	□
1008	**490**	11p multicoloured	40	40	□	□
1009	**491**	13p multicoloured	50	50	□	□
		Set of 4	1·25	1·25	□	□
		First Day Cover		2·50		□
		Presentation Pack	2·50		□	
		PHQ Cards (set of 4)	25·00	30·00	□	□
		Set of 4 Gutter Pairs	3·00		□	
		Set of 4 Traffic Light Gutter Pairs	7·00		□	

1176 1176

Eisteddfod Genedlaethol Frenhinol Cymru
Royal National Eisteddfod of Wales

492 Archdruid

Morris Dancing

493 Morris Dancing

Highland Gathering
Na Geamannan

494 Scots Piper

1176 1176

Eisteddfod Genedlaethol Frenhinol Cymru
Royal National Eisteddfod of Wales

495 Welsh Harpist

British Cultural Traditions

1976 (4 Aug.) *'All-over' phosphor*

1010	**492**	8½p multicoloured	15	10	□	□
1011	**493**	10p multicoloured	30	30	□	□
1012	**494**	11p multicoloured	35	35	□	□
1013	**495**	13p multicoloured	40	40	□	□
		Set of 4	1·10	1·10	□	□
		First Day Cover		3·00	□	
		Presentation Pack	2·50		□	
		PHQ Cards (set of 4)	15·00	20·00	□	□
		Set of 4 Gutter Pairs	2·75		□	
		Set of 4 Traffic Light Gutter Pairs	6·50		□	

William Caxton 1476   8½p

496 The Canterbury
Tales

William Caxton 1476   10p

497 The Tretyse of Love

For full information on all future British issues, collectors should write to Royal Mail, Freepost EH3647, 21 South Gyle Crescent, Edinburgh EH12 9PE.

William Caxton 1476   **11p**

498 Game and Playe
of Chesse

William Caxton 1476   **13p**

499 Early Printing Press

500th Anniversary of British Printing

1976 (29 Sept.) *'All-over' phosphor*

1014	**496**	8½p black, blue and gold .	15	10 □ □
1015	**497**	10p black, olive-green and gold	30	30 □ □
1016	**498**	11p black, grey and gold .	35	35 □ □
1017	**499**	13p brown, ochre and gold .	35	40 □ □
		Set of 4	1·00	1·00 □ □
		First Day Cover		3·00 □
		Presentation Pack	2·50	□
		PHQ Cards (set of 4)	12·00	20·00 □ □
		Set of 4 Gutter Pairs	2·75	□
		Set of 4 Traffic Light Gutter Pairs	6·50	□

English Embroidery c.1272   6½p

500 Virgin and Child

English Embroidery c.1340   8½p

501 Angel with Crown

English Embroidery c.1320   11p

502 Angel appearing to
Shepherds

English Embroidery c.1340   13p

503 The Three Kings

Christmas

1976 (24 Nov.) *Designs show English medieval embroidery. One phosphor band (6½p) or 'all-over' phosphor (others)*

1018	**500**	6½p multicoloured	15	15 □ □
1019	**501**	8½p multicoloured	25	15 □ □
1020	**502**	11p multicoloured	30	35 □ □

1021	**503**	13p multicoloured	35	40	☐	☐
		Set of 4	95	95	☐	☐
		First Day Cover		3·50		☐
		Presentation Pack	2·50		☐	
		PHQ Cards (set of 4)	4·50	20·00	☐	☐
		Set of 4 Gutter Pairs	2·25		☐	
		Set of 4 Traffic Light Gutter Pairs	6·00		☐	

Collectors Pack 1976
1976 (24 Nov.) *Comprises Nos.* 997/1021

| | | Collectors Pack . . . . | 12·00 | | ☐ | |

8½p

504 Lawn Tennis

10p

505 Table Tennis

11p

506 Squash

13p

507 Badminton

Racket Sports
1977 (12 Jan.) *Phosphorised paper*

1022	**504**	8½p multicoloured	15	10	☐	☐
1023	**505**	10p multicoloured	30	30	☐	☐
1024	**506**	11p multicoloured	35	35	☐	☐
1025	**507**	13p multicoloured	35	40	☐	☐
		Set of 4	1·00	1·00	☐	☐
		First Day Cover		3·50		☐
		Presentation Pack	2·25		☐	
		PHQ Cards (set of 4)	7·00	20·00	☐	☐
		Set of 4 Gutter Pairs	2·50		☐	
		Set of 4 Traffic Light Gutter Pairs	6·00		☐	

£1

508

1977 (2 Feb.)–87 *Type* **508** *Ordinary paper*

1026	£1 green and olive	2·75	25	☐	☐
1026*b*	£1·30 drab and deep greenish blue	5·50	6·00	☐	☐
1026*c*	£1·33 pale mauve and grey-black	7·50	7·00	☐	☐
1026*d*	£1·41 drab and deep greenish blue	8·00	8·50	☐	☐
1026*e*	£1·50 pale mauve and grey-black	6·00	5·00	☐	☐
1026*f*	£1·60 drab and deep greenish blue	6·50	7·00	☐	☐
1027	£2 green and brown	6·00	50	☐	☐
1028	£5 pink and blue	14·00	3·00	☐	☐
	Set of 8	50·00	32·00	☐	☐
	Presentation Pack (*P.O. Pack No.* 91 (*small size*)) (*Nos.* 1026, 1027/8)	24·00		☐	
	Presentation Pack (*P.O. Pack No.*13 (*large size*)) (*Nos.* 1026, 1027/8)	90·00		☐	
	Presentation Pack (*P.O. Pack No.* 14) (*No.* 1026*f*)	12·00		☐	
	Set of 8 Gutter Pairs	£110		☐	
	Set of 8 Traffic Light Gutter Pairs	£160		☐	

First Day Covers

2 Feb. 1977	Nos. 1026, 1027/8	8·00	☐
3 Aug. 1983	No. 1026*b*	6·50	☐
28 Aug. 1984	No. 1026*c*	8·00	☐
17 Sept. 1985	No. 1026*d*	8·50	☐
2 Sept. 1986	No. 1026*e*	5·50	☐
15 Sept. 1987	No. 1026*f*	8·00	☐

8½P
2

509 Steroids — Conformational Analysis

10P

510 Vitamin C — Synthesis

11P

511 Starch — Chromatography

13P

512 Salt — Crystallography

Centenary of Royal Institute of Chemistry
1977 (2 Mar.) *'All-over' phosphor*

1029	**509**	8½p multicoloured	15	10	☐	☐
1030	**510**	10p multicoloured	35	35	☐	☐
1031	**511**	11p multicoloured	35	35	☐	☐

1032	**512**	13p multicoloured	35	35	☐	☐
		Set of 4	1·10	1·00	☐	☐
		First Day Cover		2·50		☐
		Presentation Pack	2·25		☐	
		PHQ Cards (set of 4)	7·00	15·00	☐	☐
		Set of 4 Gutter Pairs	2·50		☐	
		Set of 4 Traffic Light Gutter Pairs	6·00		☐	

513

Silver Jubilee
1977 (11 May–15 June) *'All-over' phosphor*

1033	**513**	8½p multicoloured	15	15	☐	☐
1034		9p multicoloured (15 June)	25	15	☐	☐
1035		10p multicoloured	25	25	☐	☐
1036		11p multicoloured	35	35	☐	☐
1037		13p multicoloured	40	40	☐	☐
		Set of 5	1·25	1·10	☐	☐
		First Day Covers (2)		4·00		☐
		Presentation Pack (ex 9p)	1·90		☐	
		Souvenir Book (ex 9p)	4·50		☐	
		PHQ Cards (set of 5)	12·00	16·00	☐	☐
		Set of 5 Gutter Pairs	3·00		☐	
		Set of 5 Traffic Light Gutter Pairs	4·00		☐	

517 *'Gathering of Nations'*

Commonwealth Heads of Government Meeting, London
1977 (8 June) *'All-over' phosphor*

1038	**517**	13p black, deep green, rose				
		and silver	35	35	☐	☐
		First Day Cover		1·00		☐
		Presentation Pack	1·00		☐	
		PHQ Card	4·00	5·00	☐	☐
		Gutter Pair	80		☐	
		Traffic Light Gutter Pair	1·25		☐	

518 Hedgehog   **519** Brown Hare

520 Red Squirrel   **521** Otter

522 Badger

T **518/22** were printed together, *se-tenant*, throughout the sheet.

British Wildlife
1977 (5 Oct.) *'All-over' phosphor*

1039	**518**	9p multicoloured	20	20	☐	☐
		a. Strip of 5. Nos.				
		1039/43	1·40	2·00	☐	☐
1040	**519**	9p multicoloured	20	20	☐	☐
1041	**520**	9p multicoloured	20	20	☐	☐
1042	**521**	9p multicoloured	20	20	☐	☐
1043	**522**	9p multicoloured	20	20	☐	☐
		Set of 5	1·40	90	☐	☐
		First Day Cover		3·50		☐
		Presentation Pack	2·50		☐	
		PHQ Cards (set of 5)	4·00	6·00	☐	☐
		Gutter Strip of 10	3·50		☐	
		Traffic Light Gutter Strip of 10 .	4·00		☐	

| 523 | 'Three French Hens, Two Turtle Doves and a Partridge in a Pear Tree' | 524 | 'Six Geese a laying, Five Gold Rings, Four Colly Birds' |

| 525 | 'Eight Maids a-milking, Seven Swans a-swimming' | 526 | 'Ten Pipers piping, Nine Drummers drumming' |

| 527 | 'Twelve Lords a-leaping, Eleven Ladies dancing' | 528 | 'A Partridge in a Pear Tree' |

T **523/8** depict the carol 'The Twelve Days of Christmas'.
T **523/7** were printed horizontally *se-tenant* throughout the sheet.

Christmas

1977 (23 Nov.) *One centre phosphor band* (7*p*) *or 'all-over' phosphor* (9*p*)

1044	523	7p multicoloured	20	15 □ □
		a. Strip of 5. Nos. 1044/8	1·40	2·00 □ □
1045	524	7p multicoloured	20	15 □ □
1046	525	7p multicoloured	20	15 □ □
1047	526	7p multicoloured	20	15 □ □
1048	527	7p multicoloured	20	15 □ □
1049	528	9p multicoloured	25	20 □ □
		Set of 6	1·10	85 □ □
		First Day Cover		3·50 □
		Presentation Pack	2·25	□
		PHQ Cards (set of 6)	3·00	5·00 □ □
		Set of 6 Gutter Pairs	3·50	□
		Set of 6 Traffic Light Gutter Pairs	5·00	□

Collectors Pack 1977

1977 (23 Nov.) *Comprises Nos.* 1022/5 1029/49

| | Collectors Pack . . . . | 8·00 | □ |

| 529 | Oil — North Sea Production Platform | 530 | Coal — Modern Pithead |

| 531 | Natural Gas — Flame Rising from Sea | 532 | Electricity — Nuclear Power Station and Uranium Atom |

Energy Resources

1978 (25 Jan.) *'All-over' phosphor*

1050	529	9p multicoloured	20	10 □ □
1051	530	10½p multicoloured	20	25 □ □
1052	531	11p multicoloured	30	35 □ □
1053	532	13p multicoloured	35	40 □ □
		Set of 4	95	1·00 □ □
		First Day Cover		1·50 □
		Presentation Pack	2·00	□
		PHQ Cards (set of 4)	2·00	4·00 □ □
		Set of 4 Gutter Pairs	2·25	□
		Set of 4 Traffic Light Gutter Pairs	3·75	□

| 533 | Tower of London | 534 | Holyroodhouse |

| 535 | Caernarvon Castle | 536 | Hampton Court Palace |

British Architecture (Historic Buildings)

1978 (1 Mar.) *'All-over' phosphor*

1054	**533**	9p multicoloured	20	10	□	□
1055	**534**	10½p multicoloured	20	30	□	□
1056	**535**	11p multicoloured	25	30	□	□
1057	**536**	13p multicoloured	25	30	□	□
		Set of 4	80	90	□	□
		First Day Cover		1·50	□	
		Presentation Pack	2·00		□	
		PHQ Cards (set of 4)	2·00	4·00	□	□
		Set of 4 Gutter Pairs	2·25		□	
		Set of 4 Traffic Light Gutter Pairs	4·00		□	
MS1058		121 × 90 mm. Nos. 1054/7 . .	1·25	1·40	□	□
		First Day Cover		1·75	□	

No. **MS**1058 was sold at 53½p, the premium being used for
the London 1980 Stamp Exhibition.

537 State Coach

538 St Edward's Crown

539 The Sovereign's Orb

540 Imperial State Crown

25th Anniversary of Coronation

1978 (31 May) *'All-over' phosphor*

1059	**537**	9p gold and blue	25	15	□	□
1060	**538**	10½p gold and red	30	35	□	□
1061	**539**	11p gold and green	30	35	□	□
1062	**540**	13p gold and violet	40	45	□	□
		Set of 4	1·10	1·10	□	□
		First Day Cover		1·50	□	
		Presentation Pack	2·00		□	
		Souvenir Book	5·00		□	
		PHQ Cards (set of 4)	3·00	4·00	□	□
		Set of 4 Gutter Pairs	2·25		□	
		Set of 4 Traffic Light Gutter Pairs	3·75		□	

541 Shire Horse

542 Shetland Pony

543 Welsh Pony

544 Thoroughbred

Horses

1978 (5 July) *'All-over' phosphor*

1063	**541**	9p multicoloured	20	10	□	□
1064	**542**	10½p multicoloured	35	40	□	□
1065	**543**	11p multicoloured	35	45	□	□
1066	**544**	13p multicoloured	45	50	□	□
		Set of 4	1·25	1·25	□	□
		First Day Cover		1·60	□	
		Presentation Pack	1·75		□	
		PHQ Cards (set of 4)	2·00	5·00	□	□
		Set of 4 Gutter Pairs	2·75		□	
		Set of 4 Traffic Light Gutter Pairs	4·00		□	

545 Penny-farthing and
1884 Safety Bicycle

546 1920 Touring Bicycles

547 Modern Small-wheel
Bicycles

548 1978 Road-racers

Centenaries of Cyclists Touring Club and British Cycling Federation

1978 (2 Aug.) *'All-over' phosphor*

1067	**545**	9p multicoloured	20	10	☐	☐
1068	**546**	10½p multicoloured	30	35	☐	☐
1069	**547**	11p multicoloured	30	35	☐	☐
1070	**548**	13p multicoloured	35	40	☐	☐
		Set of 4	1·00	1·10	☐	☐
		First Day Cover		1·75		☐
		Presentation Pack	1·75		☐	
		PHQ Cards (set of 4)	2·00	4·50	☐	☐
		Set of 4 Gutter Pairs	2·50		☐	
		Set of 4 Traffic Light Gutter Pairs	4·00		☐	

549 Singing Carols round the Christmas Tree

550 The Waits

551 18th-Century Carol Singers

552 'The Boar's Head Carol'

Christmas

1978 (22 Nov.) *One centre phosphor band (7p) or 'all-over' phosphor (others)*

1071	**549**	7p multicoloured	15	10	☐	☐
1072	**550**	9p multicoloured	25	15	☐	☐
1073	**551**	11p multicoloured	30	35	☐	☐
1074	**552**	13p multicoloured	35	40	☐	☐
		Set of 4	95	90	☐	☐
		First Day Cover		1·50		☐
		Presentation Pack	1·60		☐	
		PHQ Cards (set of 4)	2·75	4·50	☐	☐
		Set of 4 Gutter Pairs	2·25		☐	
		Set of 4 Traffic Light Gutter Pairs	3·50		☐	

Collectors Pack 1978

1978 (22 Nov.) *Comprises Nos. 1050/7, 1059/74*

	Collectors Pack	8·00	☐

553 Old English Sheepdog   **554** Welsh Springer Spaniel

555 West Highland Terrier   **556** Irish Setter

Dogs

1979 (7 Feb.) *'All-over' phosphor*

1075	**553**	9p multicoloured	15	10	☐	☐
1076	**554**	10½p multicoloured	30	30	☐	☐
1077	**555**	11p multicoloured	30	40	☐	☐
1078	**556**	13p multicoloured	30	40	☐	☐
		Set of 4	95	1·10	☐	☐
		First Day Cover		1·60		☐
		Presentation Pack	1·60		☐	
		PHQ Cards (set of 4)	3·00	5·50	☐	☐
		Set of 4 Gutter Pairs	2·25		☐	
		Set of 4 Traffic Light Gutter Pairs	3·50		☐	

557 Primrose   **558** Daffodil

559 Bluebell   **560** Snowdrop

Spring Wild Flowers

1979 (21 Mar.) *'All-over' phosphor*

1079	557	9p multicoloured	15	10	☐	☐
1080	558	10½p multicoloured	25	35	☐	☐
1081	559	11p multicoloured	30	35	☐	☐
1082	560	13p multicoloured	30	30	☐	☐
		Set of 4	90	1·00	☐	☐
		First Day Cover		1·75		☐
		Presentation Pack	1·90		☐	
		PHQ Cards (set of 4)	3·00	4·50	☐	☐
		Set of 4 Gutter Pairs	2·25		☐	
		Set of 4 Traffic Light Gutter Pairs	3·50		☐	

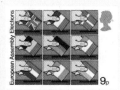
561

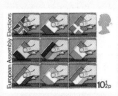
562

563

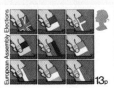
564

T **561/4** show hands placing the flags of the member nations into ballot boxes.

First Direct Elections to European Assembly

1979 (9 May) *Phosphorised paper*

1083	561	9p multicoloured	15	10	☐	☐
1084	562	10½p multicoloured	25	25	☐	☐
1085	563	11p multicoloured	30	30	☐	☐
1086	564	13p multicoloured	35	30	☐	☐
		Set of 4	95	85	☐	☐
		First Day Cover		1·75		☐
		Presentation Pack	1·90		☐	
		PHQ Cards (set of 4)	1·75	4·50	☐	☐
		Set of 4 Gutter Pairs	2·25		☐	
		Set of 4 Traffic Light Gutter Pairs	3·50		☐	

565 'Saddling "Mahmoud" for the Derby, 1936' (Sir Alfred Munnings)

566 'The Liverpool Great National Steeple Chase, 1839' (aquatint by F. C. Turner)

567 'The First Spring Meeting, Newmarket, 1793' (J. N. Sartorius)

568 'Racing at Dorsett Ferry, Windsor, 1684' (Francis Barlow)

Horseracing Paintings and Bicentenary of The Derby (9p)

1979 (6 June) *'All-over' phosphor*

1087	565	9p multicoloured	15	10	☐	☐
1088	566	10½p multicoloured	25	25	☐	☐
1089	567	11p multicoloured	30	30	☐	☐
1090	568	13p multicoloured	30	30	☐	☐
		Set of 4	90	85	☐	☐
		First Day Cover		1·75		☐
		Presentation Pack	1·90		☐	
		PHQ Cards (set of 4)	1·90	4·00	☐	☐
		Set of 4 Gutter Pairs	2·25		☐	
		Set of 4 Traffic Light Gutter Pairs	3·50		☐	

569 The Tale of Peter Rabbit (Beatrix Potter)

570 The Wind in the Willows (Kenneth Grahame)

571 Winnie-the-Pooh (A. A. Milne)

572 Alice's Adventures in in Wonderland (Lewis Carroll)

T **569/72** depict original illustrations from the four books.

International Year of the Child

1979 (11 JULY) *'All-over' phosphor*

1091	**569**	9p multicoloured	25	20 ☐ ☐
1092	**570**	10½p multicoloured	30	35 ☐ ☐
1093	**571**	11p multicoloured	35	35 ☐ ☐
1094	**572**	13p multicoloured	55	55 ☐ ☐
		Set of 4	1·25	1·25 ☐ ☐
		First Day Cover		2·00 ☐
		Presentation Pack	2·25	☐
		PHQ Cards (set of 4)	2·50	4·50 ☐ ☐
		Set of 4 Gutter Pairs	3·00	☐
		Set of 4 Traffic Light Gutter Pairs	4·00	☐

573 Sir Rowland Hill, 1795–1879

574 General Post, *c* 1839

575 London Post, *c* 1839

576 Uniform Postage, 1840

Death Centenary of Sir Rowland Hill (postal reformer)

1979 (22 AUG.–24 OCT.) *'All-over' phosphor*

1095	**573**	10p multicoloured	15	10 ☐ ☐
1096	**574**	11½p multicoloured	20	25 ☐ ☐
1097	**575**	13p multicoloured	30	35 ☐ ☐
1098	**576**	15p multicoloured	50	40 ☐ ☐
		Set of 4	1·00	1·00 ☐ ☐
		First Day Cover		1·75 ☐
		Presentation Pack	1·90	☐
		PHQ Cards (set of 4)	2·00	3·50 ☐ ☐
		Set of 4 Gutter Pairs	2·40	☐
		Set of 4 Traffic Light Gutter Pairs	3·75	☐
MS1099	89 × 121 mm. Nos. 1095/8 . .		1·25	1·25 ☐ ☐
		First Day Cover (24 Oct.) . .		2·00 ☐

No. **MS**1099 was sold at 59½p, the premium being used for the London 1980 Stamp Exhibition.

10ᴾ

11½ᴾ

577 Policeman on the Beat

578 Policeman directing Traffic

13ᴾ

15ᴾ

579 Mounted Policewoman

580 River Patrol Boat

150th Anniversary of Metropolitan Police

1979 (26 SEPT.) *Phosphorised paper*

1100	**577**	10p multicoloured	20	10 ☐ ☐
1101	**578**	11½p multicoloured	25	35 ☐ ☐
1102	**579**	13p multicoloured	30	40 ☐ ☐
1103	**580**	15p multicoloured	50	40 ☐ ☐
		Set of 4	1·10	1·10 ☐ ☐
		First Day Cover		1·75 ☐
		Presentation Pack	1·90	☐
		PHQ Cards (set of 4)	1·75	3·50 ☐ ☐
		Set of 4 Gutter Pairs	2·50	☐
		Set of 4 Traffic Light Gutter Pairs	3·75	☐

8ᴾ

10ᴾ

581 The Three Kings

582 Angel appearing to the Shepherds

11½ᴾ

13ᴾ

583 The Nativity

584 Mary and Joseph travelling to Bethlehem

585 The Annunciation

Christmas

1979 (21 Nov.) *One centre phosphor band* (8p) *or phosphorised paper* (*others*)

1104	581	8p multicoloured	15	10	☐	☐
1105	582	10p multicoloured	20	15	☐	☐
1106	583	11½p multicoloured	30	30	☐	☐
1107	584	13p multicoloured	45	35	☐	☐
1108	585	15p multicoloured	50	40	☐	☐
		Set of 5	1·40	1·25	☐	☐
		First Day Cover		1·75		☐
		Presentation Pack	2·00		☐	
		PHQ Cards (set of 5)	1·50	3·50	☐	☐
		Set of 5 Gutter Pairs	3·00		☐	
		Set of 5 Traffic Light Gutter Pairs	4·00		☐	

Collectors Pack 1979

1979 (21 Nov.) *Comprises Nos.* 1075/98, 1100/8

	Collectors Pack	10·00	☐

586 Common Kingfisher

587 Dipper

588 Moorhen

589 Yellow Wagtails

Centenary of Wild Bird Protection Act

1980 (16 Jan.) *Phosphorised paper*

1109	586	10p multicoloured	20	10	☐	☐
1110	587	11½p multicoloured	40	35	☐	☐

1111	588	13p multicoloured	50	45	☐	☐
1112	589	15p multicoloured	50	45	☐	☐
		Set of 4	1·50	1·25	☐	☐
		First Day Cover		1·75		☐
		Presentation Pack	2·00		☐	
		PHQ Cards (set of 4)	1·60	4·00	☐	☐
		Set of 4 Gutter Pairs	3·75		☐	

590 *Rocket* approaching Moorish Arch, Liverpool

591 First and Second Class Carriages passing through Olive Mount Cutting

592 Third Class Carriage and Sheep Truck crossing Chat Moss

593 Horsebox and Carriage Truck near Bridgewater Canal

594 Goods Truck and Mail-coach at Manchester

T 590/4 were printed together, *se-tenant,* in horizontal strips of 5 throughout the sheet.

150th Anniversary of Liverpool and Manchester Railway

1980 (12 Mar.) *Phosphorised paper*

1113	590	12p multicoloured	20	20	☐	☐
		a. Strip of 5. Nos. 1113/17	1·40	1·75	☐	☐
1114	591	12p multicoloured	20	20	☐	☐
1115	592	12p multicoloured	20	20	☐	☐
1116	593	12p multicoloured	20	20	☐	☐
1117	594	12p multicoloured	20	20	☐	☐
		Set of 5	1·40	90	☐	☐
		First Day Cover		1·75		☐
		Presentation Pack	2·40		☐	
		PHQ Cards (set of 5)	1·60	4·00	☐	☐
		Gutter block of 10	3·50		☐	

INTERNATIONAL STAMP EXHIBITION

595 Montage of London Buildings

'London 1980' International Stamp Exhibition

1980 (9 APR.–7 MAY) *Phosphorised paper. Perf* 14½ × 14

1118	**595**	50p agate	1·25	1·00	☐	☐
		First Day Cover		2·00		☐
		Presentation Pack	2·25			☐
		PHQ Card	80	2·25		☐
		Gutter Pair	3·25			☐
MS1119		90 × 123 mm. No. 1118	1·25	1·50	☐	☐
		First Day Cover (7 May)		2·25		☐

No. **MS**1119 was sold at 75p, the premium being used for the exhibition.

596 Buckingham Palace

597 The Albert Memorial

598 Royal Opera House

599 Hampton Court

600 Kensington Palace

London Landmarks

1980 (7 MAY) *Phosphorised paper*

1120	**596**	10½p multicoloured	20	10	☐	☐
1121	**597**	12p multicoloured	20	10	☐	☐
1122	**598**	13½p multicoloured	30	35	☐	☐
1123	**599**	15p multicoloured	40	45	☐	☐
1124	**600**	17½p multicoloured	50	45	☐	☐
		Set of 5	1·40	1·25	☐	☐
		First Day Cover		1·75		☐
		Presentation Pack	2·00			☐
		PHQ Cards (set of 5)	1·60	2·75	☐	☐
		Set of 5 Gutter Pairs	3·50			☐

601 Charlotte Brontë (*Jane Eyre*)

602 George Eliot (*The Mill on the Floss*)

603 Emily Brontë (*Wuthering Heights*)

604 Mrs Gaskell (*North and South*)

T **601/4** show authoresses and scenes from their novels. T **601/2** also include the 'Europa' C.E.P.T. emblem.

Famous Authoresses

1980 (9 JULY) *Phosphorised paper*

1125	**601**	12p multicoloured	25	10	☐	☐
1126	**602**	13½p multicoloured	30	35	☐	☐
1127	**603**	15p multicoloured	40	35	☐	☐
1128	**604**	17½p multicoloured	50	40	☐	☐
		Set of 4	1·25	1·10	☐	☐
		First Day Cover		1·75		☐
		Presentation Pack	2·00			☐
		PHQ Cards (set of 4)	2·50	2·75	☐	☐
		Set of 4 Gutter Pairs	3·25			☐

605 Queen Elizabeth the Queen Mother

80th Birthday of Queen Elizabeth the Queen Mother

1980 (4 Aug.) *Phosphorised paper*

1129	**605**	12p multicoloured	75	75	☐	☐
		First Day Cover		1·50		☐
		PHQ Card	1·00	1·75	☐	☐
		Gutter Pair	1·90		☐	

606 Sir Henry Wood

607 Sir Thomas Beecham

608 Sir Malcolm Sargent

609 Sir John Barbirolli

British Conductors

1980 (10 Sept.) *Phosphorised paper*

1130	**606**	12p multicoloured	20	10	☐	☐
1131	**607**	13½p multicoloured	35	35	☐	☐
1132	**608**	15p multicoloured	40	40	☐	☐
1133	**609**	17½p multicoloured	45	40	☐	☐
		Set of 4	1·25	1·10	☐	☐
		First Day Cover		1·90		☐
		Presentation Pack	2·00		☐	
		PHQ Cards (set of 4)	1·60	3·25	☐	☐
		Set of 4 Gutter Pairs	3·50		☐	

For full information on all future British issues, collectors should write to Royal Mail, Freepost EH3647, 21 South Gyle Crescent, Edinburgh EH12 9PE.

610 Running

611 Rugby

612 Boxing

613 Cricket

Sports Centenaries

1980 (10 Oct.) *Phosphorised paper. Perf* 14 × 14½

1134	**610**	12p multicoloured	20	10	☐	☐
1135	**611**	13½p multicoloured	40	40	☐	☐
1136	**612**	15p multicoloured	35	35	☐	☐
1137	**613**	17½p multicoloured	45	40	☐	☐
		Set of 4	1·25	1·10	☐	☐
		First Day Cover		1·90		☐
		Presentation Pack	2·00		☐	
		PHQ Cards (set of 4)	1·60	3·25	☐	☐
		Set of 4 Gutter Pairs	3·50		☐	

Centenaries:—12p Amateur Athletics Association; 13½p Welsh Rugby Union; 15p Amateur Boxing Association; 17½p First England v Australia Test Match.

614 Christmas Tree

615 Candles

616 Apples and Mistletoe

617 Crown, Chains and Bell

17½P

618 Holly

Christmas

1980 (19 Nov.) *One centre phosphor band* (10p) *or phosphorised paper* (*others*)

1138	**614**	10p multicoloured	20	10 □ □
1139	**615**	12p multicoloured	20	20 □ □
1140	**616**	13½p multicoloured	40	40 □ □
1141	**617**	15p multicoloured	55	55 □ □
1142	**618**	17½p multicoloured	55	55 □ □
		Set of 5	1·75	1·60 □ □
		First Day Cover		1·90
		Presentation Pack	2·00	□
		PHQ Cards (*set of 5*)	1·60	4·50 □ □
		Set of 5 Gutter Pairs	4·25	□

Collectors Pack 1980

1980 (19 Nov.) *Comprises Nos.* 1109/18, 1120/42

Collectors Pack . . . . 14·00 □

619 St Valentine's Day

620 Morris Dancers

621 Lammastide

622 Medieval Mummers

T **619/20** also include the 'Europa' C.E.P.T. emblem.

Folklore

1981 (6 Feb.) *Phosphorised paper*

1143	**619**	14p multicoloured	25	10 □ □
1144	**620**	18p multicoloured	35	50 □ □
1145	**621**	22p multicoloured	60	55 □ □
1146	**622**	25p multicoloured	70	65 □ □
		Set of 4	1·75	1·60 □
		First Day Cover		2·00 □
		Presentation Pack	2·25	□
		PHQ Cards (*set of 4*)	1·60	3·00 □ □
		Set of 4 Gutter Pairs	4·25	□

623 Blind Man with Guide Dog

624 Hands spelling 'Deaf' in Sign Language

625 Disabled Man in Wheelchair

626 Disabled Artist painting with Foot

International Year of the Disabled

1981 (25 Mar.) *Phosphorised paper*

1147	**623**	14p multicoloured	25	10 □ □
1148	**624**	18p multicoloured	35	50 □ □
1149	**625**	22p multicoloured	50	60 □ □
1150	**626**	25p multicoloured	55	70 □ □
		Set of 4	1·50	1·75 □ □
		First Day Cover		2·25 □
		Presentation Pack	2·25	□
		PHQ Cards (*set of 4*)	1·60	3·00 □ □
		Set of 4 Gutter Pairs	3·75	□

Small Tortoiseshell

627 *Aglais urticae*

Large Blue

628 *Maculinea arion*

Peacock

629 *Inachis io*

Chequered Skipper

630 *Carterocephalus palaemon*

Butterflies

1981 (13 MAY) *Phosphorised paper*

1151	**627**	14p multicoloured	25	10	☐	☐
1152	**628**	18p multicoloured	55	55	☐	☐
1153	**629**	22p multicoloured	65	60	☐	☐
1154	**630**	25p multicoloured	70	65	☐	☐
		Set of 4	1·90	1·75	☐	☐
		First Day Cover		2·75	☐	
		Presentation Pack	2·25		☐	
		PHQ Cards (set of 4)	1·75	5·00	☐	☐
		Set of 4 Gutter Pairs	4·75		☐	

631 Glenfinnan, Scotland

632 Derwentwater, England

633 Stackpole Head, Wales

634 Giant's Causeway, N. Ireland

635 St Kilda, Scotland

50th Anniversary of National Trust for Scotland

1981 (24 JUNE) *Phosphorised paper*

1155	**631**	14p multicoloured	25	10	☐	☐
1156	**632**	18p multicoloured	45	40	☐	☐
1157	**633**	20p multicoloured	65	65	☐	☐
1158	**634**	22p multicoloured	70	70	☐	☐
1159	**635**	25p multicoloured	80	80	☐	☐
		Set of 5	2·50	2·40	☐	☐
		First Day Cover		2·75	☐	
		Presentation Pack	3·00		☐	
		PHQ Cards (set of 5)	2·50	5·00	☐	☐
		Set of 5 Gutter Pairs	6·00		☐	

636 Prince Charles and Lady Diana Spencer

Royal Wedding

1981 (22 JULY) *Phosphorised paper*

1160	**636**	14p multicoloured	65	40	☐	☐
1161		25p multicoloured	1·25	1·60	☐	☐
		Set of 2	1·90	2·00	☐	☐
		First Day Cover		3·50	☐	
		Presentation Pack	3·50		☐	
		Souvenir Book	5·00		☐	
		PHQ Cards (set of 2)	3·00	5·00	☐	☐
		Set of 2 Gutter Pairs	4·75		☐	

637 'Expeditions'

638 'Skills'

639 'Service'

640 'Recreation'

25th Anniversary of Duke of Edinburgh Award Scheme

1981 (12 AUG.) *Phosphorised paper. Perf* 14

1162	**637**	14p multicoloured	25	10	☐	☐
1163	**638**	18p multicoloured	45	50	☐	☐
1164	**639**	22p multicoloured	70	70	☐	☐
1165	**640**	25p multicoloured	80	80	☐	☐
		Set of 4	2·00	1·90	☐	☐
		First Day Cover		2·40	☐	
		Presentation Pack	2·75		☐	
		PHQ Cards (set of 4)	1·75	4·00	☐	☐
		Set of 4 Gutter Pairs	5·00		☐	

641 Cockle-dredging from Linsey II   **642** Hauling Trawl Net

643 Lobster Potting   **644** Hoisting Seine Net

Fishing Industry

1981 (23 SEPT.) *Phosphorised paper*

1166	**641**	14p multicoloured	25	10	☐	☐
1167	**642**	18p multicoloured	45	50	☐	☐
1168	**643**	22p multicoloured	65	50	☐	☐
1169	**644**	25p multicoloured	75	60	☐	☐
		Set of 4	1·90	1·50	☐	☐
		First Day Cover		2·40		☐
		Presentation Pack	2·75		☐	
		PHQ Cards (set of 4)	1·75	4·00	☐	☐
		Set of 4 Gutter Pairs	4·75		☐	

Nos. 1166/9 were issued on the occasion of the centenary of Royal National Mission to Deep Sea Fishermen.

645 Father Christmas   **646** Jesus Christ

647 Flying Angel   **648** Joseph and Mary arriving at Bethlehem

649 Three Kings approaching Bethlehem

Christmas. Children's Pictures

1981 (18 NOV.) *One phosphor band (11½p) or phosphorised paper (others)*

1170	**645**	11½p multicoloured	20	10	☐	☐
1171	**646**	14p multicoloured	30	10	☐	☐
1172	**647**	18p multicoloured	45	50	☐	☐
1173	**648**	22p multicoloured	65	60	☐	☐
1174	**649**	25p multicoloured	75	65	☐	☐
		Set of 5	2·10	1·75	☐	☐
		First Day Cover		2·25		☐
		Presentation Pack	3·00		☐	
		PHQ Cards (set of 5)	2·00	5·00	☐	☐
		Set of 5 Gutter Pairs	5·25		☐	

Collectors Pack 1981

1981 (18 NOV.) *Comprises Nos. 1143/74*

	Collectors Pack	16·00	☐

650 Charles Darwin and Giant Tortoises   **651** Darwin and Marine Iguanas

652 Darwin, Cactus Ground Finch and Large Ground Finch   **653** Darwin and Prehistoric Skulls

Death Centenary of Charles Darwin

1982 (10 FEB.) *Phosphorised paper*

1175	**650**	15½p multicoloured	35	10	☐	☐
1176	**651**	19½p multicoloured	45	50	☐	☐
1177	**652**	26p multicoloured	60	75	☐	☐
1178	**653**	29p multicoloured	65	80	☐	☐
		Set of 4	1·90	2·00	☐	☐
		First Day Cover		2·50		☐
		Presentation Pack	3·00		☐	
		PHQ Cards (set of 4)	2·50	6·50	☐	☐
		Set of 4 Gutter Pairs	4·75		☐	

654 Boys' Brigade

655 Girls' Brigade

660 Hamlet

661 Opera Singer

Europa. British Theatre

1982 (28 APR.) *Phosphorised paper*

1183	**658**	15½p multicoloured	. . . . .	25	15	☐	☐
1184	**659**	19½p multicoloured	. . . . .	40	50	☐	☐
1185	**660**	26p multicoloured	. . . . .	70	70	☐	☐
1186	**661**	29p multicoloured	. . . . .	75	90	☐	☐
		Set of 4	. . . .	1·90	2·00	☐	☐
		First Day Cover	. . . .		2·75		☐
		Presentation Pack	. . . .	3·00		☐	
		PHQ Cards (set of 4)	. . . . .	2·50	6·50	☐	☐
		Set of 4 Gutter Pairs	. . . . . .	5·00		☐	

656 Boy Scout Movement

657 Girl Guide Movement

Youth Organizations

1982 (24 MAR.) *Phosphorised paper*

1179	**654**	15½p multicoloured	. . . . .	25	15	☐	☐
1180	**655**	19½p multicoloured	. . . . .	45	55	☐	☐
1181	**656**	26p multicoloured	. . . . .	60	75	☐	☐
1182	**657**	29p multicoloured	. . . . .	75	80	☐	☐
		Set of 4	. . . .	1·90	2·00	☐	☐
		First Day Cover	. . . .		2·75		☐
		Presentation Pack	. . . .	3·00		☐	
		PHQ Cards (set of 4)	. . . . .	2·50	6·50	☐	☐
		Set of 4 Gutter Pairs	. . . . . .	5·00		☐	

Nos. 1179/82 were issued on the occasion of the 75th anniversary of the Boy Scout Movement, the 125th birth anniversary of Lord Baden-Powell and the centenary of the Boys' Brigade (1983).

662 Henry VIII and *Mary Rose*

663 Admiral Blake and *Triumph*

658 Ballerina

659 Harlequin

664 Lord Nelson and HMS *Victory*

665 Lord Fisher and HMS *Dreadnought*

666 Viscount Cunningham and HMS *Warspite*

Maritime Heritage

1982 (16 JUNE) *Phosphorised paper*

1187	**662**	15½p multicoloured	35	10 □ □
1188	**663**	19½p multicoloured	50	45 □ □
1189	**664**	24p multicoloured	65	65 □ □
1190	**665**	26p multicoloured	75	75 □ □
1191	**666**	29p multicoloured	80	80 □ □
		Set of 5	2·75	2·50 □ □
		First Day Cover		3·00 □
		Presentation Pack	3·50	□
		PHQ Cards (set of 5)	3·00	7·00 □ □
		Set of 5 Gutter Pairs	7·00	□

667 'Strawberry Thief' (William Morris)

668 Untitled (Steiner and Co)

669 'Cherry Orchard' (Paul Nash)

670 'Chevron' (Andrew Foster)

British Textiles

1982 (23 JULY) *Phosphorised paper*

1192	**667**	15½p multicoloured	25	10 □ □
1193	**668**	19½p multicoloured	50	55 □ □
1194	**669**	26p multicoloured	65	75 □ □
1195	**670**	29p multicoloured	75	90 □ □
		Set of 4	1·90	2·00 □ □
		First Day Cover		2·50 □
		Presentation Pack	2·75	□
		PHQ Cards (set of 4)	3·00	6·50 □ □
		Set of 4 Gutter Pairs	5·00	□

Nos 1192/5 were issued on the occasion of the 250th birth anniversary of Sir Richard Arkwright (inventor of spinning machine).

For full information on all future British issues, collectors should write to Royal Mail, Freepost EH3647, 21 South Gyle Crescent, Edinburgh EH12 9PE.

671 Development of Communications

672 Modern Technological Aids

Information Technology

1982 (8 SEPT.) *Phosphorised paper. Perf* 14 × 15

1196	**671**	15½p multicoloured	40	10 □ □
1197	**672**	26p multicoloured	60	90 □ □
		Set of 2	1·00	1·00 □ □
		First Day Cover		1·75 □
		Presentation Pack	1·60	□
		PHQ Cards (set of 2)	1·50	4·50 □ □
		Set of 2 Gutter Pairs	2·50	□

673 Austin 'Seven' and 'Metro'

674 Ford 'Model T' and 'Escort'

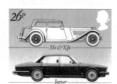

675 Jaguar 'SS1' and 'XJ6'

676 Rolls-Royce 'Silver Ghost' and 'Silver Spirit'

British Motor Industry

1982 (13 OCT.) *Phosphorised paper. Perf* 14½ × 14

1198	**673**	15½p multicoloured	30	10 □ □
1199	**674**	19½p multicoloured	55	55 □ □
1200	**675**	26p multicoloured	65	70 □ □
1201	**676**	29p multicoloured	1·00	90 □ □
		Set of 4	2·25	2·00 □ □
		First Day Cover		2·50 □
		Presentation Pack	3·00	□
		PHQ Cards (set of 4)	3·00	6·75 □ □
		Set of 4 Gutter Pairs	5·75	□

677 'While Shepherds Watched'

678 'The Holly and the Ivy'

679 'I Saw Three Ships'

680 'We Three Kings'

681 'Good King Wenceslas'

Christmas. Carols

1982 (17 Nov.) *One phosphor band (12½p) or phosphorised paper (others).*

1202	**677**	12½p multicoloured	20	10	☐	☐
1203	**678**	15½p multicoloured	30	10	☐	☐
1204	**679**	19½p multicoloured	60	65	☐	☐
1205	**680**	26p multicoloured	70	75	☐	☐
1206	**681**	29p multicoloured	75	80	☐	☐
		Set of 5	2·25	2·10	☐	☐
		First Day Cover		2·75		☐
		Presentation Pack	3·00		☐	
		PHQ Cards (set of 5)	3·00	7·00	☐	☐
		Set of 5 Gutter Pairs	5·75		☐	

Collectors Pack 1982

1982 (17 Nov.) *Comprises Nos. 1175/1206*

	Collectors Pack	22·00		☐

682 Atlantic Salmon

683 Northern Pike

684 Brown Trout

685 Eurasian Perch

British River Fishes

1983 (26 Jan.) *Phosphorised paper*

1207	**682**	15½p multicoloured	30	10	☐	☐
1208	**683**	19½p multicoloured	60	60	☐	☐
1209	**684**	26p multicoloured	75	75	☐	☐
1210	**685**	29p multicoloured	90	90	☐	☐
		Set of 4	2·25	2·10	☐	☐
		First Day Cover		2·75		☐
		Presentation Pack	3·00		☐	
		PHQ Cards (set of 4)	3·00	7·00	☐	☐
		Set of 4 Gutter Pairs	5·75		☐	

686 Tropical Island

687 Desert

688 Temperate Farmland

689 Mountain Range

Commonwealth Day. Geographical Regions

1983 (9 Mar.) *Phosphorised paper*

1211	**686**	15½p multicoloured	30	10	☐	☐
1212	**687**	19½p multicoloured	55	60	☐	☐
1213	**688**	26p multicoloured	70	75	☐	☐
1214	**689**	29p multicoloured	80	80	☐	☐
		Set of 4	2·10	2·00	☐	☐
		First Day Cover		2·50		☐
		Presentation Pack	3·00		☐	
		PHQ Cards (set of 4)	3·00	6·50	☐	☐
		Set of 4 Gutter Pairs	5·25		☐	

690   Humber Bridge

691   Thames Flood Barrier

692   *Iolair* (oilfield emergency support vessel)

Europa. Engineering Achievements

1983 (25 MAY) *Phosphorised paper*

1215	690	16p multicoloured	30	10 ☐ ☐
1216	691	20½p multicoloured	80	1·00 ☐ ☐
1217	692	28p multicoloured	90	1·00 ☐ ☐
	Set of 3	1·75	1·90 ☐ ☐
	First Day Cover		2·40 ☐
	Presentation Pack	3·00	☐
	PHQ Cards (set of 3)	2·50	5·00 ☐ ☐
	Set of 3 Gutter Pairs	4·50	☐

693   Musketeer and Pikeman, The Royal Scots (1633)

694   Fusilier and Ensign, The Royal Welch Fusiliers (mid-18th century)

695   Riflemen, 95th Rifles (The Royal Green Jackets) (1805)

696   Sergeant (khaki service uniform) and Guardsman full dress), The Irish Guards (1900).

697   Paratroopers, The Parachute Regiment (1983)

British Army Uniforms

1983 (6 JULY) *Phosphorised paper*

1218	693	16p multicoloured	30	10 ☐ ☐
1219	694	20½p multicoloured	45	60 ☐ ☐
1220	695	26p multicoloured	70	90 ☐ ☐
1221	696	28p multicoloured	75	90 ☐ ☐
1222	697	31p multicoloured	75	80 ☐ ☐
	Set of 5	2·75	3·00 ☐ ☐
	First Day Cover		3·00 ☐
	Presentation Pack	4·00	☐
	PHQ Cards (set of 5)	3·00	7·50 ☐ ☐
	Set of 5 Gutter Pairs	7·00	☐

Nos. 1218/22 were issued on the occasion of the 350th anniversary of The Royal Scots, the senior line regiment of the British Army.

SISSINGHURST

698   20th-Century Garden, Sissinghurst

BIDDULPH GRANGE

699   19th-Century Garden, Biddulph Grange

BLENHEIM

700   18th-Century Garden, Blenheim

PITMEDDEN

701   17th-Century Garden, Pitmedden

British Gardens

1983 (24 Aug.) *Phosphorised paper. Perf* 14

1223	**698**	16p multicoloured	30	10 ☐ ☐
1224	**699**	20½p multicoloured	40	55 ☐ ☐
1225	**700**	28p multicoloured	75	90 ☐ ☐
1226	**701**	31p multicoloured	80	90 ☐ ☐
		Set of 4	2·00	2·25 ☐ ☐
		First Day Cover		2·75 ☐
		Presentation Pack	3·25	☐
		PHQ Cards (set of 4)	3·00	6·00 ☐ ☐
		Set of 4 Gutter Pairs	5·00	☐

702 Merry-go-round

703 Big Wheel, Helter-skelter and Performing Animals

704 Side-shows

705 Early Produce Fair

British Fairs

1983 (5 Oct.) *Phosphorised paper*

1227	**702**	16p multicoloured	30	10 ☐ ☐
1228	**703**	20½p multicoloured	55	65 ☐ ☐
1229	**704**	28p multicoloured	65	75 ☐ ☐
1230	**705**	31p multicoloured	75	75 ☐ ☐
		Set of 4	2·00	2·00 ☐ ☐
		First Day Cover		2·50 ☐
		Presentation Pack	3·25	☐
		PHQ Cards (set of 4)	3·00	6·00 ☐ ☐
		Set of 4 Gutter Pairs	5·00	☐

Nos. 1227/30 were issued to mark the 850th anniversary of St Bartholomew's Fair, Smithfield, London.

706 'Christmas Post' (pillar-box)

707 'The Three Kings' (chimney-pots)

708 'World at Peace' (Dove and Blackbird)

709 'Light of Christmas' (street lamp)

710 'Christmas Dove' (hedge sculpture)

Christmas

1983 (16 Nov.) *One phosphor band* (12½p) *or phosphorised paper* (*others*)

1231	**706**	12½p multicoloured	25	10 ☐ ☐
1232	**707**	16p multicoloured	30	10 ☐ ☐
1233	**708**	20½p multicoloured	55	75 ☐ ☐
1234	**709**	28p multicoloured	75	80 ☐ ☐
1235	**710**	31p multicoloured	90	1·00 ☐ ☐
		Set of 5	2·50	2·50 ☐ ☐
		First Day Cover		3·00 ☐
		Presentation Pack	3·50	☐
		PHQ Cards (set of 5)	3·00	6·00 ☐ ☐
		Set of 5 Gutter Pairs	6·25	☐

Collectors Pack 1983

1983 (16 Nov.) *Comprises Nos.* 1207/35

	Collectors Pack	27·00	☐

711 Arms of the College of Arms

712 Arms of King Richard III (founder)

713 Arms of the Earl Marshal of England

714 Arms of the City of London

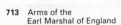

500th Anniversary of College of Arms

1984 (17 Jan.) *Phosphorised paper. Perf 14½*

1236	711	16p multicoloured	30	10	☐	☐
1237	712	20½p multicoloured	40	60	☐	☐
1238	713	28p multicoloured	80	80	☐	☐
1239	714	31p multicoloured	90	90	☐	☐
		Set of 4	2·25	2·25	☐	☐
		First Day Cover		3·25		☐
		Presentation Pack	3·25		☐	
		PHQ Cards (set of 4)	3·00	7·50	☐	☐
		Set of 4 Gutter Pairs	5·75		☐	

715 Highland Cow

716 Chillingham Wild Bull

717 Hereford Bull

718 Welsh Black Bull

719 Irish Moiled Cow

British Cattle

1984 (6 Mar.) *Phosphorised paper*

1240	715	16p multicoloured	35	10	☐	☐
1241	716	20½p multicoloured	55	55	☐	☐
1242	717	26p multicoloured	75	70	☐	☐
1243	718	28p multicoloured	75	75	☐	☐
1244	719	31p multicoloured	1·00	80	☐	☐
		Set of 5	3·00	2·75	☐	☐
		First Day Cover		3·75		☐
		Presentation Pack	4·00		☐	
		PHQ Cards (set of 5)	3·00	7·00	☐	☐
		Set of 5 Gutter Pairs	7·50		☐	

Nos. 1240/4 marked the centenary of the Highland Cattle Society and the bicentenary of the Royal Highland and Agricultural Society of Scotland.

720 Festival Hall, Liverpool

721 Milburngate Shopping Centre, Durham

722 Bush House, Bristol

723 Commercial Street Housing Scheme, Perth

Urban Renewal

1984 (10 Apr.) *Phosphorised paper*

1245	720	16p multicoloured	30	10	☐	☐
1246	721	20½p multicoloured	50	60	☐	☐
1247	722	28p multicoloured	90	1·00	☐	☐
1248	723	31p multicoloured	1·00	1·00	☐	☐
		Set of 4	2·40	2·40	☐	☐
		First Day Cover		3·00		☐
		Presentation Pack	3·00		☐	
		PHQ Cards (set of 4)	3·00	6·00	☐	☐
		Set of 4 Gutter Pairs	6·00		☐	

Nos. 1245/8 marked the opening of the International Gardens Festival, Liverpool, and the 150th anniversaries of the Royal Institute of British Architects and the Chartered Institute of Building.

724 C.E.P.T. 25th Anniversary Logo

725 Abduction of Europa

Nos. 1249/50 and 1251/2 were each printed together, *se-tenant*, in horizontal pairs throughout the sheets.

For full information on all future British issues, collectors should write to Royal Mail, Freepost EH3647, 21 South Syle Crescent, Edinburgh EH12 9PE.

Europa. 25th Anniversary of C.E.P.T. and 2nd European Parliamentary Elections

1984 (15 MAY) *Phosphorised paper*

1249	**724**	16p greenish slate, deep blue and gold	30	15	☐	☐
		a. Horiz pair. Nos. 1249/50	1·00	1·25	☐	☐
1250	**725**	16p greenish slate, deep blue, black and gold .	30	15	☐	☐
1251	**724**	20½p Venetian red, deep magenta and gold . .	70	75	☐	☐
		a. Horiz pair. Nos. 1251/2	2·00	2·50	☐	☐
1252	**725**	20½p Venetian red, deep magenta, black and gold	70	75	☐	☐
		Set of 4	2·75	1·60	☐	☐
		First Day Cover		4·00		☐
		Presentation Pack	4·50		☐	
		PHQ Cards (set of 4)	3·00	6·00	☐	☐
		Set of 2 Gutter Blocks of 4 . . .	6·75		☐	

726   Lancaster House

London Economic Summit Conference

1984 (5 JUNE) *Phosphorised paper*

1253	**726**	31p multicoloured	80	80	☐	☐
		First Day Cover		2·00		☐
		PHQ Card	1·00	3·25	☐	☐
		Gutter Pair	2·00		☐	

727   View of Earth from 'Apollo 11'

728   Navigational Chart of English Channel

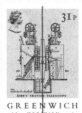

729   Greenwich Observatory

730   Sir George Airey's Transit Telescope

Centenary of Greenwich Meridian

1984 (26 JUNE) *Phosphorised paper. Perf* 14 × 14½

1254	**727**	16p multicoloured	35	10	☐	☐
1255	**728**	20½p multicoloured	55	55	☐	☐
1256	**729**	28p multicoloured	75	75	☐	☐
1257	**730**	31p multicoloured	1·00	90	☐	☐
		Set of 4	2·40	2·10	☐	☐
		First Day Cover		2·50		☐
		Presentation Pack	3·25		☐	
		PHQ Cards (set of 4)	3·00	6·00	☐	☐
		Set of 4 Gutter Pairs	6·00		☐	

731   Bath Mail Coach, 1784

732   Attack on Exeter Mail, 1816

733   Norwich Mail in Thunderstorm, 1827

734   Holyhead and Liverpool Mails leaving London, 1828

735   Edinburgh Mail Snowbound, 1831

T **731/5** were printed together, *se-tenant,* in horizontal strips of 5 throughout the sheet.

Bicentenary of First Mail Coach Run, Bath and Bristol to London

1984 (31 July) *Phosphorised paper*

1258	**731**	16p multicoloured	40	35	☐	☐
		a. Horiz strip of 5. Nos.				
		1258/62	2·50	2·75	☐	☐
1259	**732**	16p multicoloured	40	35	☐	☐
1260	**733**	16p multicoloured	40	35	☐	☐
1261	**734**	16p multicoloured	40	35	☐	☐
1262	**735**	16p multicoloured	40	35	☐	☐
		Set of 5	2·50	1·60	☐	☐
		First Day Cover		3·50		☐
		Presentation Pack	3·50		☐	
		Souvenir Book	7·00		☐	
		PHQ Cards (set of 5)	3·00	7·50	☐	☐
		Gutter Block of 10	6·00		☐	

736 Nigerian Clinic

737 Violinist and Acropolis, Athens

738 Building Project, Sri Lanka

739 British Council Library

50th Anniversary of The British Council

1984 (25 Sept.) *Phosphorised paper*

1263	**736**	17p multicoloured	35	10	☐	☐
1264	**737**	22p multicoloured	55	75	☐	☐
1265	**738**	31p multicoloured	70	1·00	☐	☐
1266	**739**	34p multicoloured	75	90	☐	☐
		Set of 4	2·10	2·50	☐	☐
		First Day Cover		3·00		☐
		Presentation Pack	3·25		☐	
		PHQ Cards (set of 4)	3·00	6·00	☐	☐
		Set of 4 Gutter Pairs	5·25		☐	

For full information on all future British issues, collectors should write to Royal Mail, Freepost EH3647, 21 South Gyle Crescent, Edinburgh EH12 9PE.

740 The Holy Family   **741** Arrival in Bethlehem

742 Shepherd and Lamb   **743** Virgin and Child

744 Offering of Frankincense

Christmas

1984 (20 Nov.) *One phosphor band (13p) or phosphorised paper (others)*

1267	**740**	13p multicoloured	20	15	☐	☐
1268	**741**	17p multicoloured	40	20	☐	☐
1269	**742**	22p multicoloured	50	70	☐	☐
1270	**743**	31p multicoloured	70	90	☐	☐
1271	**744**	34p multicoloured	90	1·00	☐	☐
		Set of 5	2·40	2·75	☐	☐
		First Day Cover		3·25		☐
		Presentation Pack	3·50		☐	
		PHQ Cards (set of 5)	3·00	6·00	☐	☐
		Set of 5 Gutter Pairs	6·00		☐	

Collectors Pack 1984

1984 (20 Nov.) *Comprises Nos. 1236/71*

	Collectors Pack	35·00		☐

Post Office Yearbook

1984 *Comprises Nos. 1236/71 in hardbound book with slip case*

	Yearbook	90·00		☐

745 'Flying Scotsman'

746 'Golden Arrow'

Wart-Biter Bush-Cricket

752 *Decticus verrucivorus* (bush-cricket)

Stag Beetle

753 *Lucanus cervus* (stag beetle)

CHELTENHAM FLYER

747 'Cheltenham Flyer'

ROYAL SCOT

748 'Royal Scot'

Emperor Dragonfly

754 *Anax imperator* (dragonfly)

Insects

1985 (12 Mar.) *Phosphorised paper*

1277	750	17p multicoloured	. . . . .	35	10	☐	☐
1278	751	22p multicoloured	. . . . .	55	55	☐	☐
1279	752	29p multicoloured	. . . . .	80	90	☐	☐
1280	753	31p multicoloured	. . . . .	1·00	1·00	☐	☐
1281	754	34p multicoloured	. . . . .	1·00	90	☐	☐
		Set of 5	. . . .	3·50	3·25	☐	☐
		First Day Cover	. . . .		4·00		☐
		Presentation Pack	. . . .	4·50		☐	
		PHQ Cards (set of 5)	. . . .	3·00	8·00	☐	☐
		Set of 5 Gutter Pairs	. . . . .	8·75		☐	

Nos. 1277/81 were issued on the occasion of the centenaries of the Royal Entomological Society of London's Royal Charter and of the Selborne Society.

CORNISH RIVIERA

749 'Cornish Riviera'

Famous Trains

1985 (22 Jan.) *Phosphorised paper*

1272	745	17p multicoloured	. . . . .	40	10	☐	☐
1273	746	22p multicoloured	. . . . .	70	75	☐	☐
1274	747	29p multicoloured	. . . . .	80	90	☐	☐
1275	748	31p multicoloured	. . . . .	1·00	1·10	☐	☐
1276	749	34p multicoloured	. . . . .	1·25	1·10	☐	☐
		Set of 5	. . . .	3·75	3·50	☐	☐
		First Day Cover	. . . .		6·00		☐
		Presentation Pack	. . . .	6·00		☐	
		PHQ Cards (set of 5)	. . . .	5·50	16·00	☐	☐
		Set of 5 Gutter Pairs	. . . . .	9·25		☐	

Nos. 1272/6 were issued on the occasion of the 150th anniversary of the Great Western Railway Company.

Buff Tailed Bumble Bee

750 *Bombus terrestris* (bee)

Seven Spotted Ladybird

751 *Coccinella septempunctata* (ladybird)

WATER·MUSIC
George Frideric Handel

755 'Water Music', by Handel

THE·PLANETS·SUITE
Gustav Holst

756 'The Planets', by Holst

THIRTY-ONE-PENCE

THE FIRST CUCKOO
Frederick Delius

THIRTY-FOUR-PENCE

SEA PICTURES
Edward Elgar

757 'The First Cuckoo',
by Delius

758 'Sea Pictures',
by Elgar

Europa. European Music Year

1985 (14 MAY) *Phosphorised paper. Perf* 14½

1282	**755**	17p multicoloured	. . . .	55	10	□ □
1283	**756**	22p multicoloured	. . . .	75	90	□ □
1284	**757**	31p multicoloured	. . . .	1·25	1·25	□ □
1285	**758**	34p multicoloured	. . . .	1·25	1·25	□ □
		Set of 4	. . . .	3·50	3·25	□ □
		First Day Cover	. . . .		4·50	□
		Presentation Pack	. . . .	4·75		□
		PHQ Cards (set of 4)	. . . . . .	3·00	6·00	□ □
		Set of 4 Gutter Pairs	. . . . . .	8·75		□

Nos. 1282/5 were issued on the occasion of the 300th birth anniversary of Handel.

759 R.N.L.I. Lifeboat and
Signal Flags

760 Beachy Head Lighthouse
and Chart

761 'Marecs A'
Communications Satelite
and Dish Aerials

762 Buoys

Safety at Sea

1985 (18 JUNE) *Phosphorised paper. Perf* 14

1286	**759**	17p multicoloured	. . . .	35	10	□ □
1287	**760**	22p multicoloured	. . . .	55	65	□ □
1288	**761**	31p multicoloured	. . . .	80	90	□ □
1289	**762**	34p multicoloured	. . . .	90	1·10	□ □
		Set of 4	. . . .	2·40	2·50	□ □
		First Day Cover	. . . .		3·25	□
		Presentation Pack	. . . .	4·00		□
		PHQ Cards (set of 4)	. . . . . .	3·00	6·00	□ □
		Set of 4 Gutter Pairs	. . . . . .	6·00		□

Nos. 1286/9 were issued to mark the bicentenary of the unimmersible lifeboat and the 50th anniversary of Radar.

763 Datapost Motorcyclist,
City of London

764 Rural Postbus

765 Parcel Delivery
in Winter

766 Town Letter Delivery

350 Years of Royal Mail Public Postal Service

1985 (30 JULY) *Phosphorised paper*

1290	**763**	17p multicoloured	. . . .	35	10	□ □
1291	**764**	22p multicoloured	. . . .	55	70	□ □
1292	**765**	31p multicoloured	. . . .	80	1·00	□ □
1293	**766**	34p multicoloured	. . . .	1·00	1·00	□ □
		Set of 4	. . . .	2·40	2·50	□ □
		First Day Cover	. . . .		3·25	□
		Presentation Pack	. . . .	3·75		□
		PHQ Cards (set of 4)	. . . . . .	3·00	6·00	□ □
		Set of 4 Gutter Pairs	. . . . . .	6·00		□

767 King Arthur and Merlin

768 The Lady of the Lake

769   Queen Guinevere and Sir Lancelot

770   Sir Galahad

Arthurian Legends

1985 (3 SEPT.) *Phosphorised paper*

1294	**767**	17p multicoloured	35	10	□	□
1295	**768**	22p multicoloured	55	70	□	□
1296	**769**	31p multicoloured	90	1·10	□	□
1297	**770**	34p multicoloured	1·00	1·10	□	□
		Set of 4	2·50	2·75	□	□
		First Day Cover		3·50		□
		Presentation Pack	4·50		□	
		PHQ Cards (set of 4)	3·00	7·00	□	□
		Set of 4 Gutter Pairs	6·25		□	

Nos. 1294/7 were issued to mark the 500th anniversary of the printing of Sir Thomas Malory's *Morte d'Arthur*.

771   Peter Sellers (from photo by Bill Brandt)

772   David Niven (from photo by Cornell Lucas)

773   Charlie Chaplin (from photo by Lord Snowdon)

774   Vivien Leigh (from photo by Angus McBean)

775   Alfred Hitchcock (from photo by Howard Coster)

British Film Year

1985 (8 OCT.) *Phosphorised paper. Perf 14½*

1298	**771**	17p multicoloured	45	10	□	□
1299	**772**	22p multicoloured	60	70	□	□
1300	**773**	29p multicoloured	1·00	1·10	□	□
1301	**774**	31p multicoloured	1·10	1·25	□	□
1302	**775**	34p multicoloured	1·40	1·40	□	□
		Set of 5	4·00	4·00	□	□
		First Day Cover		5·00		□
		Presentation Pack	6·00		□	
		Souvenir Book	10·00		□	
		PHQ Cards (set of 5)	3·00	9·50	□	□
		Set of 5 Gutter Pairs	9·25		□	

776   Principal Boy

777   Genie

778   Dame

779   Good Fairy

780   Pantomime Cat

Christmas. Pantomime Characters

1985 (19 NOV.) *One phosphor band (12p) or phosphorised paper (others)*

1303	**776**	12p multicoloured	35	15	□	□
1304	**777**	17p multicoloured	40	25	□	□
1305	**778**	22p multicoloured	65	90	□	□
1306	**779**	31p multicoloured	1·00	1·10	□	□
1307	**780**	34p multicoloured	1·10	1·25	□	□
		Set of 5	3·00	3·25	□	□
		First Day Cover		3·75		□
		Presentation Pack	4·25		□	
		PHQ Cards (Set of 5)	3·00	8·00	□	□
		Set of 5 Gutter Pairs	7·00		□	

Collectors Pack 1985

1985 (19 Nov.) *Comprises Nos. 1272/1307*
  Collectors Pack . . . . 35·00 ☐

Post Office Yearbook

1985 *Comprises Nos. 1272/1307 in hardbound book with slip case*
  Yearbook . . . . 80·00 ☐

17 PENCE · INDUSTRY YEAR 1986

781 Light Bulb and North Sea Oil Drilling Rig (Energy)

22 PENCE · INDUSTRY YEAR 1986

782 Thermometer and Pharmaceutical Laboratory (Health)

31 PENCE · INDUSTRY YEAR 1986

783 Garden Hoe and Steel Works (Steel)

34 PENCE · INDUSTRY YEAR 1986

784 Loaf of Bread and and Cornfield (Agriculture)

Industry Year

1986 (14 Jan.) *Phosphorised paper. Perf* $14\frac{1}{2} \times 14$

1308	**781**	17p multicoloured	35	10	☐ ☐
1309	**782**	22p multicoloured	55	70	☐ ☐
1310	**783**	31p multicoloured	1·00	1·10	☐ ☐
1311	**784**	34p multicoloured	1·25	1·25	☐ ☐
		Set of 4	2·75	2·75	☐ ☐
		First Day Cover		3·75	☐
		Presentation Pack	3·75		☐
		PHQ Cards (set of 4)	3·00	6·00	☐ ☐
		Set of 4 Gutter Pairs	6·75		☐

17p

785 Dr Edmond Halley as Comet

22p

786 *Giotto* Spacecraft approaching Comet

'Twice in a Lifetime' 31p

787 'Twice in a Lifetime'

34p

788 Comet orbiting Sun and Planets

Appearance of Halley's Comet

1986 (18 Feb.) *Phosphorised paper*

1312	**785**	17p multicoloured	35	10	☐ ☐
1313	**786**	22p multicoloured	60	75	☐ ☐
1314	**787**	31p multicoloured	90	1·00	☐ ☐
1315	**788**	34p multicoloured	1·10	1·10	☐ ☐
		Set of 4	2·75	2·75	☐ ☐
		First Day Cover		4·00	☐
		Presentation Pack	3·75		☐
		PHQ Cards (set of 4)	4·00	6·00	☐ ☐
		Set of 4 Gutter Pairs	6·75		☐

HER MAJESTY THE QUEEN

Sixtieth Birthday 17p

789 Queen Elizabeth II in 1928, 1942 and 1952

HER MAJESTY THE QUEEN

Sixtieth Birthday 17p

790 Queen Elizabeth II in 1958, 1973 and 1982

Nos. 1316/17 and 1318/19 were each printed together, *se-tenant*, in horizontal pairs throughout the sheets.

60th Birthday of Queen Elizabeth II

1986 (21 Apr.) *Phosphorised paper*

1316	**789**	17p multicoloured	60	50	☐ ☐
		a. Horiz pair. Nos. 1316/17	1·50	1·50	☐ ☐
1317	**790**	17p multicoloured	60	50	☐ ☐
1318	**789**	34p multicoloured	1·40	1·75	☐ ☐
		a. Horiz pair. Nos. 1318/19	3·00	3·75	☐ ☐
1319	**790**	34p multicoloured	1·40	1·75	☐ ☐
		Set of 4	4·50	4·00	☐ ☐
		First Day Cover		4·50	☐
		Presentation Pack	6·50		☐
		Souvenir Book	9·00		☐
		PHQ Cards (set of 4)	3·00	7·00	☐ ☐
		Set of 2 Gutter Blocks of 4 . . .	11·00		☐

For full information on all future British issues, collectors should write to Royal Mail, Freepost EH3647, 21 South Gyle Crescent, Edinburgh EH12 9PE.

791 Barn Owl

792 Pine Marten

793 Wild Cat

794 Natterjack Toad

Europa. Nature Conservation. Endangered Species

1986 (20 May) *Phosphorised paper. Perf* $14\frac{1}{2} \times 14$

1320	791	17p multicoloured	40	10 □ □
1321	792	22p multicoloured	80	1·00 □ □
1322	793	31p multicoloured	1·25	1·25 □ □
1323	794	34p multicoloured	1·40	1·40 □ □
		Set of 4	3·50	3·50 □ □
		First Day Cover		4·25 □
		Presentation Pack	4·25	□
		PHQ Cards (set of 4)	3·00	7·00 □ □
		Set of 4 Gutter Pairs	8·75	□

795 Peasants Working in Fields

796 Freemen working at Town Trades

797 Knight and Retainers

798 Lord at Banquet

900th Anniversary of Domesday Book

1986 (17 June) *Phosphorised paper*

1324	795	17p multicoloured	40	10 □ □
1325	796	22p multicoloured	70	85 □ □
1326	797	31p multicoloured	1·10	1·40 □ □
1327	798	34p multicoloured	1·25	1·40 □ □
		Set of 4	3·00	3·50 □ □
		First Day Cover		4·25 □
		Presentation Pack	4·00	□
		PHQ Cards (set of 4)	3·00	6·00 □ □
		Set of 4 Gutter Pairs	7·00	□

799 Athletics

800 Rowing

801 Weightlifting

802 Rifle-shooting

803 Hockey

Thirteenth Commonwealth Games, Edinburgh (Nos. 1328/31) and World Men's Hockey Cup, London (No. 1332)

1986 (15 July) *Phosphorised paper*

1328	799	17p multicoloured	40	10 □ □
1329	800	22p multicoloured	55	70 □ □
1330	801	29p multicoloured	75	80 □ □
1331	802	31p multicoloured	1·00	1·10 □ □
1332	803	34p multicoloured	1·25	1·25 □ □
		Set of 5	3·50	3·50 □ □
		First Day Cover		4·75 □
		Presentation Pack	4·50	□
		PHQ Cards (set of 5)	4·00	8·00 □ □
		Set of 5 Gutter Pairs	8·75	□

No. 1332 also marked the centenary of the Hockey Association.

804   Prince Andrew and Miss Sarah Ferguson **805**

Royal Wedding

1986 (22 July) *One side band* (12p) *or phosphorised paper* (17p)
1333	**804**	12p multicoloured	50	30	□	□
1334	**805**	17p multicoloured	1·00	95	□	□
		Set of 2	1·50	1·25	□	□
		First Day Cover		2·25		□
		Presentation Pack	2·00		□	
		PHQ Cards (set of 2)	1·75	5·00	□	□
		Set of 2 Gutter Pairs	3·50		□	

806   Stylised Cross on Ballot Paper

2nd Commonwealth Parliamentary Conference, London

1986 (19 Aug.) *Phosphorised paper. Perf* 14 × 14½
1335	**806**	34p multicoloured	1·00	1·00	□	□
		First Day Cover		1·60		□
		PHQ Card	1·00	2·50	□	□
		Gutter Pair	2·50		□	

807   Lord Dowding and
       Hawker Hurricane Mk. I

808   Lord Tedder and
       Hawker Typhoon 1B

809   Lord Trenchard and   810   Sir Arthur Harris and
       De Havilland D.H.9A   Avro Type 683 Lancaster

811   Lord Portal and De
       Havilland D.H.98 Mosquito

History of the Royal Air Force

1986 (16th Sept.) *Phosphorised paper. Perf* 14½ × 14
1336	**807**	17p multicoloured	70	10	□	□
1337	**808**	22p multicoloured	90	95	□	□
1338	**809**	29p multicoloured	1·25	1·10	□	□
1339	**810**	31p multicoloured	1·50	1·40	□	□
1340	**811**	34p multicoloured	1·75	1·50	□	□
		Set of 5	5·50	4·50	□	□
		First Day Cover		5·25		□
		Presentation Pack	6·00		□	
		PHQ Cards (set of 5)	4·00	10·00	□	□
		Set of 5 Gutter Pairs	13·00		□	

Nos. 1336/40 were issued to celebrate the 50th anniversary of the first R.A.F. Commands.

812   The Glastonbury Thorn   813   The Tanad Valley Plygain

814   The Hebrides Tribute   815   The Dewsbury Church
                                         Knell

816 The Hereford Boy Bishop

Christmas. Folk Customs

1986 (18 Nov.–2 Dec.) *One phosphor band (12p, 13p) or phosphorised paper (others)*

1341	**812**	12p multicoloured (2 Dec.)	50	30	☐	☐
1342		13p multicoloured	25	10	☐	☐
1343	**813**	18p multicoloured	45	10	☐	☐
1344	**814**	22p multicoloured	80	95	☐	☐
1345	**815**	31p multicoloured	90	1·00	☐	☐
1346	**816**	34p multicoloured	1·10	1·10	☐	☐
		Set of 6	3·50	3·25	☐	☐
		First Day Covers (2)		5·75		☐
		Presentation Pack (Nos. 1342/6)	5·00			☐
		PHQ Cards (set of 5) (Nos. 1342/6)	3·00	7·00	☐	☐
		Set of 6 Gutter Pairs	8·50			☐

Collectors Pack 1986

1986 (18 Nov.) *Comprises Nos. 1308/40, 1342/6*

Collectors Pack . . . . 35·00 ☐

Post Office Yearbook

1986 *Comprises Nos. 1308/40, 1342/6 in hardbound book with slip case*

Yearbook . . . . 75·00 ☐

817 North American Blanket Flower

818 Globe Thistle

819 Echeveria

820 Autumn Crocus

Flower Photographs by Alfred Lammer

1987 (20 Jan.) *Phosphorised paper. Perf 14½ × 14*

1347	**817**	18p multicoloured	40	10	☐	☐
1348	**818**	22p multicoloured	70	85	☐	☐
1349	**819**	31p multicoloured	1·00	1·25	☐	☐
1350	**820**	34p multicoloured	1·10	1·25	☐	☐
		Set of 4	3·00	3·25	☐	☐
		First Day Cover		3·75		☐
		Presentation Pack	4·50			☐
		PHQ Cards (set of 4)	3·00	7·00	☐	☐
		Set of 4 Gutter Pairs	7·50			☐

821 The Principia Mathematica

822 Motion of Bodies in Ellipses

823 Optick Treatise

824 The System of the World

300th Anniversary of The Principia Mathematica by Sir Isaac Newton

1987 (24 Mar.) *Phosphorised paper*

1351	**821**	18p multicoloured	60	15	☐	☐
1352	**822**	22p multicoloured	85	90	☐	☐
1353	**823**	31p multicoloured	1·40	1·60	☐	☐
1354	**824**	34p multicoloured	1·50	1·50	☐	☐
		Set of 4	4·00	3·75	☐	☐
		First Day Cover		4·25		☐
		Presentation Pack	4·50			☐
		PHQ Cards (set of 4)	3·00	6·25	☐	☐
		Set of 4 Gutter Pairs	9·00			☐

For full information on all future British issues, collectors should write to Royal Mail, Freepost EH3647, 21 South Gyle Crescent, Edinburgh EH12 9PE.

825 Willis Faber and Dumas Building, Ipswich   **826** Pompidou Centre, Paris

827 Staatsgalerie, Stuttgart   **828** European Investment Bank, Luxembourg

Europa. British Architects in Europe
1987 (12 May) *Phosphorised paper*

1355	**825**	18p multicoloured	55	15	☐	☐
1356	**826**	22p multicoloured	80	90	☐	☐
1357	**827**	31p multicoloured	1·40	1·50	☐	☐
1358	**828**	34p multicoloured	1·50	1·50	☐	☐
		Set of 4	3·75	3·75	☐	☐
		First Day Cover		4·25		☐
		Presentation Pack	4·50		☐	
		PHQ Cards (set of 4)	3·00	6·25	☐	☐
		Set of 4 Gutter Pairs	8·50		☐	

829 Brigade Members with Ashford Litter, 1887

830 Bandaging Blitz Victim, 1940

831 Volunteer with fainting Girl, 1965

832 Transport of Transplant Organ by Air Wing, 1987

Centenary of St John Ambulance Brigade
1987 (16 June) *Phosphorised paper. Perf* 14 × 14½

1359	**829**	18p multicoloured	40	10	☐	☐
1360	**830**	22p multicoloured	60	70	☐	☐
1361	**831**	31p multicoloured	1·00	1·10	☐	☐
1362	**832**	34p multicoloured	1·25	1·25	☐	☐
		Set of 4	3·00	3·00	☐	☐
		First Day Cover		3·75		☐
		Presentation Pack	4·50		☐	
		PHQ Cards (set of 4)	3·00	6·25	☐	☐
		Set of 4 Gutter Pairs	7·50		☐	

833 Arms of the Lord Lyon King of Arms   **834** Scottish Heraldic Banner of Prince Charles

835 Arms of Royal Scottish Academy of Painting, Sculpture and Architecture   **836** Arms of Royal Society of Edinburgh

300th Anniversary of Revival of Order of the Thistle
1987 (21 July) *Phosphorised paper. Perf* 14½

1363	**833**	18p multicoloured	50	10	☐	☐
1364	**834**	22p multicoloured	75	90	☐	☐
1365	**835**	31p multicoloured	1·40	1·40	☐	☐
1366	**836**	34p multicoloured	1·50	1·40	☐	☐
		Set of 4	3·75	3·50	☐	☐
		First Day Cover		4·00		☐
		Presentation Pack	4·50		☐	
		PHQ Cards (set of 4)	3·00	7·50	☐	☐
		Set of 4 Gutter Pairs	9·00		☐	

For full information on all future British issues, collectors should write to Royal Mail, Freepost EH3647, 21 South Gyle Crescent, Edinburgh EH12 9PE.

837 Crystal Palace, 'Monarch of the Glen' (Landseer) and Grace Darling

838 Great Eastern, Beeton's Book of Household Management and Prince Albert

839 Albert Memorial, Ballot Box and Disraeli

840 Diamond Jubilee Emblem, Morse Key and Newspaper Placard for Relief of Mafeking

150th Anniversary of Queen Victoria's Accession

1987 (8 SEPT.) *Phosphorised paper*

1367	**837**	18p multicoloured	. . . . .	50		10	☐	☐
1368	**838**	22p multicoloured	. . . . .	80		90	☐	☐
1369	**839**	31p multicoloured	. . . . .	1·50		1·50	☐	☐
1370	**840**	34p multicoloured	. . . . .	1·60		1·60	☐	☐
		Set of 4	. . . .	4·00		3·75	☐	☐
		First Day Cover	. . . .			4·00		☐
		Presentation Pack	. . . .	4·50			☐	
		PHQ Cards (set of 4)	. . . . . .	3·00		7·00	☐	☐
		Set of 4 Gutter Pairs	. . . . . .	10·00			☐	

841 Pot by Bernard Leach

842 Pot by Elizabeth Fritsch

843 Pot by Lucie Rie

844 Pot by Hans Coper

Studio Pottery

1987 (13 OCT.) *Phosphorised paper. Perf* $14\frac{1}{2} \times 14$

1371	**841**	18p multicoloured	. . . . .	50		10	☐	☐
1372	**842**	26p multicoloured	. . . . .	70		70	☐	☐
1373	**843**	31p multicoloured	. . . . .	1·25		1·10	☐	☐
1374	**844**	34p multicoloured	. . . . .	1·40		1·40	☐	☐
		Set of 4	. . . .	3·50		3·00	☐	☐
		First Day Cover	. . . .			3·50		☐
		Presentation Pack	. . . .	4·50			☐	
		PHQ Cards (set of 4)	. . . . . .	3·00		6·00	☐	☐
		Set of 4 Gutter Pairs	. . . . . .	8·50			☐	

Nos. 1371/4 also mark the birth centenary of Bernard Leach, the potter.

845 Decorating the Christmas Tree

846 Waiting for Father Christmas

847 Sleeping Child and Father Christmas in Sleigh

848 Child reading

849 Child playing Flute and Snowman

Christmas

1987 (17 NOV.) *One phosphor band (13p) or phosphorised paper (others)*

1375	**845**	13p multicoloured	. . . . .	30		10	☐	☐
1376	**846**	18p multicoloured	. . . . .	40		20	☐	☐
1377	**847**	26p multicoloured	. . . . .	80		1·00	☐	☐
1378	**848**	31p multicoloured	. . . . .	1·10		1·50	☐	☐
1379	**849**	34p multicoloured	. . . . .	1·25		1·50	☐	☐
		Set of 5	. . . .	3·50		4·00	☐	☐
		First Day Cover	. . . .			4·50		☐
		Presentation Pack	. . . .	4·50			☐	
		PHQ Cards (set of 5)	. . . . . .	3·00		6·00	☐	☐
		Set of 5 Gutter Pairs	. . . . . .	8·50			☐	

Collectors Pack 1987

1987 (17 Nov.) *Comprises Nos. 1347/79*
     Collectors Pack . . . . 40·00 ☐

Post Office Yearbook

1987 *Comprises Nos. 1347/79 in hardbound book with slip case*
     Yearbook . . . . 40·00 ☐

850 Short-spined Seascorpion ('Bull-rout') (Jonathan Couch)

851 Yellow Waterlily (Major Joshua Swatkin)

852 Whistling ('Bewick's') Swan (Edward Lear)

853 Morchella esculenta (James Sowerby)

Bicentenary of Linnean Society. Archive Illustrations

1988 (19 Jan.) *Phosphorised paper*

1380	850	18p multicoloured	55	10 ☐ ☐
1381	851	26p multicoloured	85	1·00 ☐ ☐
1382	852	31p multicoloured	1·10	1·25 ☐ ☐
1383	853	34p multicoloured	1·25	1·40 ☐ ☐
		Set of 4	3·25	3·25 ☐ ☐
		First Day Cover		3·75 ☐
		Presentation Pack	4·50	☐
		PHQ Cards (set of 4)	3·00	6·00 ☐ ☐
		Set of 4 Gutter Pairs	8·00	☐

854 Revd William Morgan (Bible translator, 1588)

855 William Salesbury (New Testament translator, 1567)

856 Bishop Richard Davies (New Testament translator, 1567)

857 Bishop Richard Parry (editor of Revised Welsh Bible, 1620)

400th Anniversary of Welsh Bible

1988 (1 Mar.) *Phosphorised paper. Perf 14½ × 14*

1384	854	18p multicoloured	40	10 ☐ ☐
1385	855	26p multicoloured	70	95 ☐ ☐
1386	856	31p multicoloured	1·25	1·25 ☐ ☐
1387	857	34p multicoloured	1·40	1·25 ☐ ☐
		Set of 4	3·25	3·25 ☐ ☐
		First Day Cover		3·75 ☐
		Presentation Pack	4·50	☐
		PHQ Cards (set of 4)	3·00	6·00 ☐ ☐
		Set of 4 Gutter Pairs	8·00	☐

858 Gymnastics (Centenary of British Amateur Gymnastics Association)

859 Downhill Skiing (Ski Club of Great Britain)

860 Tennis (Centenary of Lawn Tennis Association)

861 Football (Centenary of Football League)

Sports Organizations

1988 (22 Mar.) *Phosphorised paper. Perf* 14½

1388	858	18p multicoloured	40		15	□	□
1389	859	26p multicoloured	70		80	□	□
1390	860	31p multicoloured	1·10		1·25	□	□
1391	861	34p multicoloured	1·25		1·25	□	□
		Set of 4	3·25		3·25	□	□
		First Day Cover			3·50		□
		Presentation Pack	4·25			□	
		PHQ Cards (set of 4)	2·50		6·00	□	□
		Set of 4 Gutter Pairs	8·00			□	

862 *Mallard* and Mailbags on Pick-up Arms

863 Loading Transatlantic Mail on Liner *Queen Elizabeth*

864 Glasgow Tram No. 1173 and Pillar Box

865 Imperial Airways Handley Page H.P.45 *Horatius* and Airmail Van

Europa. Transport and Mail Services in 1930's

1988 (10 May) *Phosphorised paper*

1392	862	18p multicoloured	50		15	□	□
1393	863	26p multicoloured	1·00		1·00	□	□
1394	864	31p multicoloured	1·25		1·60	□	□
1395	865	34p multicoloured	1·60		1·75	□	□
		Set of 4	4·00		4·00	□	□
		First Day Cover			4·50		□
		Presentation Pack	5·00			□	
		PHQ Cards (set of 4)	2·00		5·00	□	□
		Set of 4 Gutter Pairs	9·00			□	

866 Early Settler and Sailing Clipper

867 Queen Elizabeth II with British and Australian Parliament Buildings

868 W. G. Grace (cricketer) and Tennis Racquet

869 Shakespeare, John Lennon (entertainer) and Sydney Landmarks

Nos. 1396/7 and 1398/9 were each printed together, *se-tenant,* in horizontal pairs throughout the sheets, each pair showing a background design of the Australian flag.

Bicentenary of Australian Settlement

1988 (21 June) *Phosphorised paper. Perf* 14½

1396	866	18p multicoloured	50		25	□	□
		a. Horiz pair. Nos. 1396/7	1·25		1·50	□	□
1397	867	18p multicoloured	50		25	□	□
1398	868	34p multicoloured	1·00		80	□	□
		a. Horiz pair. Nos. 1398/9	2·25		2·75	□	□
1399	869	34p multicoloured	1·00		80	□	□
		Set of 4	3·50		1·90	□	□
		First Day Cover			3·50		□
		Presentation Pack	4·25			□	
		Souvenir Book	10·00			□	
		PHQ Cards (set of 4)	2·00		6·50	□	□
		Set of 2 Gutter Blocks of 4 . . .	8·75			□	

Stamps in similar designs were also issued by Australia. These are included in the Souvenir Book.

870 Spanish Galeasse off The Lizard

871 English Fleet leaving Plymouth

872 Engagement off Isle of Wight

873 Attack of English Fire-ships, Calais

ARMADA · NORTH SEA · 30 JULY – 2 AUG 1588

874　Armada in Storm, North Sea

Nos. 1400/4 were printed together, *se-tenant*, in horizontal strips of 5 throughout the sheet, forming a composite design.

400th Anniversary of Spanish Armada

1988 (19 July) *Phosphorised paper*

1400	870	18p multicoloured	70	40	☐	☐
		a. Horiz strip of 5. Nos. .				
		1400/4	3·50	3·75	☐	☐
1401	871	18p multicoloured	70	40	☐	☐
1402	872	18p multicoloured	70	40	☐	☐
1403	873	18p multicoloured	70	40	☐	☐
1404	874	18p multicoloured	70	40	☐	☐
		Set of 5	3·50	1·75	☐	☐
		First Day Cover		3·75		☐
		Presentation Pack	3·75		☐	
		PHQ Cards (set of 5)	2·75	8·00	☐	☐
		Gutter Block of 10	8·75		☐	

The Owl and the Pussy-cat went to sea
In a beautiful pea-green boat,

EDWARD LEAR • 1812-1888

EDWARD LEAR • 1812-1888

875　'The Owl and the Pussy-cat'

876　'Edward Lear as a Bird' (self-portrait)

C is a lovely Pussy Cat; its eyes were large,
And in it back it had a stripe, and...

EDWARD LEAR • 1812-1888

There was a Young Lady whose bonnet,
Came untied when the birds sate upon it;

EDWARD LEAR • 1812-1888

877　'Cat' (from alphabet book)

878　'There was a Young Lady whose Bonnet . . .' (limerick)

Death Centenary of Edward Lear (artist and author)

1988 (6–27 Sept.) *Phosphorised paper*

1405	875	19p black, pale cream and carmine	65	20	☐	☐
1406	876	27p black, pale cream and yellow	1·00	1·00	☐	☐
1407	877	32p black, pale cream and emerald	1·25	1·40	☐	☐
1408	878	35p black, pale cream and blue	1·40	1·40	☐	☐
		Set of 4	4·00	3·50	☐	☐
		First Day Cover		4·00		☐
		Presentation Pack	4·50		☐	
		PHQ Cards (set of 4)	2·00	7·00	☐	☐
		Set of 4 Gutter Pairs	10·00		☐	
MS1409		122 × 90 mm. Nos. 1405/8 . .	7·00	7·50	☐	☐
		First Day Cover (27 Sept.) . . .		7·50		☐

No. MS1409 was sold at £1·35, the premium being used for the 'Stamp World London 90' International Stamp Exhibition.

CARRICKFERGUS CASTLE

CAERNARFON CASTLE

879　Carrickfergus Castle

880　Caernarvon Castle

EDINBURGH CASTLE

WINDSOR CASTLE

881　Edinburgh Castle

882　Windsor Castle

1988 (18 Oct.) *Ordinary paper*

1410	879	£1 deep green	3·25	60	☐	☐
1411	880	£1·50 maroon	4·00	1·25	☐	☐
1412	881	£2 indigo	6·50	1·50	☐	☐
1413	882	£5 deep brown	20·00	5·50	☐	☐
		Set of 4	30·00	8·00	☐	☐
		First Day Cover		35·00		☐
		Presentation Pack	35·00		☐	
		Set of 4 Gutter pairs	65·00		☐	

For similar designs, but with silhouette of Queen's head see Nos. 1611/14 and 1993/6.

Minimum Price. The minimum price quoted is 10p. This represents a handling charge rather than a basis for valuing common stamps. Where the actual value of a stamp is less than 10p this may be apparent when set prices are shown, particularly for sets including a number of 10p stamps. It therefore follows that in valuing common stamps the 10p catalogue price should not be reckoned automatically since it covers a variation in real scarcity.

883 Journey to Bethlehem

884 Shepherds and Star

885 Three Wise Men

886 Nativity

887 The Annunciation

Christmas

1988 (15 Nov.) *One phosphor band (14p) or phosphorised paper (others)*

1414	**883**	14p multicoloured	45	20	☐	☐
1415	**884**	19p multicoloured	50	20	☐	☐
1416	**885**	27p multicoloured	90	1·00	☐	☐
1417	**886**	32p multicoloured	1·10	1·10	☐	☐
1418	**887**	35p multicoloured	1·40	1·10	☐	☐
		Set of 5	4·00	3·25	☐	☐
		First Day Cover		4·25	☐	
		Presentation Pack	4·50		☐	
		PHQ Cards (set of 5)	2·50	7·00	☐	☐
		Set of 5 Gutter Pairs	10·00		☐	

Collectors Pack 1988

1988 (15 Nov.) *Comprises Nos.* 1380/1408, 1414/18
    Collectors Pack . . . . 40·00   ☐

Post Office Yearbook

1988 *Comprises Nos.* 1380/1404, **MS**1409, 1414/18 *in hardbound book with slip case*
    Yearbook . . . . 40·00   ☐

888 Atlantic Puffin

889 Avocet

890 Oystercatcher

891 Northern Gannet

Centenary of Royal Society for the Protection of Birds

1989 (17 JAN.) *Phosphorised paper*

1419	**888**	19p multicoloured	45	20	☐	☐
1420	**889**	27p multicoloured	1·25	1·25	☐	☐
1421	**890**	32p multicoloured	1·25	1·25	☐	☐
1422	**891**	35p multicoloured	1·40	1·40	☐	☐
		Set of 4	4·00	3·75	☐	☐
		First Day Cover		4·25	☐	
		Presentation Pack	4·50		☐	
		PHQ Cards (set of 4)	2·50	8·00	☐	☐
		Set of 4 Gutter Pairs	10·00		☐	

892 Rose

893 Cupid

894 Yachts

895 Fruit

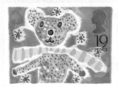

896 Teddy Bear

Nos. 1423/7 were printed together, *se-tenant*, in horizontal strips of five, two such strips forming the booklet pane with twelve half stamp-size labels.

Greetings Booklet Stamps

1989 (31 JAN.) *Phosphorised paper*

1423	892	19p multicoloured	5·50	3·75 ☐	☐
		a. Booklet pane. Nos.			
		1423/7 × 2	50·00		☐
1424	893	19p multicoloured	5·50	3·75 ☐	☐
1425	894	19p multicoloured	5·50	3·75 ☐	☐
1426	895	19p multicoloured	5·50	3·75 ☐	☐
1427	896	19p multicoloured	5·50	3·75 ☐	☐
		Set of 5	25·00	17·00 ☐	☐
		First Day Cover		25·00	☐

897 Fruit and Vegetables   **898** Meat Products

899 Dairy Produce   **900** Cereal Products

Food and Farming Year

1989 (7 MAR.) *Phosphorised paper. Perf* 14 × 14½

1428	897	19p multicoloured	45	15 ☐	☐
1429	898	27p multicoloured	90	85 ☐	☐
1430	899	32p multicoloured	1·25	1·40 ☐	☐
1431	900	35p multicoloured	1·40	1·50 ☐	☐
		Set of 4	3·50	3·50 ☐	☐
		First Day Cover		4·00	☐
		Presentation Pack	4·50		☐
		PHQ Cards (set of 4)	2·00	7·50 ☐	☐
		Set of 4 *Gutter Pairs*	8·50		☐

901 Mortar Board (150th Anniv of Public Education in England)   **902** Cross on Ballot Paper (3rd Direct Elections to European Parliament)

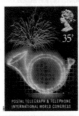

903 Posthorn (26th Postal, Telegraph and Telephone International Congress, Brighton)   **904** Globe (Inter-Parliamentary Union Centenary Conference, London)

Nos. 1432/3 and 1434/5 were each printed together, *se-tenant,* in horizontal pairs throughout the sheets.

Anniversaries

1989 (11 APR.) *Phosphorised paper. Perf* 14 × 14½

1432	901	19p multicoloured	1·00	50 ☐	☐
		a. Horiz pair. Nos. 1432/3	2·00	2·00 ☐	☐
1433	902	19p multicoloured	1·00	50 ☐	☐
1434	903	35p multicoloured	1·50	1·75 ☐	☐
		a. Horiz pair. Nos. 1434/5	3·00	4·00 ☐	☐
1435	904	35p multicoloured	1·50	1·75 ☐	☐
		Set of 4	4·50	4·00 ☐	☐
		First Day Cover		4·50	☐
		Presentation Pack	6·00		☐
		PHQ Cards (set of 4)	2·00	6·50 ☐	☐
		Set of 2 *Gutter Strips of* 4 . . .	11·00		☐

905 Toy Train and Airplane Airplane   **906** Building Bricks

907 Dice and Board Games   908 Toy Robot, Boat and Doll's House

Europa. Games and Toys

1989 (16 MAY) *Phosphorised paper*

1436	**905**	19p multicoloured	65	20	☐	☐
1437	**906**	27p multicoloured	95	1·00	☐	☐
1438	**907**	32p multicoloured	1·40	1·40	☐	☐
1439	**908**	35p multicoloured	1·50	1·50	☐	☐
		Set of 4	4·00	3·75	☐	☐
		First Day Cover		4·25		☐
		Presentation Pack	4·50		☐	
		PHQ Cards (set of 4)	2·00	7·00	☐	☐
		Set of 4 Gutter Pairs	10·00		☐	

909 Ironbridge, Shropshire   910 Tin Mine. St Agnes Head, Cornwall

911 Cotton Mills, New Lanark, Strathclyde   912 Pontcysylite Aqueduct, Clwyd

912a

Industrial Archaeology

1989 (4–25 JULY) *Phosphorised paper*

1440	**909**	19p multicoloured	60	15	☐	☐
1441	**910**	27p multicoloured	1·00	1·10	☐	☐
1442	**911**	32p multicoloured	1·10	1·25	☐	☐
1443	**912**	35p multicoloured	1·25	1·50	☐	☐
		Set of 4	3·50	3·50	☐	☐
		First Day Cover		4·00		☐
		Presentation Pack	4·50		☐	
		PHQ Cards (set of 4)	2·25	6·50	☐	☐
		Set of 4 Gutter Pairs	8·50		☐	
MS1444		122 × 90 mm. **912a** As Nos.				
		1440/3 but designs horizontal .	5·00	5·50	☐	☐
		First Day Cover (25 July)		6·00		☐

No. **MS**1444 was sold at £1·40, the premium being used for the 'Stamp World London 90' International Stamp Exhibition.

913   914

Booklet Stamps

1989 (22 AUG.)–**92** (*a*) *Printed in photogravure by Harrison and Sons. Perf* 15 × 14

1445	**913**	(2nd) bright blue (1 centre band)	1·00	1·00	☐	☐
1446		(2nd) bright blue (1 side band) (20.3.90)	3·00	3·25	☐	☐
1447	**914**	(1st) black (phosphorised paper)	1·75	1·75	☐	☐
1448		(1st) brownish black (2 bands (20.3.90)	3·25	3·25	☐	☐

(*b*) *Printed in lithography by Walsall. Perf* 14

1449	**913**	(2nd) bright blue (1 centre band)	90	90	☐	☐
1450	**914**	(1st) black (2 bands)	2·50	2·40	☐	☐

(c) Printed in lithography by Questa. Perf 15 × 14

1451	**913**	(2nd) bright blue (1 centre band) (19.9.89)	1·00	1·00	☐	☐
1451*a*		(2nd) bright blue (1 side band) (25.2.92)	3·00	3·00	☐	☐
1452	**914**	(1st) black (phosphorised paper) (19.9.89)	2·50	2·50	☐	☐
		First Day Cover (Nos. 1445, 1447)		5·00		☐

For similar stamps showing changed colours see Nos. 1511/16, for those with elliptical perforations Nos. 1663*a*/6 and 1979 and for self-adhesive versions Nos. 2039/40.

No. 1451*a* exists with the phosphor band at the left or right of the stamp.

915 Snowflake (×10)

916 *Calliphora erythrocephala* (fly) (×5)

917 Blood Cells (×500)

918 Microchip (×600)

150th Anniversary of Royal Microscopical Society

1989 (5 Sept.) *Phosphorised paper. Perf 14½ × 14*

1453	**915**	19p multicoloured	45	15	☐	☐
1454	**916**	27p multicoloured	95	1·10	☐	☐
1455	**917**	32p multicoloured	1·10	1·40	☐	☐
1456	**918**	35p multicoloured	1·25	1·40	☐	☐
		Set of 4	3·50	3·75	☐	☐
		First Day Cover		4·00		☐
		Presentation Pack	4·50			☐
		PHQ Cards (set of 4)	2·00	6·00	☐	☐
		Set of 4 Gutter Pairs	8·50			☐

919 Royal Mail Coach   **920** Escort of Blues and Royals

921 Lord Mayor's Coach   **922** Coach Team passing St Paul's

923 Blues and Royals Drum Horse

Nos. 1457/61 were printed together, *se-tenant*, in horizontal strips of 5 throughout the sheet, forming a composite design.

Lord Mayor's Show, London

1989 (17 Oct.) *Phosphorised paper*

1457	**919**	20p multicoloured	70	40	☐	☐
		a. Horiz strip of 5. Nos.				
		1457/61	3·25	3·50	☐	☐
1458	**920**	20p multicoloured	70	40	☐	☐
1459	**921**	20p multicoloured	70	40	☐	☐
1460	**922**	20p multicoloured	70	40	☐	☐
1461	**923**	20p multicoloured	70	40	☐	☐
		Set of 5	3·25	1·75	☐	☐
		First Day Cover		4·00		☐
		Presentation Pack	3·75			☐
		PHQ Cards (set of 5)	2·50	7·00	☐	☐
		Gutter Strip of 10	8·00			☐

Nos. 1457/61 commemorate the 800th anniversary of the installation of the first Lord Mayor of London.

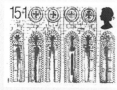

| 924 | 14th-century Peasants from Stained-glass Window | 925 | Arches and Roundels, West Front |

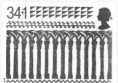

| 926 | Octagon Tower | 927 | Arcade from West Transept |

928   Triple Arch from West Front

Christmas. 800th Anniversary of Ely Cathedral

1989 (14 Nov.) *One phosphor band (Nos. 1462/3) or phosphorised paper (others)*

1462	924	15p gold, silver and blue .	40	15	□ □
1463	925	15p + 1p gold, silver and blue	50	40	□ □
1464	926	20p + 1p gold, silver and rosine	65	80	□ □
1465	927	34p + 1p gold, silver and emerald	1·25	1·75	□ □
1466	928	37p + 1p gold, silver and yellow-olive	1·40	1·90	□ □
		Set of 5	3·75	4·50	□ □
		First Day Cover		4·50	□
		Presentation Pack	5·00		□
		PHQ Cards (set of 5)	2·50	7·00	□ □
		Set of 5 Gutter Pairs	8·50		□

Collectors Pack 1989

1989 (14 Nov.) *Comprises Nos. 1419/22, 1428/43 and 1453/66*

| | *Collectors Pack* . . . . | 42·00 | | □ |

Post Office Yearbook

1989 (14 Nov.) *Comprises Nos. 1419/22, 1428/44 and 1453/66 in hardback book with slip case*

| | *Yearbook* . . . . | 42·00 | | □ |

929   Queen Victoria and Queen Elizabeth II

150th Anniversary of the Penny Black

1990 (10 JAN.–17 APR.) (*a*) *Printed in photogravure by Harrison and Sons (Nos. 1468, 1470, 1472 from booklets only). Perf 15 × 14*

1467	929	15p bright blue (1 centre band)	80	80	□ □
1468		15p bright blue (1 side band) (30 Jan.)	3·75	3·50	□ □
1469		20p brownish black and cream (phosphorised paper)	80	80	□ □
1470		20p brownish black and cream (2 bands) (30 Jan.)	2·75	2·75	□ □
1471		29p deep mauve (phosphorised paper)	1·75	1·75	□ □
1472		29p deep mauve (2 bands) (20 Mar.)	9·00	9·00	□ □
1473		34p deep bluish grey (phosphorised paper)	2·00	2·00	□ □
1474		37p rosine (phosphorised paper)	2·25	2·25	□ □
		Set of 5 (*Nos. 1467, 1469, 1471, 1473/4*)	7·00	7·00	□ □
		First Day Cover (*Nos. 1467, 1469, 1471, 1473/4*)		7·00	□
		Presentation Pack (*Nos. 1467, 1469, 1471, 1473/4*)	9·00		□

(*b*) *Litho Walsall* (*booklets*). *Perf 14* (30 Jan.)

| 1475 | 929 | 15p bright blue (1 centre band) . . . . | 1·50 | 1·75 | □ □ |
| 1476 | | 20p brownish black and cream (phosphorised paper) . . . . | 1·60 | 1·60 | □ □ |

(*c*) *Litho Questa* (*booklets*). *Perf 15 × 14* (17 Apr.)

| 1477 | 929 | 15p bright blue (1 centre band) . . . . | 2·25 | 2·25 | □ □ |
| 1478 | | 20p brownish black (phosphorised paper) . . . . . . | 1·75 | 2·00 | □ □ |

No. 1468 exists with the phosphor band at the left or right of the stamp.

For Type **929** redrawn with "1st" face value see No. 2133.

Minimum Price. The minimum price quoted is 10p. This represents a handling charge rather than a basis for valuing common stamps. Where the actual value of a stamp is less than 10p this may be apparent when set prices are shown, particularly for sets including a number of 10p stamps. It therefore follows that in valuing common stamps the 10p catalogue price should not be reckoned automatically since it covers a variation in real scarcity.

930   Kitten

931   Rabbit

932   Duckling

933   Puppy

150th Anniversary of Royal Society for Prevention of Cruelty to Animals

1990 (23 Jan.) *Phosphorised paper. Perf* 14 × 14½

1479	930	20p multicoloured	60	15	☐	☐
1480	931	29p multicoloured	1·10	1·10	☐	☐
1481	932	34p multicoloured	1·25	1·25	☐	☐
1482	933	37p multicoloured	1·40	1·40	☐	☐
		Set of 4	4·00	3·50	☐	☐
		First Day Cover		4·00		☐
		Presentation Pack	5·00		☐	
		PHQ Cards (set of 4)	3·00	8·00	☐	☐
		Set of 4 Gutter Pairs	8·00		☐	

934   Teddy Bear

935   Dennis the Menace

936   Punch

937   Cheshire Cat

938   The Man in the Moon

939   The Laughing Policeman

940   Clown

941   Mona Lisa

942   Queen of Hearts

943   Stan Laurel (comedian)

T **934/43** were printed together, *se-tenant*, in booklet panes of 10.

Greetings Booklet Stamps. 'Smiles'

1990 (6 Feb.) *Two phosphor bands*

1483	934	20p multicoloured	3·50	2·50	☐	☐
		a. Booklet pane. Nos.				
		1483/92	30·00		☐	
1484	935	20p multicoloured	3·50	2·50	☐	☐
1485	936	20p multicoloured	3·50	2·50	☐	☐
1486	937	20p multicoloured	3·50	2·50	☐	☐
1487	938	20p multicoloured	3·50	2·50	☐	☐
1488	939	20p multicoloured	3·50	2·50	☐	☐
1489	940	20p multicoloured	3·50	2·50	☐	☐
1490	941	20p multicoloured	3·50	2·50	☐	☐
1491	942	20p multicoloured	3·50	2·50	☐	☐
1492	943	20p gold and grey-black .	3·50	2·50	☐	☐
		Set of 10	30·00	22·00	☐	☐
		First Day Cover		25·00		☐

For these designs with the face value expressed as '1st' see Nos. 1550/9.

For full information on all future British issues, collectors should write to Royal Mail, Freepost EH3647, 21 South Gyle Crescent, Edinburgh EH12 9PE.

944 Alexandra Palace
('Stamp World London
90' Exhibition)

945 Glasgow School
of Art

946 British Philatelic
Bureau, Edinburgh

947 Templeton Carpet
Factory, Glasgow

Europa (Nos. 1493 and 1495) and 'Glasgow 1990 European City of Culture' (Nos. 1494 and 1496)

1990 (6 Mar.) *Phosphorised paper*

1493	944	20p multicoloured	60	20	□	□
1494	945	20p multicoloured	60	20	□	□
1495	946	29p multicoloured	1·40	1·60	□	□
1496	947	37p multicoloured	1·50	1·60	□	□
		Set of 4	3·75	3·25	□	□
		First Day Cover		3·50	□	
		Presentation Pack	4·00		□	
		PHQ Cards (set of 4)	2·50	6·50	□	□
		Set of 4 Gutter Pairs	9·50		□	

948 Export Achievement
Award

949 Technological
Achievement Award

Nos. 1497/8 and 1499/500 were each printed together, *se-tenant*, in horizontal pairs throughout the sheets.

25th Anniversary of Queen's Awards for Export and Technology

1990 (10 Apr.) *Phosphorised paper. Perf* 14 × 14½

1497	948	20p multicoloured	70	45	□	□
		a. Horiz pair. Nos. 1497/8	1·40	1·60	□	□
1498	949	20p multicoloured	70	45	□	□
1499	948	37p multicoloured	1·25	1·25	□	□
		a. Horiz pair. Nos. 1499/1500	2·50	3·25	□	□
1500	949	37p multicoloured	1·25	1·25	□	□
		Set of 4	3·50	3·00	□	□
		First Day Cover		4·25		□
		Presentation Pack	4·50		□	
		PHQ Cards (set of 4)	2·50	6·50	□	□
		Set of 2 Gutter Strips of 4 . . .	8·50		□	

949a

'Stamp World 90' International Stamp Exhibition, London

1990 (3 May) *Sheet* 122 × 90 *mm. Phosphorised paper*

MS1501	949a	20p brownish black and cream	4·50	4·50	□ □
		First Day Cover		5·50	□
		Souvenir Book (Nos. 1467, 1469, 1471, 1473/4 and MS1501 . .	22·00		□

No. **MS**1501 was sold at £1, the premium being used for the exhibition.

950 Cycad and Sir Joseph
Banks Building

951 Stone Pine and Princess
of Wales Conservatory

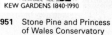

KEW GARDENS 1840-1990   KEW GARDENS 1840-1990

952   Willow Tree and   **953**   Cedar Tree and Pagoda
Palm House

150th Anniversary of Kew Gardens
1990 (5 JUNE) *Phosphorised paper*

1502	**950**	20p multicoloured	55	15	☐	☐
1503	**951**	29p multicoloured	90	1·00	☐	☐
1504	**952**	34p multicoloured	1·40	1·60	☐	☐
1505	**953**	37p multicoloured	1·60	1·50	☐	☐
		Set of 4	4·00	3·75	☐	☐
		First Day Cover		4·00		☐
		Presentation Pack	4·50		☐	
		PHQ Cards (set of 4)	2·50	6·50	☐	☐
		Set of 4 Gutter Pairs	10·00		☐	

954   Thomas Hardy and Clyffe Clump, Dorset

150th Birth Anniversary of Thomas Hardy (author)
1990 (10 JULY) *Phosphorised paper*

1506	**954**	20p multicoloured	80	70	☐	☐
		First Day Cover		1·50		☐
		Presentation Pack	1·50		☐	
		PHQ Card	1·00	2·00	☐	☐
		Gutter Pair	2·00		☐	

955   Queen Elizabeth the   **956**   Queen Elizabeth
Queen Mother

957   Elizabeth, Duchess   **958**   Lady Elizabeth
of York   Bowes-Lyon

90th Birthday of Queen Elizabeth the Queen Mother
1990 (2 AUG.) *Phosphorised paper*

1507	**955**	20p multicoloured	95	20	☐	☐
1508	**956**	29p silver, indigo and grey-blue	1·40	1·40	☐	☐
1509	**957**	34p multicoloured	2·00	2·00	☐	☐
1510	**958**	37p silver, sepia and stone	2·25	2·10	☐	☐
		Set of 4	6·00	5·25	☐	☐
		First Day Cover		6·50		☐
		Presentation Pack	7·00		☐	
		PHQ Cards (set of 4)	5·00	8·00	☐	☐
		Set of 4 Gutter Pairs	14·00		☐	

For these designs with Queen's head and frame in black see Nos. 2280/3.

Booklet Stamps
1990 (7 AUG.)–**92** *As Types* **913/14**, *but colours changed*

(*a*) *Photo Harrison. Perf* 15 × 14

1511	**913**	(2nd) deep blue (1 centre band)	1·25	1·25	☐	☐
1512	**914**	(1st) bright orange-red (phosphorised paper)	1·10	1·10	☐	☐

(*b*) *Litho Questa. Perf* 15 × 14

1513	**913**	(2nd) deep blue (1 centre band)	2·50	2·50	☐	☐
1514	**914**	(1st) bright orange-red (phosphorised paper)	90	1·00	☐	☐
1514a		(1st) bright orange-red (2 bands) (25.2.92)	2·25	2·25	☐	☐

(*c*) *Litho Walsall. Perf* 14

1515	**913**	(2nd) deep blue (1 centre band)	80	80	☐	☐
1516	**914**	(1st) bright orange-red (phosphorised paper)	90	90	☐	☐
		c. Perf 13	2·75	3·00	☐	☐
		First Day Cover (*Nos.* 1515/16) .		5·00		☐

For similar stamps with elliptical perforations see Nos. 1663*a*/6.

For full information on all future British issues, collectors should write to Royal Mail, Freepost EH3647, 21 South Syle Crescent, Edinburgh EH12 9PE.

959 Victoria Cross

960 George Cross

961 Distinguished Service Cross and Distinguished Service Medal

962 Military Cross and Military Medal

963 Distinguished Flying Cross and Distinguished Flying Medal

Gallantry Awards

1990 (11 SEPT.) *Phosphorised paper*

1517	**959**	20p multicoloured	80	65	☐	☐
1518	**960**	20p multicoloured	80	65	☐	☐
1519	**961**	20p multicoloured	80	65	☐	☐
1520	**962**	20p multicoloured	80	65	☐	☐
1521	**963**	20p multicoloured	80	65	☐	☐
		Set of 5	3·75	3·00	☐	☐
		First Day Cover		3·75		☐
		Presentation Pack	4·00		☐	
		PHQ Cards (set of 5)	3·00	8·00	☐	☐
		Set of 5 Gutter Pairs	8·50		☐	

964 Armagh Observatory, Jodrell Bank Radio Telescope and La Palma Telescope

965 Newton's Moon and Tides Diagram with Early Telescopes

966 Greenwich Old Observatory and Early Astronomical Equipment

967 Stonehenge, Gyroscope and Navigating by Stars

Astronomy

1990 (16 OCT.) *Phosphorised paper. Perf* 14 × 14½

1522	**964**	22p multicoloured	65	15	☐	☐
1523	**965**	26p multicoloured	1·00	1·10	☐	☐
1524	**966**	31p multicoloured	1·25	1·40	☐	☐
1525	**967**	37p multicoloured	1·50	1·40	☐	☐
		Set of 4	4·00	3·75	☐	☐
		First Day Cover		4·25		☐
		Presentation Pack	4·50		☐	
		PHQ Cards (set of 4)	2·50	7·00	☐	☐
		Set of 4 Gutter Pairs	9·00		☐	

Nos. 1522/5 commemorate the centenary of the British Astronomical Association and the bicentenary of the Armagh Observatory.

968 Building a Snowman

969 Fetching the Christmas Tree

970 Carol Singing

971 Tobogganing

972 Ice-skating

Christmas

1990 (13 Nov.) *One phosphor band (17p) or phosphorised paper (others)*

1526	**968**	17p multicoloured	50	15	☐	☐
1527	**969**	22p multicoloured	70	20	☐	☐
1528	**970**	26p multicoloured	95	1·10	☐	☐
1529	**971**	31p multicoloured	1·25	1·50	☐	☐
1530	**972**	37p multicoloured	1·40	1·50	☐	☐
		Set of 5	4·50	4·00	☐	☐
		First Day Cover		4·25		☐
		Presentation Pack	4·75		☐	
		PHQ Cards (set of 5)	3·25	7·00	☐	☐
		Set of 5 Gutter Pairs	10·00		☐	

Collectors Pack 1990

1990 (13 Nov.) *Comprises Nos. 1479/82, 1493/1510 and 1517/30*

	Collectors Pack	55·00	☐

Post Office Yearbook

1990 *Comprises Nos. 1479/82, 1493/1500, 1502/10 and 1517/30 in hardback book with slip case*

	Yearbook	55·00	☐

973 'King Charles Spaniel'

974 'A Pointer'

975 'Two Hounds in a Landscape'

976 'A Rough Dog'

977 'Fino and Tiny'

Dogs. Paintings by George Stubbs

1991 (8 Jan.) *Phosphorised paper. Perf 14 × 14½*

1531	**973**	22p multicoloured	85	15	☐	☐
1532	**974**	26p multicoloured	1·10	1·25	☐	☐

1533	**975**	31p multicoloured	1·25	1·25	☐	☐
1534	**976**	33p multicoloured	1·40	1·40	☐	☐
1535	**977**	37p multicoloured	1·50	1·40	☐	☐
		Set of 5	5·50	5·00	☐	☐
		First Day Cover		5·25		☐
		Presentation Pack	6·00		☐	
		PHQ Cards (set of 5)	3·50	7·00	☐	☐
		Set of 5 Gutter Pairs	12·00		☐	

978 Thrush's Nest

979 Shooting Star and Rainbow

980 Magpies and Charm Bracelet

981 Black Cat

982 Common Kingfisher with Key

983 Mallard and Frog

984 Four-leaf Clover in Boot and Match Box

985 Pot of Gold at End of Rainbow

986 Heart-shaped Butterflies

987 Wishing Well and Sixpence

T **978/87** were printed together, *se-tenant,* in booklet panes of 10 stamps and 12 half stamp-size labels, the backgrounds of the stamps forming a composite design.

Greetings Booklet Stamps. 'Good Luck'

1991 (5 Feb.) *Two phosphor bands*

1536	**978**	(1st) multicoloured	1·90	1·90	☐	☐
		a. Booklet pane. Nos.				
		1536/45	17·00		☐	
1537	**979**	(1st) multicoloured	1·90	1·90	☐	☐
1538	**980**	(1st) multicoloured	1·90	1·90	☐	☐
1539	**981**	(1st) multicoloured	1·90	1·90	☐	☐
1540	**982**	(1st) multicoloured	1·90	1·90	☐	☐
1541	**983**	(1st) multicoloured	1·90	1·90	☐	☐
1542	**984**	(1st) multicoloured	1·90	1·90	☐	☐
1543	**985**	(1st) multicoloured	1·90	1·90	☐	☐
1544	**986**	(1st) multicoloured	1·90	1·90	☐	☐
1545	**987**	(1st) multicoloured	1·90	1·90	☐	☐
		Set of 10	17·00	17·00	☐	☐
		First Day Cover		19·00		☐

988 Michael Faraday (inventor of electric motor) (Birth Bicentenary)

989 Charles Babbage (computer science pioneer) (Birth Bicentenary)

990 Radar Sweep of East Anglia (50th Anniv of Discovery by Sir Robert Watson-Watt)

991 Gloster Whittle E28/39 Aircraft over East Anglia (50th Anniv of First Flight of Sir Frank Whittle's Jet Engine

Scientific Achievements

1991 (5 Mar.) *Phosphorised paper*

1546	**988**	22p multicoloured	55	20	☐	☐
1547	**989**	22p multicoloured	55	20	☐	☐
1548	**990**	31p multicoloured	1·10	1·25	☐	☐
1549	**991**	37p multicoloured	1·25	1·60	☐	☐
		Set of 4	3·00	3·00	☐	☐
		First Day Cover		3·75		☐
		Presentation Pack	4·00			☐
		PHQ Cards (set of 4)	3·00	6·50	☐	☐
		Set of 4 Gutter Pairs	7·50			☐

992 Teddy Bear

Nos. 1550/9 were originally printed together, *se-tenant,* in booklet panes of 10 stamps and 12 half stamp-size labels.

Greetings Booklet Stamps. 'Smiles'

1991 (26 Mar.) *As Nos. 1483/92, but inscribed '1st' as T* **992.** *Two phosphor bands. Perf* 15 × 14

1550	**992**	(1st) multicoloured	1·25	1·50	☐	☐
		a. Booklet pane. Nos.				
		1550/9	11·00		☐	
1551	**935**	(1st) multicoloured	1·25	1·50	☐	☐
1552	**936**	(1st) multicoloured	1·25	1·50	☐	☐
1553	**937**	(1st) multicoloured	1·25	1·50	☐	☐
1554	**938**	(1st) multicoloured	1·25	1·50	☐	☐
1555	**939**	(1st) multicoloured	1·25	1·50	☐	☐
1556	**940**	(1st) multicoloured	1·25	1·50	☐	☐
1557	**941**	(1st) multicoloured	1·25	1·50	☐	☐
1558	**942**	(1st) multicoloured	1·25	1·50	☐	☐
1559	**943**	(1st) multicoloured	1·25	1·50	☐	☐
		Set of 10	11·00	13·50	☐	☐
		First Day Cover		14·00		☐

The stamps were re-issued in sheets of 10 each with *se-tenant* label on 22 May 2000 in connection with 'customised' stamps available at 'Stamp Show 2000'. The labels show either a pattern of ribbons or a personal photograph.

A similar sheet, but in lithography instead of photogravure, and perforated 14½ × 14, appeared on 3 July 2001 with the labels showing either greetings or a personal photograph.

Three further sheets, also in lithography, appeared on 1 October 2002. One contained Nos. 1550/1 each ×10 with greetings labels. Both designs were also available in sheets of 20 with personal photographs.

993 Man looking at Space   **994**

995 Space looking at Man **996**

Nos. 1560/1 and 1562/3 were each printed together, *se-tenant*, in horizontal pairs throughout the sheets, each pair forming a composite design.

Europa. Europe in Space

1991 (23 APR.) *Phosphorised paper*

1560	**993**	22p multicoloured	75	50	□	□
		a. Horiz pair. Nos. 1560/1	1·50	1·50	□	□
1561	**994**	22p multicoloured	75	50	□	□
1562	**995**	37p multicoloured	2·00	1·40	□	□
		a. Horiz pair. Nos. 1562/3	4·00	2·75	□	□
1563	**996**	37p multicoloured	2·00	1·40	□	□
		Set of 4	5·00	3·25	□	□
		First Day Cover		4·00		□
		Presentation Pack	5·50		□	
		PHQ Cards (set of 4)	3·00	6·50	□	□
		Set of 2 Gutter Strips of 4 . . .	12·00		□	

997 Fencing

998 Hurdling

999 Diving

1000 Rugby

World Student Games, Sheffield (Nos. 1564/6) and World Cup Rugby Championship, London (No. 1567)

1991 (11 JUNE) *Phosphorised paper. Perf* 14½ × 14

1564	**997**	22p multicoloured	60	20	□	□
1565	**998**	26p multicoloured	1·00	1·00	□	□
1566	**999**	31p multicoloured	1·25	1·25	□	□
1567	**1000**	37p multicoloured	1·50	1·50	□	□
		Set of 4	4·00	3·50	□	□
		First Day Cover		4·00		□
		Presentation Pack	4·50		□	
		PHQ Cards (set of 4)	2·50	6·50	□	□
		Set of 4 Gutter Pairs	10·00		□	

1001 'Silver Jubilee'

1002 'Mme Alfred Carrière'

1003 *Rosa moyesii*

1004 'Harvest Fayre'

1005 'Mutabilis'

9th World Congress of Roses, Belfast

1991 (16 JULY) *Phosphorised paper. Perf* 14½ × 14

1568	**1001**	22p multicoloured	95	20	□	□
1569	**1002**	26p multicoloured	1·10	1·25	□	□
1570	**1003**	31p multicoloured	1·25	1·25	□	□
1571	**1004**	33p multicoloured	1·50	1·50	□	□
1572	**1005**	37p multicoloured	1·60	1·50	□	□
		Set of 5	5·75	5·00	□	□
		First Day Cover		6·00		□
		Presentation Pack	6·25		□	
		PHQ Cards (set of 5)	3·00	8·50	□	□
		Set of 5 Gutter Pairs	12·00		□	

1006 Iguanodon

1007 Stegosaurus

1008 Tyrannosaurus

1009 Protoceratops

1010 Triceratops

150th Anniversary of Dinosaurs' Identification by Owen

1991 (20 Aug.) *Phosphorised paper. Perf* 14½ × 14

1573	**1006**	22p multicoloured	. . . .	90	20	☐	☐
1574	**1007**	26p multicoloured	. . . .	1·10	1·25	☐	☐
1575	**1008**	31p multicoloured	. . . .	1·25	1·25	☐	☐
1576	**1009**	33p multicoloured	. . . .	1·50	1·50	☐	☐
1577	**1010**	37p multicoloured	. . . .	1·60	1·50	☐	☐
		Set of 5	. . . .	5·75	5·00	☐	☐
		First Day Cover	. . . .		6·00		☐
		Presentation Pack	. . . .	6·50		☐	
		PHQ Cards (set of 5)	. . . . . .	3·25	8·50	☐	☐
		Set of 5 Gutter Pairs	. . . . . .	12·00		☐	

1011 Map of 1816

1012 Map of 1906

1013 Map of 1959

1014 Map of 1991

Bicentenary of Ordnance Survey. Maps of Hamstreet, Kent

1991 (17 Sept.) *Phosphorised paper. Perf* 14½ × 14

1578	**1011**	24p multicoloured	. . . .	60	20	☐	☐
1579	**1012**	28p multicoloured	. . . .	1·00	95	☐	☐
1580	**1013**	33p multicoloured	. . . .	1·25	1·40	☐	☐
1581	**1014**	39p multicoloured	. . . .	1·50	1·40	☐	☐
		Set of 4	. . . .	4·00	3·50	☐	☐
		First Day Cover	. . . .		4·25		☐
		Presentation Pack	. . . .	4·50		☐	
		PHQ Cards (set of 4)	. . . . . .	3·00	6·00	☐	☐
		Set of 4 Gutter Pairs	. . . . . .	10·00		☐	

1015 Adoration of the Magi

1016 Mary and Baby Jesus in Stable

1017 Holy Family and Angel

1018 The Annunciation

1019 The Flight into Egypt

Christmas. Illuminated Manuscripts from the Bodleian Library, Oxford

1991 (12 Nov.) *One phosphor band* (18p) *or phosphorised paper* (*others*)

1582	**1015**	18p multicoloured	75	10	☐	☐
1583	**1016**	24p multicoloured	90	10	☐	☐
1584	**1017**	28p multicoloured	95	1·25	☐	☐
1585	**1018**	33p multicoloured	1·10	1·40	☐	☐
1586	**1019**	39p multicoloured	1·25	1·60	☐	☐
		Set of 5	4·50	4·00	☐	☐
		First Day Cover		5·00		☐
		Presentation Pack	5·00			☐
		PHQ Cards (*set of* 5)	3·00	7·50	☐	☐
		Set of 5 *Gutter Pairs*	11·00			☐

Collectors Pack 1991

1991 (12 Nov.) *Comprises Nos.* 1531/5, 1546/9 *and* 1560/86
    Collectors Pack . . . . 55·00   ☐

Post Office Yearbook

1991 *Comprises Nos.* 1531/5, 1546/9 *and* 1560/86 *in hardback book with slip case*
    Yearbook . . . . 60·00   ☐

1020 Fallow Deer in Scottish Forest

1021 Hare on North Yorkshire Moors

1022 Fox in the Fens

1023 Redwing and Home Counties Village

1024 Welsh Mountain Sheep in Snowdonia

The Four Seasons. Wintertime

1992 (14 Jan.) *One phosphor band* (18p) *or phosphorised paper* (*others*)

1587	**1020**	18p multicoloured	55	15	☐	☐
1588	**1021**	24p multicoloured	75	20	☐	☐
1589	**1022**	28p multicoloured	1·00	1·10	☐	☐
1590	**1023**	33p multicoloured	1·25	1·40	☐	☐
1591	**1024**	39p multicoloured	1·40	1·60	☐	☐
		Set of 5	4·50	4·00	☐	☐
		First Day Cover		4·75		☐
		Presentation Pack	4·75			☐
		PHQ Cards (*set of* 5)	3·50	8·00	☐	☐
		Set of 5 *Gutter Pairs*	11·00			☐

1025 Flower Spray

1026 Double Locket

1027 Key

1028 Model Car and Cigarette Cards

1029 Compass and Map

1030 Pocket Watch

1031 1854 1d. Red Stamp and Pen

1032 Pearl Necklace

1033 Marbles

1034 Bucket, Spade and Starfish

1039 Queen Elizabeth and Commonwealth Emblem

T **1025/34** were printed together, *se-tenant*, in booklet panes of 10 stamps and 12 half stamp-size labels, the backgrounds of the stamps forming a composite design.

Nos. 1602/6 were printed together, *se-tenant*, in horizontal strips of 5 throughout the sheet.

Greetings Stamps. 'Memories'

1992 (28 JAN.) *Two phosphor bands*

1592	**1025**	(1st) multicoloured	1·10	1·10	☐	☐
		a. Booklet pane. Nos.				
		1592/1601	10·00		☐	
1593	**1026**	(1st) multicoloured	1·10	1·10	☐	☐
1594	**1027**	(1st) multicoloured	1·10	1·10	☐	☐
1595	**1028**	(1st) multicoloured	1·10	1·10	☐	☐
1596	**1029**	(1st) multicoloured	1·10	1·10	☐	☐
1597	**1030**	(1st) multicoloured	1·10	1·10	☐	☐
1598	**1031**	(1st) multicoloured	1·10	1·10	☐	☐
1599	**1032**	(1st) multicoloured	1·10	1·10	☐	☐
1600	**1033**	(1st) multicoloured	1·10	1·10	☐	☐
1601	**1034**	(1st) multicoloured	1·10	1·10	☐	☐
		Set of 10	10·00	10·00	☐	☐
		First Day Cover		12·00		☐
		Presentation Pack	15·00		☐	

40th Anniversary of Accession

1992 (6 FEB.) *Two phosphor bands. Perf* $14\frac{1}{2} \times 14$

1602	**1035**	24p multicoloured	1·10	1·10	☐	☐
		a. Horiz strip of 5. Nos.				
		1602/6	6·00	7·00	☐	☐
1603	**1036**	24p multicoloured	1·10	1·10	☐	☐
1604	**1037**	24p multicoloured	1·10	1·10	☐	☐
1605	**1038**	24p multicoloured	1·10	1·10	☐	☐
1606	**1039**	24p multicoloured	1·10	1·10	☐	☐
		Set of 5	6·00	5·00	☐	☐
		First Day Cover		7·00		☐
		Presentation Pack	7·00		☐	
		PHQ Cards (set of 5)	3·50	7·50	☐	☐
		Gutter Block of 10	13·00		☐	

1035 Queen Elizabeth in Coronation Robes and Parliamentary Emblem

1036 Queen Elizabeth in Garter Robes and Archiepiscopal Arms

1040 Tennyson in 1888 and 'The Beguiling of Merlin' (Sir Edward Burne-Jones)

1041 Tennyson in 1856 and 'April Love' (Arthur Hughes)

1037 Queen Elizabeth with Baby Prince Andrew and Royal Arms

1038 Queen Elizabeth at Trooping the Colour and Service Emblems

1042 Tennyson in 1864 and 'I am Sick of the Shadows' (John Waterhouse)

1043 Tennyson as a Young Man and 'Mariana' (Dante Gabriel Rossetti)

Death Centenary of Alfred, Lord Tennyson (poet)

1992 (10 Mar.) *Phosphorised paper. Perf* 14½ × 14

1607	**1040**	24p multicoloured	60	20 □ □
1608	**1041**	28p multicoloured	85	85 □ □
1609	**1042**	33p multicoloured	1·40	1·60 □ □
1610	**1043**	39p multicoloured	1·50	1·60 □ □
		Set of 4	4·00	3·75 □ □
		First Day Cover		4·25 □
		Presentation Pack	4·50	□
		PHQ Cards (set of 4)	3·00	6·50 □ □
		Set of 4 Gutter Pairs	10·00	□

£1

CARRICKFERGUS CASTLE

1044 Carrickfergus Castle

1992 (24 Mar.)–95. *Designs as Nos. 1410/13, but showing Queen's head in silhouette as T* **1044.** *Perf* 15 × 14 *(with one elliptical hole on each vertical side)*

1611	**1044**	£1 bottle green and gold†	5·50	1·00 □ □
1612	**880**	£1·50 maroon and gold†	5·00	1·00 □ □
1613	**881**	£2 indigo and gold† ...	6·75	1·00 □ □
1613a	**1044**	£3 reddish violet and gold†	20·00	3·00 □ □
1614	**882**	£5 deep brown and gold†	17·00	3·00 □ □
		Set of 5	48·00	8·00 □ □
		First Day Cover (Nos. 1611/13, 1614)		35·00 □
		First Day Cover (22 Aug. 1995) (No. 1613a)		10·00 □
		Presentation Pack (P.O. Pack No. 27) (Nos. 1611/13, 1614) ...	38·00	□
		Presentation Pack (P.O. Pack No. 33) (No. 1613a)	20·00	□
		PHQ Cards (Nos. 1611/14) ...	12·00	□
		PHQ Card (No. 1613a)	6·00	22·00 □ □
		Set of 5 Gutter Pairs	95·00	□

†The Queen's head on these stamps is printed in optically variable ink which changes colour from gold to green when viewed from different angles.

PHQ cards for Nos. 1611/13 and 1614 were not issued until 16 February 1993.

Nos. 1611/14 were printed by Harrison. For stamps with different lettering by Enschedé see Nos. 1993/6.

For full information on all future British issues, collectors should write to Royal Mail, Freepost EH3647, 21 South Gyle Crescent, Edinburgh EH12 9PE.

1045 British Olympic Association Logo (Olympic Games, Barcelona)

1046 British Paralympic Association Symbol (Paralympics '92, Barcelona)

1047 Santa Maria (500th Anniv of Discovery of America by Columbus)

1048 Kaisei (Japanese cadet brigantine) (Grand Regatta Columbus, 1992)

1049 British Pavilion, 'EXPO 92', Seville

Nos. 1615/16 were printed together, *se-tenant*, in horizontal pairs throughout the sheet.

Europa. International Events

1992 (7 Apr.) *Phosphorised paper. Perf* 14 × 14½

1615	**1045**	24p multicoloured	1·00	60 □ □
		a. Horiz pair. Nos. 1615/16	2·25	1·75 □ □
1616	**1046**	24p multicoloured	1·00	60 □ □
1617	**1047**	24p multicoloured	1·00	50 □ □
1618	**1048**	39p multicoloured	1·40	1·25 □ □
1619	**1049**	39p multicoloured	1·40	1·25 □ □
		Set of 5	5·50	3·75 □ □
		First Day Cover		5·00 □
		Presentation Pack	5·75	□
		PHQ Cards (set of 5)	3·50	6·50 □ □
		Set of 3 Gutter Pairs and a Gutter Strip of 4	11·50	□

1050 Pikeman

1051 Drummer

1052 Musketeer

1053 Standard Bearer

350th Anniversary of the Civil War

1992 (16 JUNE) *Phosphorised paper. Perf 14½ × 14*

1620	**1050**	24p multicoloured	. . . .	60	20	☐	☐
1621	**1051**	28p multicoloured	. . . .	85	85	☐	☐
1622	**1052**	33p multicoloured	. . . .	1·40	1·40	☐	☐
1623	**1053**	39p multicoloured	. . . .	1·50	1·50	☐	☐
		Set of 4	. . . .	4·00	3·50	☐	☐
		First Day Cover	. . . .		4·00		☐
		Presentation Pack	. . . .	4·50		☐	
		PHQ Cards (set of 4)	. . . . . .	3·50	6·00	☐	☐
		Set of 4 Gutter Pairs	. . . . . .	10·00		☐	

1054 The Yeomen of the Guard

1055 The Gondoliers

1056 The Mikado

1057 The Pirates of Penzance

1058 Iolanthe

150th Birth Anniversary of Sir Arthur Sullivan (composer). Gilbert and Sullivan Operas

1992 (21 JULY) *One phosphor band* (18p) *or phosphorised paper* (*others*). *Perf 14½ × 14*

1624	**1054**	18p multicoloured	. . . .	50	20	☐	☐
1625	**1055**	24p multicoloured	. . . .	80	20	☐	☐
1626	**1056**	28p multicoloured	. . . .	95	1·00	☐	☐
1627	**1057**	33p multicoloured	. . . .	1·50	1·60	☐	☐
1628	**1058**	39p multicoloured	. . . .	1·60	1·60	☐	☐
		Set of 5	. . . .	4·75	4·25	☐	☐
		First Day Cover	. . . .		4·75		☐
		Presentation Pack	. . . .	5·00		☐	
		PHQ Cards (set of 5)	. . . . . .	3·50	6·00	☐	☐
		Set of 5 Gutter Pairs	. . . . . .	10·50		☐	

1059 'Acid Rain Kills'

1060 'Ozone Layer'

1061 'Greenhouse Effect'

1062 'Bird of Hope'

Protection of the Environment. Children's Paintings

1992 (15 SEPT.) *Phosphorised paper. Perf 14 × 14½*

1629	**1059**	24p multicoloured	. . . .	70	20	☐	☐
1630	**1060**	28p multicoloured	. . . .	1·10	1·10	☐	☐
1631	**1061**	33p multicoloured	. . . .	1·25	1·25	☐	☐
1632	**1062**	39p multicoloured	. . . .	1·40	1·25	☐	☐
		Set of 4	. . . .	4·00	3·50	☐	☐
		First Day Cover	. . . .		4·50		☐
		Presentation Pack	. . . .	4·75		☐	
		PHQ Cards (set of 4)	. . . . . .	3·50	5·50	☐	☐
		Set of 4 Gutter Pairs	. . . . . .	10·00		☐	

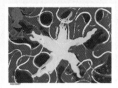

1063 European Star

Single European Market

1992 (13 OCT.) *Phosphorised paper*

1633	**1063**	24p multicoloured	90	80	☐	☐
		First Day Cover		1·90		☐
		Presentation Pack	1·90		☐	
		PHQ Card	90	3·50	☐	☐
		Gutter Pair	2·00		☐	

1064 'Angel Gabriel',
St James's, Pangbourne

1065 'Madonna and Child',
St. Mary's, Bibury

1066 'King with Gold', Our Lady
and St Peter, Leatherhead

1067 'Shepherds', All Saints,
Porthcawl

1068 'Kings with Frankincense
and Myrrh', Our Lady and
St Peter, Leatherhead

Christmas. Stained Glass Windows

1992 (10 Nov.) *One phosphor band* (18p) *or phosphorised paper* (others)

1634	**1064**	18p multicoloured	45	15	☐	☐
1635	**1065**	24p multicoloured	75	15	☐	☐
1636	**1066**	28p multicoloured	90	1·10	☐	☐
1637	**1067**	33p multicoloured	1·10	1·50	☐	☐
1638	**1068**	39p multicoloured	1·25	1·40	☐	☐
		Set of 5	4·00	4·00	☐	☐
		First Day Cover		4·75		☐
		Presentation Pack	4·75		☐	
		PHQ Cards (set of 5)	3·50	7·50	☐	☐
		Set of 5 Gutter Pairs	10·00		☐	

Collectors Pack 1992

1992 (10 Nov.) *Comprises Nos. 1587/91, 1602/10 and 1615/38*

Collectors Pack	55·00		☐

Post Office Yearbook

1992 (11 Nov.) *Comprises Nos. 1587/91, 1602/10 and 1615/38 in hardback book with slip case*

Yearbook	60·00		☐

1069 Mute Swan Cob
and St Catherine's,
Abbotsbury

1070 Cygnet and Decoy

1071 Swans and Cygnet

1072 Eggs in Nest and Tithe
Barn, Abbotsbury

1073 Young Swan and the Fleet

100

600th Anniversary of Abbotsbury Swannery

1993 (19 JAN.) *One phosphor band (18p) or phosphorised paper (others)*

1639	**1069**	18p multicoloured	1·25	25	☐	☐
1640	**1070**	24p multicoloured	1·10	25	☐	☐
1641	**1071**	28p multicoloured	1·40	1·75	☐	☐
1642	**1072**	33p multicoloured	1·75	2·40	☐	☐
1643	**1073**	39p multicoloured	1·90	2·40	☐	☐
		Set of 5	6·50	6·25	☐	☐
		First Day Cover		7·00		☐
		Presentation Pack	8·00		☐	
		PHQ Cards (set of 5)	4·00	9·00	☐	☐
		Set of 5 Gutter Pairs	16·00		☐	

1074 Long John Silver and Parrot (*Treasure Island*)

1075 Tweedledum and Tweedledee (*Alice Through the Looking-Glass*)

1076 William (*William* books)

1077 Mole and Toad (*The Wind in the Willows*)

1078 Teacher and Wilfrid ('The Bash Street Kids')

1079 Peter Rabbit and Mrs Rabbit (*The Tale of Peter Rabbit*)

1080 Snowman (*The Snowman*) and Father Christmas (*Father Christmas*)

1081 The Big Friendly Giant and Sophie (*The BFG*)

1082 Bill Badger and Rupert Bear

1083 Aladdin and the Genie

T **1074/83** were printed together, *se-tenant*, in booklet panes of 10 stamps and 20 half stamp-size labels.

Greetings Stamps. 'Gift Giving'

1993 (2 FEB.) *Two phosphor bands. Perf 15 × 14 (with one elliptical hole on each vertical side)*

1644	**1074**	(1st) multicoloured	1·25	1·10	☐	☐
		a. Booklet pane. Nos.				
		1644/53	11·00		☐	
1645	**1075**	(1st) gold, cream and black	1·25	1·10	☐	☐
1646	**1076**	(1st) multicoloured	1·25	1·10	☐	☐
1647	**1077**	(1st) multicoloured	1·25	1·10	☐	☐
1648	**1078**	(1st) multicoloured	1·25	1·10	☐	☐
1649	**1079**	(1st) multicoloured	1·25	1·10	☐	☐
1650	**1080**	(1st) multicoloured	1·25	1·10	☐	☐
1651	**1081**	(1st) multicoloured	1·25	1·10	☐	☐
1652	**1082**	(1st) multicoloured	1·25	1·10	☐	☐
1653	**1083**	(1st) multicoloured	1·25	1·10	☐	☐
		Set of 10	11·00	10·00	☐	☐
		First Day Cover		12·00		☐
		Presentation Pack	15·00		☐	
		PHQ Cards (set of 10)	7·00	20·00	☐	☐

1084 Decorated Enamel Dial

1085 Escapement, Remontoire and Fusee

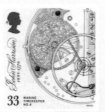

1086 Balance, Spring and Temperature Compensator

1087 Back of Movement

300th Birth Anniversary of John Harrison (inventor of the marine chronometer). Details of 'H4' Clock

1993 (16 Feb.) *Phosphorised paper. Perf* $14\frac{1}{2} \times 14$

1654	**1084**	24p multicoloured	. . . .	60	20 ☐ ☐
1655	**1085**	28p multicoloured	. . . .	1·00	1·10 ☐ ☐
1656	**1086**	33p multicoloured	. . . .	1·40	1·25 ☐ ☐
1657	**1087**	39p multicoloured	. . . .	1·50	1·40 ☐ ☐
		Set of 4	. . . .	4·00	3·50 ☐ ☐
		First Day Cover	. . . .		4·25 ☐
		Presentation Pack	. . . .	4·25	☐
		PHQ Cards (set of 4)	. . . . . .	3·50	8·00 ☐ ☐
		Set of 4 Gutter Pairs	. . . . . .	10·00	☐

1088 Britannia

1993 (2 Mar.) *Granite paper. Perf* $14 \times 14\frac{1}{2}$ *(with two elliptical holes on each horizontal side)*

1658	**1088**	£10 multicoloured	. . . .	26·00	12·00 ☐ ☐
		First Day Cover	. . . .		25·00 ☐
		Presentation Pack	. . . .	28·00	☐
		PHQ Card	. . . .	5·00	35·00 ☐ ☐

1089 Dendrobium hellwigianum

1090 Paphiopedilum Maudiae 'Magnifcum'

1091 Cymbidium lowianum

1092 Vanda Rothschildiana

1093 Dendrobium vexillarius var albiviride   **1093a**

14th World Orchid Conference, Glasgow

1993 (16 Mar.) *One phosphor band (18p) or phosphorised paper (others)*

1659	**1089**	18p multicoloured	. . . .	45	20 ☐ ☐
1660	**1090**	24p multicoloured	. . . .	75	20 ☐ ☐
1661	**1091**	28p multicoloured	. . . .	1·00	1·10 ☐ ☐
1662	**1092**	33p multicoloured	. . . .	1·25	1·50 ☐ ☐
1663	**1093**	39p multicoloured	. . . .	1·60	1·40 ☐ ☐
		Set of 5	. . . .	4·50	4·00 ☐ ☐
		First Day Cover	. . . .		5·00 ☐
		Presentation Pack	. . . .	5·50	☐
		PHQ Cards (set of 5)	. . . . . .	5·00	8·00 ☐ ☐
		Set of 5 Gutter Pairs	. . . . . .	10·00	☐

Booklet Stamps

1993 (6 Apr.)–**99** *As T* **913/14** *and* **1093a**, *but Perf* 14 (*No.* 1663b) *or* 15 × 14 (*others*) (*both with one elliptical hole on each vertical side*)

(a) *Photo*
Harrison (*No.* 1664)
Questa (*Nos.* 1663ab, 1664ab)
Walsall (*No.* 1663b)
Harrison (*later De La Rue*), Questa *or* Walsall (*No.* 1664a)
Harrison (*later De La Rue*), Enschedé, Questa *or* Walsall (*Nos.* 1663a, 1664b, 1664c)

1663a	**913**	(2nd) bright blue (1 centre band)	. . . .	30	35 ☐ ☐
		ab. Perf 14	. . . .	1·00	1·00 ☐ ☐
1663b		(2nd) bright blue (1 side band)	. . . .	1·10	1·10 ☐ ☐
1664	**914**	(1st) bright orange-red (phosphorised paper)	1·50	1·25 ☐ ☐
1664a		(1st) bright orange-red (2 phosphor bands) . .	40	45 ☐ ☐
		ab. Perf 14	. . . .	1·50	1·50 ☐ ☐
1664b		(1st) gold (2 phosphor bands) . .		45	50 ☐ ☐
1664c	**1093a**	(E) deep blue (2 phosphor bands) . .	60	65 ☐ ☐

(b) *Litho Questa or Walsall* (*No.* 1666 *also Enschedé*)

1665	**913**	(2nd) bright blue (1 centre band)	. . . .	75	75 ☐ ☐
1666	**914**	(1st) bright orange-red (2 phosphor bands) . .	90	90 ☐ ☐

First Day Covers

21 Apr. 1997	(1st), 26p (Nos 1664b, Y1683b)	£3·50	☐
19 Jan. 1999	(E) (No 1664c)	£3·50	☐

Nos. 1663a, 1664a, 1664c and 1665/6 also come from sheets.

No. 1663b exists with the phosphor band at the left or right of the stamp and was only issued in booklets.

No. 1664b was issued by Harrison in booklets and Walsall in sheets and booklets for the Queen's Golden Wedding on 21 April 1997. The gold colour was later adopted for the (1st) class rate, replacing bright orange-red.

For No. 1664b in presentation pack see Pack No. 38 listed below, No. Y1667 etc.

No. 1664c was valid for the basic European airmail rate, initially 30p.

> For self-adhesive versions in these colours see Nos. 2039/40 and 2295/8.

1993–2003 As Nos. X841 *etc*, but *perf* 14 (*No.* Y1676) *or* 15 × 14 (*others*) (*both with one elliptical hole on each vertical side*)

(a) *Photo*
Enschedé:— 20*p* (Y1677), 29*p*, 35*p* (Y1688), 36*p*, 38*p* (Y1692), 41*p* (Y1696), 43*p* (Y1699)
Harrison (*later De La Rue*):— 7*p*, 8*p*, 20*p* (Y1679/80), 25*p* (Y1681), 33*p*, 34*p*, 35*p* (Y1689), 37*p* (Y1691*a*), 41*p* (Y1697/8), 42*p*, 43*p* (Y1700), 44*p*, 45*p*, 47*p*, 68*p*
Walsall:— 10*p* (Y1674*a*), 19*p* (Y1676), 38*p* (Y1693*a*), 43*p* (Y1700*a*)
Enschedé or Harrison (*later De La Rue*):— 4*p*, 5*p*, 6*p*, 10*p* (Y1674), 25*p* (Y1682), 31*p*, 39*p*, 50*p*, £1
Enschedé, Harrison (*later De La Rue*) *or Questa:*— 1*p*, 2*p*
Enschedé, Harrison (*later De La Rue*) *or Walsall:*— 30*p*, 37*p* (Y1691), 63*p*
Harrison (*later De La Rue*) *or Questa:*— 19*p* (Y1675), 20*p* (Y1678), 26*p* (Y1683/b)
De La Rue or Walsall:— 38*p* (Y1693), 40*p*, 64*p*, 65*p*

Y1667	**367**	1p crimson (2 bands)	10	10	☐	☐
Y1668		2p deep green (2 bands)	10	10	☐	☐
Y1669		4p new blue (2 bands) .	10	10	☐	☐
Y1670		5p dull red-brown (2 bands)	10	10	☐	☐
Y1671		6p yellow-olive (2 bands)	25	30	☐	☐
Y1672		7p grey (2 bands)	30	30	☐	☐
Y1673		8p yellow (2 bands) . .	10	15	☐	☐
Y1674		10p dull orange (2 bands)	15	15	☐	☐
		a. Perf 14	2·00	2·00	☐	☐
Y1675		19p bistre (1 centre band)	30	35	☐	☐
Y1676		19p bistre (1 side band) .	2·00	2·00	☐	☐
Y1677		20p turquoise-green (2 bands)	90	90	☐	☐
Y1678		20p bright green (1 centre band)	70	70	☐	☐
Y1679		20p bright green (1 side band)	1·40	1·40	☐	☐
Y1680		20p bright green (2 bands)	30	35	☐	☐
Y1681		25p rose-red (phosphorised paper)	1·10	1·10	☐	☐

Y1682	25p rose-red (2 bands) .	1·10	1·10	☐	☐
Y1683	26p red-brown (2 bands)	1·10	1·10	☐	☐
Y1683b	26p gold (2 bands)	90	90	☐	☐
Y1684	29p grey (2 bands)	1·25	1·25	☐	☐
Y1685	30p deep olive-grey (2 bands)	1·10	1·10	☐	☐
Y1686	31p deep mauve (2 bands)	1·10	1·10	☐	☐
Y1687	33p grey-green (2 bands)	50	55	☐	☐
Y1687a	34p yellow-olive (2 bands)	55	60	☐	☐
Y1688	35p yellow (2 bands) . .	1·40	1·50	☐	☐
Y1689	35p yellow (phosphorised paper)	6·25	6·25	☐	☐
Y1690	36p bright ultramarine (2 bands)	1·50	1·50	☐	☐
Y1691	37p bright mauve (2 bands)	1·40	1·40	☐	☐
Y1691a	37p grey-black (2 bands)	60	65	☐	☐
Y1692	38p rosine (2 bands) . . .	1·50	1·50	☐	☐
Y1693	38p ultramarine (2 bands)	1·40	1·40	☐	☐
	a. Perf 14	4·25	4·50	☐	☐
Y1694	39p bright magenta (2 bands)	1·25	1·40	☐	☐
Y1695	40p deep azure (2 bands)	60	65	☐	☐
Y1696	41p grey-brown (2 bands)	1·40	1·40	☐	☐
Y1697	41p drab (phosphorised paper)	6·50	6·50	☐	☐
Y1698	41p rosine (2 bands) . . .	65	70	☐	☐
Y1698a	42p deep olive-grey (2 bands)	65	70	☐	☐
Y1699	43p deep olive-brown (2 bands)	1·75	1·75	☐	☐
Y1700	43p sepia (2 bands) . . .	1·75	1·75	☐	☐
	a. Perf 14	2·00	2·00	☐	☐
Y1701	44p grey-brown (2 bands)	1·90	1·90	☐	☐
Y1702	45p bright mauve (2 bands)	70	75	☐	☐
Y1702a	47p turquoise-green (2 bands)	75	80	☐	☐
Y1703	50p ochre (2 bands) . . .	75	80	☐	☐
Y1704	63p light emerald (2 bands)	2·00	2·00	☐	☐
Y1705	64p turquoise-green (2 bands)	2·10	2·10	☐	☐
Y1706	65p greenish blue (2 bands)	1·00	1·10	☐	☐
Y1706a	68p grey-brown (2 bands)	1·10	1·25	☐	☐
Y1707	£1 bluish violet (2 bands)	1·50	1·60	☐	☐
Y1708	£1·50 brown-red (2 bands)	2·25	2·40	☐	☐
Y1709	£2 deep blue-green (2 bands)	3·00	3·25	☐	☐
Y1710	£3 deep mauve (2 bands)	4·50	4·75	☐	☐
Y1711	£5 azure (2 bands) . . .	7·50	7·75	☐	☐

(b) *Litho Walsall* (37*p*, 60*p*, 63*p*), *Questa or Walsall* (25*p*, 35*p*, 41*p*), *Questa* (others)

Y1743	**367**	1p lake (2 bands)	40	40	☐	☐
Y1748		6p yellow-olive (2 bands)	12·00	13·00	☐	☐
Y1749		10p dull orange (2 bands)	4·50	4·50	☐	☐
Y1750		19p bistre (1 side band) .	1·90	1·75	☐	☐
Y1751		20p bright yellow-green (1 centre band) . . .	1·50	1·50	☐	☐
Y1752		25p red (2 bands)	1·00	1·00	☐	☐
Y1753		26p chestnut (2 bands) .	1·00	1·00	☐	☐
Y1754		30p olive-grey (2 bands)	4·00	4·00	☐	☐
Y1755		35p yellow (2 bands) . .	1·60	1·60	☐	☐
Y1756		37p bright mauve (2 bands)	2·40	2·40	☐	☐
Y1757		41p drab (2 bands) . . .	1·75	1·75	☐	☐
Y1758		60p dull blue-grey (2 bands)	2·50	2·50	☐	☐
Y1759		63p light emerald (2 bands)	3·00	3·00	☐	☐

(c) *Recess Enschedé or De La Rue*

Y1800	**367**	£1·50 red	2·25	2·00	☐	☐
Y1801		£2 dull blue	3·00	2·25	☐	☐
Y1802		£3 dull violet	4·50	3·00	☐	☐
Y1803		£5 brown	7·50	5·00	☐	☐

PHQ Card (*No.* Y1707) . . . . . 40 3·00 ☐ ☐

Presentation Pack (*P.O. Pack No. 30*) (*contains* 19p (Y1675), 25p (Y1681), 29p (Y1684), 36p (Y1690), 38p (Y1692), 41p (Y1696)) . .   8·00 ☐

Presentation Pack (*P.O. Pack No. 34*) (*contains* 1p (Y1667), 2p (Y1668), 4p (Y1669), 5p (Y1670), 6p (Y1671), 10p (Y1674), 19p (Y1675), 20p (Y1677), 25p (Y1682), 29p (Y1684), 30p (Y1685), 35p (Y1688), 36p (Y1690), 38p (Y1692), 41p (Y1696), 50p (Y1703), 60p (Y1758), £1 (Y1707)) . . . . . 17·00 ☐

Presentation Pack (*P.O. Pack No. 35*) (*contains* 20p (Y1678), 26p (Y1683), 31p (Y1686), 37p (Y1691), 39p (Y1694), 43p (Y1699), 63p (Y1704)) . . . .   8·00 ☐

Presentation Pack (*P.O. Pack No. 38*) (*contains* 1st (Y1664b), 26p (Y1683b)) . . . .   3·50 ☐

Presentation Pack (*P.O. Pack No. 41*) (*contains* 2nd (Y1663a), 1st (Y1664a), 1p (Y1667), 2p (Y1668), 4p (Y1669), 5p (Y1670), 6p (Y1671), 10p (Y1674), 20p (Y1678), 26p (Y1683), 30p (Y1685), 31p (Y1686), 37p (Y1691), 39p (Y1694), 43p (Y1700), 50p (Y1703), 63p (Y1704), £1 (Y1707)) . . . . 12·00 ☐

Presentation Pack (*P.O. Pack No. 43A*) (*contains* £1·50 (Y1800), £2 (Y1801), £3 (Y1802), £5 (Y1803)) 18·00 ☐

Presentation Pack (*P.O. Pack No. 44*) *contains* 7p (Y1672), 19p (Y1675), 38p (Y1693), 44p (Y1701), 64p (Y1705)) . . . . .   5·50 ☐

Presentation Pack (*P.O. Pack No. 49*) (*contains* 8p (Y1673), 33p (Y1687), 40p (Y1695), 41p (Y1698), 45p (Y1702), 65p (Y1706)) . . . .   7·50 ☐

Presentation Pack (*P.O. Pack No. 57*) (*contains* 2nd (1663a), 1st (1664a), E (1664b), 1p (Y1667), 2p (Y1668), 4p (Y1669), 5p (Y1670), 8p (Y1673), 10p (Y1674), 20p (Y1680), 33p (Y1687), 40p (Y1695), 41p (Y1698), 45p (Y1702), 50p (Y1703), 65p (Y1706), £1 (Y1707)) . . . . 12·00 ☐

Presentation Pack (*P.O. Pack No. 58*) (*contains* 37p (Y1691a), 42p (Y1698a), 47p (Y1702a), 68p (Y1706a)) . . . .   5·00 ☐

For P.O. Pack No. 37 see below SG1977.

First Day Covers

26 Oct. 1993	19*p*, 25*p*, 29*p*, 36*p*, 38*p*, 41*p* (*Nos.* Y1675, Y1681, Y1684, Y1690, Y1692, Y1696)	6·00	☐
9 Aug. 1994	60*p* (*No.* Y1758)	4·00	☐
22 Aug. 1995	£1 (*No.* Y1707)	3·50	☐
25 June 1996	20*p*, 26*p*, 31*p*, 37*p*, 39*p*, 43*p*, 63*p* (*Nos.* Y1678, Y1683, Y1686, Y1691, Y1694, Y1699, Y1704)	8·00	☐
9 Mar. 1999	£1·50, £2, £3, £5 (*Nos.* Y1800/3)	27·00	☐
20 Apr. 1999	7*p*, 38*p*, 44*p*, 64*p* (*Nos.* Y1672, Y1693, Y1701, Y1705)	5·00	☐
25 Apr. 2000	8*p*, 33*p*, 40*p*, 41*p*, 45*p*, 65*p* (*Nos.* Y1673, Y1687, Y1695, Y1698, Y1702, Y1706)	5·00	☐
4 July 2002	37*p*, 42*p*, 47*p*, 68*p*, (Nos. Y1691a, Y1698a, Y1702a, Y1706a) . . .	4·00	☐

Nos. Y1707 and Y1708/11 are printed in Iriodin ink which gives a shiny effect to the solid part of the background behind the Queen's head.

Nos. Y1689 and Y1697 were only issued in coils and Nos. Y1674a, Y1676, Y1679, Y1693a, Y1700a, Y1743 and Y1748/59 only in booklets.

No. Y1750 exists with the phosphor band at the left or right of the stamp, but Nos. Y1676 and Y1679 exist with band at right only.

For self-adhesive versions of the 42p and 68p see Nos. 2297/8.

1094 'Family Group' (bronze sculpture) (Henry Moore)

1095 'Kew Gardens' (lithograph) (Edward Bawden)

1096 'St Francis and the Birds' (Stanley Spencer)

1097 'Still Life: Odyssey I' (Ben Nicholson)

Europa. Contemporary Art

1993 (11 MAY) *Phosphorised paper. Perf* 14 × 14½

1767	**1094**	24p multicoloured	. . .	60	20	☐ ☐
1768	**1095**	28p multicoloured	. . .	90	1·00	☐ ☐
1769	**1096**	33p multicoloured	. . .	1·25	1·40	☐ ☐
1770	**1097**	39p multicoloured	. . .	1·40	1·40	☐ ☐
		Set of 4	. . . .	3·75	3·50	☐ ☐
		First Day Cover	. . . .		4·00	☐
		Presentation Pack	. . . .	4·50		☐
		PHQ Cards (set of 4)	. . . . .	4·00	6·50	☐ ☐
		Set of 4 *Gutter Pairs*	. . . . .	8·00		☐

1098 Emperor Claudius (from gold coin)

1099 Emperor Hadrian (bronze head)

1100 Goddess Roma (from gemstone)

1101 Christ (Hinton St Mary mosaic)

Roman Britain

1993 (15 JUNE) *Phosphorised paper with two phosphor bands. Perf* 14 × 14½

1771	**1098**	24p multicoloured	. . . .	60	20	☐ ☐
1772	**1099**	28p multicoloured	. . . .	90	1·00	☐ ☐
1773	**1100**	33p multicoloured	. . . .	1·25	1·40	☐ ☐
1774	**1101**	39p multicoloured	. . . .	1·40	1·40	☐ ☐
		Set of 4	. . . .	3·75	3·50	☐ ☐
		First Day Cover	. . . .		4·00	☐
		Presentation Pack	. . . .	4·50		☐
		PHQ Cards (set of 4)	. . . . .	4·00	6·50	☐ ☐
		Set of 4 *Gutter Pairs*	. . . . .	8·00		☐

1102 *Midland Maid* and other Narrow Boats, Grand Junction Canal

1103 *Yorkshire Maid* and other Humber Keels, Stainforth and Keadby Canal

1104 *Valley Princess* and other Horse-drawn Barges, Brecknock and Abergavenny Canal

1105 Steam Barges including *Pride of Scotland* and and Fishing Boats, Crinan Canal

Inland Waterways

1993 (20 JULY) *Two phosphor bands. Perf* 14½ × 14

1775	**1102**	24p multicoloured	. . . .	60	20	☐ ☐
1776	**1103**	28p multicoloured	. . . .	95	1·00	☐ ☐
1777	**1104**	33p multicoloured	. . . .	1·25	1·25	☐ ☐
1778	**1105**	39p multicoloured	. . . .	1·50	1·40	☐ ☐
		Set of 4	. . . .	4·00	3·50	☐ ☐
		First Day Cover	. . . .		4·25	☐
		Presentation Pack	. . . .	4·50		☐
		PHQ Cards (set of 4)	. . . . .	4·00	8·00	☐ ☐
		Set of 4 *Gutter Pairs*	. . . . .	9·00		☐

Nos. 1775/8 commemorate the bicentenaries of the Acts of Parliament authorising the canals depicted.

1106 Horse Chestnut

1107 Blackberry

1108 Hazel

1109 Rowan

1110 Pear

The Four Seasons. Autumn. Fruits and Leaves

1993 (14 SEPT.) *One phosphor band (18p) or phosphorised paper (others)*

1779	**1106**	18p multicoloured	50	20	☐	☐
1780	**1107**	24p multicoloured	75	20	☐	☐
1781	**1108**	28p multicoloured	1·10	1·25	☐	☐
1782	**1109**	33p multicoloured	1·40	1·50	☐	☐
1783	**1110**	39p multicoloured	1·50	1·50	☐	☐
		Set of 5	4·75	4·25	☐	☐
		First Day Cover		5·00		☐
		Presentation Pack	5·25		☐	
		PHQ Cards (set of 5)	5·00	8·00	☐	☐
		Set of 5 Gutter Pairs	10·50		☐	

1111 *The Reigate Squire*

1112 *The Hound of the Baskervilles*

1113 *The Six Napoleons*

1114 *The Greek Interpreter*

1115 *The Final Problem*

T **1111/15** were printed together, *se-tenant,* in horizontal strips of 5 throughout the sheet.

Sherlock Holmes. Centenary of the Publication of **The Final Problem**

1993 (12 OCT.) *Phosphorised paper. Perf* 14 × 14½

1784	**1111**	24p multicoloured	1·10	1·10	☐	☐
		a. Horiz strip of 5. Nos.				
		1784/8	5·00	5·00	☐	☐
1785	**1112**	24p multicoloured	1·10	1·10	☐	☐
1786	**1113**	24p multicoloured	1·10	1·10	☐	☐
1787	**1114**	24p multicoloured	1·10	1·10	☐	☐
1788	**1115**	24p multicoloured	1·10	1·10	☐	☐
		Set of 5	5·00	5·00	☐	☐
		First Day Cover		6·50		☐
		Presentation Pack	6·00		☐	
		PHQ Cards (set of 5)	5·00	10·00	☐	☐
		Gutter Strip of 10	11·00		☐	

1116

Self-adhesive Booklet Stamp

1993 (19 OCT.) *Litho Walsall. Two phosphor bands. Die-cut perf* 14 × 15 *(with one elliptical hole on each vertical side)*

1789	**1116**	(1st) orange-red	1·25	1·40	☐	☐
		First Day Cover		4·50		☐
		Presentation Pack (booklet pane of 20)	20·00		☐	
		PHQ Card	4·00	8·00	☐	☐

For similar 2nd and 1st designs printed in photogravure by Enschedé see Nos. 1976/7.

1117 Bob Cratchit and Tiny Tim

1118 Mr and Mrs Fezziwig

1119   Scrooge

1120   The Prize Turkey

1121   Mr Scrooge's Nephew

1124   Class 4 No. 43000
on Turntable at Blyth
North

1125   Class 4 No. 42455
near Wigan Central

1126   Class Castle No. 7002
Devizes Castle on Bridge
crossing Worcester and
Birmingham Canal

Christmas. 150th Anniversary of Publication of A Christmas Carol

1993 (9 Nov.) *One phosphor band* (19p) *or phosphorised paper* (*others*)

1790	**1117**	19p multicoloured	. . . .	60	15	☐ ☐
1791	**1118**	25p multicoloured	. . . .	90	15	☐ ☐
1792	**1119**	30p multicoloured	. . . .	1·25	1·50	☐ ☐
1793	**1120**	35p multicoloured	. . . .	1·40	1·60	☐ ☐
1794	**1121**	41p multicoloured	. . . .	1·50	1·60	☐ ☐
		Set of 5	. . . .	5·00	4·50	☐ ☐
		First Day Cover	. . . .		5·50	☐
		Presentation Pack	. . . .	5·75		☐
		PHQ Cards (*set of 5*)	. . . . .	5·00	9·00	☐ ☐
		Set of 5 Gutter Pairs	. . . . .	11·00		☐

Collectors Pack 1993

1993 (9 Nov.) *Comprises Nos. 1639/43, 1654/7, 1659/63, 1767/88 and 1790/4*

	Collectors Pack	. . . .	60·00	☐

Post Office Yearbook

1993 (9 Nov.) *Comprises Nos. 1639/43, 1654/7, 1659/63, 1767/88 and 1790/4 in hardback book with slip case*

	Yearbook	. . . .	65·00	☐

1122   Class 5 No. 44957
and Class B1 No.
61342 on West
Highland Line

1123   Class A1 No. 60149
Amadis at Kings Cross

The Age of Steam. Railway Photographs by Colin Gifford

1994 (18 Jan.) *One phosphor band* (19p) *or phosphorised paper with two bands* (*others*). *Perf* 14½

1795	**1122**	19p deep blue-green, grey-black and black	55	25	☐ ☐
1796	**1123**	25p slate-lilac, grey-black and black	90	95	☐ ☐
1797	**1124**	30p lake-brown, grey-black and black . . .	1·40	1·40	☐ ☐
1798	**1125**	35p deep claret, grey-black and black . . .	1·50	1·60	☐ ☐
1799	**1126**	41p indigo, grey-black and black	1·60	1·50	☐ ☐
		Set of 5	5·50	5·00	☐ ☐
		First Day Cover		5·50	☐
		Presentation Pack	6·25		☐
		PHQ Cards (*set of 5*)	5·00	9·00	☐ ☐
		Set of 5 Gutter Pairs	12·00		☐

1127   Dan Dare and the Mekon   **1128**   The Three Bears

1129   Rupert Bear

1130   Alice (*Alice in Wonderland*)

1131 Noggin and the Ice Dragon

1132 Peter Rabbit posting Letter

1137 Castell Y Waun (Chirk Castle), Clwyd, Wales

1138 Ben Arkle, Sutherland, Scotland

1133 Red Riding Hood and Wolf

1134 Orlando the Marmalade Cat

1139 Mourne Mountains, County Down, Northern Ireland

1140 Dersingham, Norfolk, England

1141 Dolwyddelan, Gwynedd, Wales

1135 Biggles

1136 Paddington Bear on Station

T **1127/36** were printed together, *se-tenant*, in booklet panes of 10 stamps and 20 half stamp-size labels.

Greeting Stamps. 'Messages'
1994 (1 Feb.) *Two phosphor bands. Perf* 15 × 14 (*with one elliptical hole on each vertical side*)

1800	**1127**	(1st) multicoloured	. . . .	1·00	90 ☐ ☐	
		a. Booklet pane. Nos.				
		1800/9	. . . .	11·00	☐	
1801	**1128**	(1st) multicoloured	. . . .	1·00	90 ☐ ☐	
1802	**1129**	(1st) multicoloured	. . . .	1·00	90 ☐ ☐	
1803	**1130**	(1st) gold, bistre-yellow				
		and black	. . . . . .	1·00	90 ☐ ☐	
1804	**1131**	(1st) multicoloured	. . . .	1·00	90 ☐ ☐	
1805	**1132**	(1st) multicoloured	. . . .	1·00	90 ☐ ☐	
1806	**1133**	(1st) multicoloured	. . . .	1·00	90 ☐ ☐	
1807	**1134**	(1st) multicoloured	. . . .	1·00	90 ☐ ☐	
1808	**1135**	(1st) multicoloured	. . . .	1·00	90 ☐ ☐	
1809	**1136**	(1st) multicoloured	. . . .	1·00	90 ☐ ☐	
		Set of 10	. . . .	11·00	8·00 ☐ ☐	
		First Day Cover	. . . .	12·00	☐	
		Presentation Pack	. . . .	20·00	☐	
		PHQ Cards (*set of* 10)	. . . . . .	10·00	22·00 ☐ ☐	

25th Anniversary of Investiture of the Prince of Wales. Paintings by Prince Charles
1994 (1 Mar.) *One phosphor band* (19p) *or phosphorised paper* (*others*)

1810	**1137**	19p multicoloured	. . . .	55	20 ☐ ☐	
1811	**1138**	25p multicoloured	. . . .	1·00	20 ☐ ☐	
1812	**1139**	30p multicoloured	. . . .	1·10	1·40 ☐ ☐	
1813	**1140**	35p multicoloured	. . . .	1·40	1·50 ☐ ☐	
1814	**1141**	41p multicoloured	. . . .	1·50	1·50 ☐ ☐	
		Set of 5	. . . .	5·00	4·50 ☐ ☐	
		First Day Cover	. . . .		5·00	☐
		Presentation Pack	. . . .	5·25	☐	
		PHQ Cards (*set of* 5)	. . . . . .	5·00	9·00 ☐ ☐	
		Set of 5 *Gutter Pairs*	. . . . . .	11·00	☐	

1142 Bather at Blackpool

1143 'Where's my Little Lad?'

1144 'Wish You were Here!'

1145 Punch and Judy Show

1146 'The Tower Crane' Machine

Centenary of Picture Postcards

1994 (12 APR.) *One side band* (19p) *or two phosphor bands* (*others*). *Perf* 14 × 14½

1815	**1142**	19p multicoloured	. . . .	60	20	□ □
1816	**1143**	25p multicoloured	. . . .	90	20	□ □
1817	**1144**	30p multicoloured	. . . .	1·10	1·25	□ □
1818	**1145**	35p multicoloured	. . . .	1·40	1·50	□ □
1819	**1146**	41p multicoloured	. . . .	1·50	1·50	□ □
		Set of 5	. . . .	5·00	4·25	□ □
		First Day Cover	. . . .		4·75	□
		Presentation Pack	. . . .	5·50		□
		PHQ Cards (set of 5)	. . . . .	5·00	9·00	□ □
		Set of 5 Gutter Pairs	. . . . .	11·00		□

1147 British Lion and French Cockerel over Tunnel

> **Minimum Price.** The minimum price quoted is 10p. This represents a handling charge rather than a basis for valuing common stamps. Where the actual value of a stamp is less than 10p this may be apparent when set prices are shown, particularly for sets including a number of 10p stamps. It therefore follows that in valuing common stamps the 10p catalogue price should not be reckoned automatically since it covers a variation in real scarcity.

1148 Symbolic Hands over Train

Nos. 1820/1 and 1822/3 were printed together, *se-tenant*, in horizontal pairs throughout the sheets.

Opening of Channel Tunnel

1994 (3 MAY) *Phosphorised paper. Perf* 14 × 14½

1820	**1147**	25p multicoloured	. . . .	80	70	□ □
		a. Horiz pair. Nos. 1820/1		1·75	1·60	□ □
1821	**1148**	25p multicoloured	. . . .	80	70	□ □
1822	**1147**	41p multicoloured	. . . .	1·50	1·50	□ □
		a. Horiz pair. Nos. 1822/3		3·25	3·25	□ □
1823	**1148**	41p multicoloured	. . . .	1·50	1·50	□ □
		Set of 4	. . . .	4·50	4·00	□ □
		First Day Cover	. . . .		5·50	□
		Presentation Pack	. . . .	5·50		□
		Souvenir Book	. . . .	27·00		□
		PHQ Cards (set of 4)	. . . . .	4·00	8·00	□ □

Stamps in similar designs were also issued by France and these are included in the Souvenir Book.

1149 Groundcrew replacing Smoke Canisters on Douglas Boston of 88 Sqn

1150 H.M.S. *Warspite* (battleship) shelling Enemy Positions

1151 Commandos landing on Gold Beach

1152 Infantry regrouping on Sword Beach

1153 Tank and Infantry advancing, Ouistreham

1158 The 9th Hole, Turnberry

Nos. 1824/8 were printed together, *se-tenant*, in horizontal strips of 5 throughout the sheet.

50th Anniversary of D-Day

1994 (6 JUNE) *Two phosphor bands. Perf* 14½ × 14

1824	**1149**	25p multicoloured	1·10	1·10	☐	☐
		a. Horiz strip of 5. Nos.				
		1824/8	5·00	5·50	☐	☐
1825	**1150**	25p multicoloured	1·10	1·10	☐	☐
1826	**1151**	25p multicoloured	1·10	1·10	☐	☐
1827	**1152**	25p multicoloured	1·10	1·10	☐	☐
1828	**1153**	25p multicoloured	1·10	1·10	☐	☐
		Set of 5	5·00	5·00	☐	☐
		First Day Cover		5·25	☐	
		Presentation Pack	5·50		☐	
		PHQ Cards (set of 5)	5·00	9·00	☐	☐
		Gutter Block of 10	11·00		☐	

Scottish Golf Courses

1994 (5 JULY) *One phosphor band* (19p) *or phosphorised paper* (*others*). *Perf* 14½ × 14

1829	**1154**	19p multicoloured	50	20	☐	☐
1830	**1155**	25p multicoloured	75	20	☐	☐
1831	**1156**	30p multicoloured	1·10	1·40	☐	☐
1832	**1157**	35p multicoloured	1·25	1·40	☐	☐
1833	**1158**	41p multicoloured	1·40	1·40	☐	☐
		Set of 5	4·50	4·25	☐	☐
		First Day Cover		5·00		☐
		Presentation Pack	5·25		☐	
		PHQ Cards (set of 5)	5·00	10·00	☐	☐
		Set of 5 Gutter Pairs	10·00		☐	

Nos. 1829/33 commemorate the 250th anniversary of golf's first set of rules produced by the Honourable Company of Edinburgh Golfers.

1154 The Old Course, St Andrews

1155 The 18th Hole, Muirfield

AMSER HAF/SUMMERTIME Llanelwedd

1159 Royal Welsh Show, Llanelwedd

SUMMERTIME Wimbledon

1160 All England Tennis Championships, Wimbledon

1156 The 15th Hole ('Luckyslap'), Carnoustie

1157 The 8th Hole ('The Postage Stamp'), Royal Troon

SUMMERTIME Cowes

1161 Cowes Week

SUMMERTIME Lord's

1162 Test Match, Lord's

| | 1163 | Braemar Gathering |

1168 Virgin Mary and Joseph   1169 Three Wise Men

The Four Seasons. Summertime. Events

1994 (2 Aug.) *One phosphor band* (19p) *or phosphorised paper* (*others*)

1834	1159	19p multicoloured	50	20	☐	☐
1835	1160	25p multicoloured	75	20	☐	☐
1836	1161	30p multicoloured	1·10	1·25	☐	☐
1837	1162	35p multicoloured	1·25	1·60	☐	☐
1838	1163	41p multicoloured	1·40	1·60	☐	☐
		Set of 5	4·50	4·25	☐	☐
		First Day Cover		4·75		☐
		Presentation Pack	5·00		☐	
		PHQ Cards (*set of 5*)	5·00	9·00	☐	☐
		Set of 5 Gutter Pairs	10·00		☐	

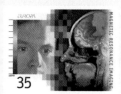

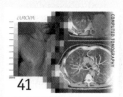

1164   Ultrasonic Imaging   1165   Scanning Electron Microscopy

1170   Virgin and Child   1171   Shepherds

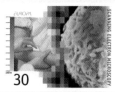

1166   Magnetic Resonance Imaging   1167   Computed Tomography

1172   Angels

Europa. Medical Discoveries

1994 (27 Sept.) *Phosphorised paper. Perf* 14 × 14½

1839	1164	25p multicoloured	80	20	☐	☐
1840	1165	30p multicoloured	1·25	1·10	☐	☐
1841	1166	35p multicoloured	1·25	1·40	☐	☐
1842	1167	41p multicoloured	1·50	1·40	☐	☐
		Set of 4	4·25	3·75	☐	☐
		First Day Cover		4·50		☐
		Presentation Pack	4·75		☐	
		PHQ Cards (*set of 4*)	4·50	8·00	☐	☐
		Set of 4 Gutter Pairs	8·50		☐	

Christmas. Children's Nativity Plays

1994 (1 Nov.) *One phosphor band* (19p) *or phosphorised paper* (*others*)

1843	1168	19p multicoloured	65	15	☐	☐
1844	1169	25p multicoloured	90	15	☐	☐
1845	1170	30p multicoloured	1·10	1·40	☐	☐
1846	1171	35p multicoloured	1·25	1·40	☐	☐
1847	1172	41p multicoloured	1·50	1·40	☐	☐
		Set of 5	4·75	4·00	☐	☐
		First Day Cover		4·50		☐
		Presentation Pack	5·25		☐	
		PHQ Cards (*set of 5*)	5·00	9·00	☐	☐
		Set of 5 Gutter Pairs	10·50		☐	

Collectors Pack 1994

1994 (14 Nov.) *Comprises Nos.* 1795/1847

| | | Collectors Pack . . . . | 55·00 | | ☐ |

Post Office Yearbook

1994 (14 Nov.) *Comprises Nos.* 1795/9 *and* 1810/47 *in hardback book with slip case*

| | | Yearbook . . . . | 60·00 | | ☐ |

1173 Sophie (black cat)

1174 Puskas (Siamese) and Tigger (tabby)

1180 Garlic Leaves

1181 Hazel Leaves

1175 Chloe (ginger cat)

1176 Kikko (tortoiseshell) and Rosie (Abyssinian)

1182 Spring Grass

The Four Seasons. Springtime. Plant Sculptures by Andy Goldsworthy

1995 (14 MAR.) *One phosphor band* (19p) *or two phosphor bands* (others)

1853	**1178**	19p multicoloured	80	15	☐	☐
1854	**1179**	25p multicoloured	95	15	☐	☐
1855	**1180**	30p multicoloured	1·25	1·40	☐	☐
1856	**1181**	35p multicoloured	1·25	1·40	☐	☐
1857	**1182**	41p multicoloured	1·60	1·60	☐	☐
		Set of 5	5·25	4·25	☐	☐
		First Day Cover		5·00		☐
		Presentation Pack	5·50		☐	
		PHQ *Cards* (*set of* 5)	6·00	8·00	☐	☐
		Set of 5 *Gutter Pairs*	11·50		☐	

1177 Fred (black and white cat)

Cats

1995 (17 JAN.) *One phosphor band* (19p) *or two phosphor bands* (others). *Perf* 14½ × 14

1848	**1173**	19p multicoloured	80	20	☐	☐
1849	**1174**	25p multicoloured	95	25	☐	☐
1850	**1175**	30p multicoloured	1·10	1·40	☐	☐
1851	**1176**	35p multicoloured	1·25	1·50	☐	☐
1852	**1177**	41p multicoloured	1·60	1·60	☐	☐
		Set of 5	5·00	4·50	☐	☐
		First Day Cover		5·00		☐
		Presentation Pack	5·50		☐	
		PHQ *Cards* (*set of* 5)	6·00	10·00	☐	☐
		Set of 5 *Gutter Pairs*	11·00		☐	

1178 Dandelions

1179 Sweet Chestnut Leaves

1183 'La Danse a la Campagne' (Renoir)

1184 'Troilus and Criseyde' (Peter Brookes)

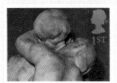

1185 'The Kiss' (Rodin)

1186 'Girls on the Town' (Beryl Cook)

| 1187 | 'Jazz' (Andrew Mockett) | 1188 | 'Girls performing a Kathal Dance' (Aurangzeb period) |

1193 Fireplace Decoration, Attingham Park, Shropshire

1194 Oak Seedling

| 1189 | 'Alice Keppel with her Daughter' (Alice Hughes) | 1190 | 'Children Playing' (L. S. Lowry) |

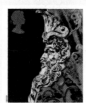

1195 Carved Table Leg, Attingham Park

1196 St David's Head, Dyfed, Wales

| 1191 | 'Circus Clowns' (Emily Firmin and Justin Mitchell) | 1192 | Decoration from 'All the Love Poems of Shakespeare' (Eric Gill) |

T **1183/92** were printed together, *se-tenant,* in booklet panes of 10 stamps and 20 half stamp-size labels.

Greetings Stamp. 'Greetings in Art'

1995 (21 Mar.) *Two phosphor bands. Perf* $14\frac{1}{2} \times 14$ (*with one elliptical hole on each vertical side*)

1858	**1183**	(1st) multicoloured	. . . .	1·00	80 □ □
		a. Booklet pane. Nos.			
		1858/67	. . . . . .	11·00	□
1859	**1184**	(1st) multicoloured	. . . .	1·00	80 □ □
1860	**1185**	(1st) multicoloured	. . . .	1·00	80 □ □
1861	**1186**	(1st) multicoloured	. . . .	1·00	80 □ □
1862	**1187**	(1st) multicoloured	. . . .	1·00	80 □ □
1863	**1188**	(1st) multicoloured	. . . .	1·00	80 □ □
1864	**1189**	(1st) purple-brown and silver	. . . .	1·00	80 □ □
1865	**1190**	(1st) multicoloured	. . . .	1·00	80 □ □
1866	**1191**	(1st) multicoloured	. . . .	1·00	80 □ □
1867	**1192**	(1st) black, greenish yellow and silver	. .	1·00	80 □ □
	Set of 10	. . . .		11·00	7·25 □
	First Day Cover	. . . .			9·00 □
	Presentation Pack	. . . .		12·00	□
	PHQ Cards (set of 10)	. . . . . .		9·00	22·00 □ □

1197 Elizabethan Window, Little Moreton Hall, Cheshire

Centenary of The National Trust

1995 (11 Apr.) *One phosphor band* (19p), *two phosphor bands* (25p, 35p) *or phosphorised paper* (30p, 41p)

1868	**1193**	19p multicoloured	. . . .	60	20 □ □
1869	**1194**	25p multicoloured	. . . .	80	20 □ □
1870	**1195**	30p multicoloured	. . . .	1·00	1·25 □ □
1871	**1196**	35p multicoloured	. . . .	1·25	1·50 □ □
1872	**1197**	41p multicoloured	. . . .	1·40	1·50 □ □
	Set of 5	. . . .		4·50	4·25 □ □
	First Day Cover	. . . .			4·75 □
	Presentation Pack	. . . .		5·25	□
	PHQ Cards (set of 5)	. . . . . .		6·00	8·00 □ □
	Set of 5 *Gutter Pairs*	. . . . . .		10·00	□

1198 British Troops and French Civilians celebrating

1199 Symbolic Hands and Red Cross

1203 The Time Machine

1204 The First Men in the Moon

1200 St Paul's Cathedral and Searchlights

1201 Symbolic Hand releasing Peace Dove

1205 The War of the Worlds

1206 The Shape of Things to Come

Science Fiction. Novels by H. G. Wells

1995 (6 JUNE) *Two phosphor bands. Perf* $14\frac{1}{2} \times 14$

1878	**1203**	25p multicoloured	95	25	☐	☐
1879	**1204**	30p multicoloured	1·40	1·50	☐	☐
1880	**1205**	35p multicoloured	1·50	1·60	☐	☐
1881	**1206**	41p multicoloured	1·60	1·60	☐	☐
		Set of 4	5·00	4·50	☐	☐
		First Day Cover		5·25		☐
		Presentation Pack	5·50			☐
		PHQ Cards (set of 4)	5·00	10·00	☐	☐
		Set of 4 Gutter Pairs	11·00			☐

Nos. 1878/81 commemorate the centenary of publication of Wells's *The Time Machine*.

1202 Symbolic Hands

Europa. Peace and Freedom

1995 (2 MAY) *One phosphor band (Nos. 1873/4) or two phosphor bands (others). Perf* $14\frac{1}{2} \times 14$

1873	**1198**	19p silver, bistre-brown and grey-black . . .	70	40	☐	☐
1874	**1199**	19p multicoloured	70	40	☐	☐
1875	**1200**	25p silver, blue and grey-black	1·00	60	☐	☐
1876	**1201**	25p multicoloured	1·00	60	☐	☐
1877	**1202**	30p multicoloured	1·25	1·75	☐	☐
		Set of 5	4·25	3·50	☐	☐
		First Day Cover		4·00		☐
		Presentation Pack	5·00			☐
		PHQ Cards (set of 5)	6·00	9·00	☐	☐
		Set of 5 Gutter Pairs	9·00			☐

Nos. 1873 and 1875 commemorate the 50th anniversary of the end of the Second World War, No. 1874 the 125th anniversary of the British Red Cross Society and Nos. 1876/7 the 50th anniversary of the United Nations.

Nos. 1876/7 include the 'EUROPA' emblem.

1207 The Swan, 1595

1208 The Rose, 1592

For full information on all future British issues, collectors should write to Royal Mail, Freepost EH3647, 21 South Gyle Crescent, Edinburgh EH12 9PE.

1209 The Globe, 1599

1210 The Hope, 1613

1211 The Globe, 1614

T **1207/11** were printed together, *se-tenant,* in horizontal strips of 5 throughout the sheet, the backgrounds forming a composite design.

Reconstruction of Shakespeare's Globe Theatre

1995 (8 AUG.) *Two phosphor bands. Perf 14½*

1882	**1207**	25p multicoloured	90	90	□	□
		a. Horiz strip of 5. Nos.				
		1882/6	4·25	4·25	□	□
1883	**1208**	25p multicoloured	90	90	□	□
1884	**1209**	25p multicoloured	90	90	□	□
1885	**1210**	25p multicoloured	90	90	□	□
1886	**1211**	25p multicoloured	90	90	□	□
		Set of 5	4·25	4·00	□	□
		First Day Cover		5·50		
		Presentation Pack	5·25		□	
		PHQ Cards (set of 5)	6·00	9·00	□	□
		Gutter Strip of 10	10·50		□	

1212 Sir Rowland Hill and Uniform Penny Postage Petition

1213 Hill and Penny Black

1214 Guglielmo Marconi and Early Wireless

1215 Marconi and Sinking of *Titanic* (liner)

Pioneers of Communications

1995 (5 SEPT.) *One phosphor band* (19p) *or phosphorised paper* (*others*). *Perf 14½ × 14*

1887	**1212**	19p silver, red and black	65	30	□	□
1888	**1213**	25p silver, brown and black	90	35	□	□
1889	**1214**	41p silver, grey-green and black	1·50	1·60	□	□
1890	**1215**	60p silver, deep ultra-marine and black . .	1·75	1·90	□	□
		Set of 4	4·25	3·75	□	□
		First Day Cover		4·50		□
		Presentation Pack	5·00		□	
		PHQ Cards (set of 4)	5·00	9·00	□	□
		Set of 4 Gutter Pairs	9·50		□	

Nos. 1887/8 mark the birth bicentenary of Sir Rowland Hill and Nos. 1889/90 the centenary of the first radio transmissions.

1216 Harold Wagstaff

1217 Gus Risman

1218 Jim Sullivan

1219 Billy Batten

1220 Brian Bevan

Centenary of Rugby League

1995 (3 Oct.) *One phosphor band* (19p) *or two phosphor bands*
(*others*). *Perf* 14 × 14½

1891	**1216**	19p multicoloured	85	25	☐	☐
1892	**1217**	25p multicoloured	1·00	30	☐	☐
1893	**1218**	30p multicoloured	1·25	1·50	☐	☐
1894	**1219**	35p multicoloured	1·25	1·60	☐	☐
1895	**1220**	41p multicoloured	1·60	1·75	☐	☐
		Set of 5	5·25	5·00	☐	☐
		First Day Cover		5·50		☐
		Presentation Pack	6·00		☐	
		PHQ Cards (set of 5)	6·00	9·00	☐	☐
		Set of 5 Gutter Pairs	11·00		☐	

1221 European Robin in Mouth of Pillar Box

1222 European Robin on Railings and Holly

1223 European Robin on Snow-covered Milk Bottles

1224 European Robin on Road Sign

1225 European Robin on Door Knob and Christmas Wreath

Christmas. Christmas Robins

1995 (30 Oct.) *One phosphor band* (19p) *or two phosphor
bands* (*others*)

1896	**1221**	19p multicoloured	60	20	☐	☐
1897	**1222**	25p multicoloured	85	30	☐	☐
1898	**1223**	30p multicoloured	1·25	1·40	☐	☐
1899	**1224**	41p multicoloured	1·60	1·60	☐	☐
1900	**1225**	60p multicoloured	1·75	1·90	☐	☐
		Set of 5	5·50	4·75	☐	☐
		First Day Cover		5·25		☐
		Presentation Pack	6·00		☐	
		PHQ Cards (set of 5)	6·00	9·00	☐	☐
		Set of 5 Gutter Pairs	12·00		☐	

The 19p value was re-issued on 3 October 2000 in sheets of 20 each with *se-tenant* label, in connection with 'customised' stamps available from the Philatelic Bureau. The labels show either Christmas greetings or a personal photograph.

Collectors Pack 1995

1995 (30 Oct.) *Comprises Nos.* 1848/1900

		Collectors Pack	55·00		☐

Post Office Yearbook

1995 (30 Oct.) *Comprises Nos.* 1848/57 *and* 1868/1900 *in
hardback book with slip case*

		Yearbook	60·00		☐

1226 Opening Lines of 'To a Mouse' and Fieldmouse

1227 'O my Luve's like a red, red rose' and Wild Rose

1228 'Scots, wha hae wi Wallace bled' and Sir William Wallace

1229 'Auld Lang Syne' and Highland Dancers

Death Bicentenary of Robert Burns (Scottish poet)

1996 (25 Jan.) *One phosphor band* (19p) *or two phosphor bands* (others). *Perf* 14½

1901	**1226**	19p cream, bistre-brown and black	60	25 □ □
1902	**1227**	25p multicoloured	90	30 □ □
1903	**1228**	41p multicoloured	1·40	1·50 □ □
1904	**1229**	60p multicoloured	1·75	1·90 □ □
		Set of 4	4·25	3·50 □ □
		First Day Cover		5·00 □
		Presentation Pack	5·00	□
		PHQ Cards (set of 4)	6·00	7·00 □ □
		Set of 4 Gutter Pairs	9·50	□

1230 'MORE! LOVE' (Mel Calman)

1231 'Sincerely' (Charles Barsotti)

1232 'Do you have something for the HUMAN CONDITION?' (Mel Calman)

1233 'MENTAL FLOSS (Leo Cullum)

1234 '4.55 P.M.' (Charles Barsotti)

1235 'Dear lottery prize winner (Larry)

1236 'I'm writing to you because...' (Mel Calman)

1237 'FETCH THIS, FETCH THAT' (Charles Barsotti)

1238 'My day starts before I'm ready for it' (Mel Calman)

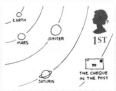

1239 'THE CHEQUE IN THE POST' (Jack Ziegler)

T **1230/9** were printed together, *se-tenant*, in booklet panes of 10 stamps and 20 half stamp-size labels.

Greetings Stamps. Cartoons

1996 (26 Feb.–11 Nov.) *'All-over' phosphor. Perf* 14½ × 14 (*with one elliptical hole on each vertical side*)

1905	**1230**	(1st) black and bright mauve	80	75 □ □
		a. Booklet pane. Nos. 1905/14	9·00	□
		p. Two phosphor bands	1·25	1·25 □ □
		pa. Booklet pane. Nos. 1905p/14p (11 Nov.)	15·00	□
1906	**1231**	(1st) black and blue-green	80	75 □ □
		p. Two phosphor bands	1·25	1·25 □ □
1907	**1232**	(1st) black and new blue	80	75 □ □
		p. Two phosphor bands	1·25	1·25 □ □
1908	**1233**	(1st) black and bright violet	80	75 □ □
		p. Two phosphor bands	1·25	1·25 □ □
1909	**1234**	(1st) black and vermilion	80	75 □ □
		p. Two phosphor bands	1·25	1·25 □ □
1910	**1235**	(1st) black and new blue	80	75 □ □
		p. Two phosphor bands	1·25	1·25 □ □
1911	**1236**	(1st) black and vermilion	80	75 □ □
		p. Two phosphor bands	1·25	1·25 □ □
1912	**1237**	(1st) black and bright violet	80	75 □ □
		p. Two phosphor bands	1·25	1·25 □ □
1913	**1238**	(1st) black and blue-green	80	75 □ □
		p. Two phosphor bands	1·25	1·25 □ □
1914	**1239**	(1st) black and bright mauve	80	75 □ □
		p. Two phosphor bands	1·25	1·25 □ □
		Set of 10 (Nos. 1905/14)	9·00	6·75 □ □
		Set of 10 (Nos. 1905p/14p)	15·00	11·00 □ □
		First Day Cover (Nos. 1905/14)		8·00 □
		Presentation Pack (Nos. 1905/14)	10·00	□
		PHQ Cards (set of 10)	10·00	20·00 □ □

Nos. 1905/14 were re-issued on 18 December 2001 in sheets of 10, each stamp with a *se-tenant* label showing cartoon titles. They were again issued on 29 July 2003 in sheets of 20 containing two of each design, each stamp accompanied by a half stamp size label showing a crossword grid or personal photograph. Such sheets are perforated without elliptical holes.

For full information on all future British issues, collectors should write to Royal Mail, Freepost EH3647, 21 South Gyle Crescent, Edinburgh EH12 9PE.

1240 'Muscovy Duck'

1241 'Lapwing'

1242 'White-fronted Goose'

1243 'Bittern'

1244 'Whooper Swan'

50th Anniversary of the Wildfowl and Wetlands Trust. Bird Paintings by C. F. Tunnicliffe

1996 (12 MAR.) *One phosphor band* (19p) *or phosphorised paper* (others). *Perf* 14 × 14½

1915	**1240**	19p multicoloured	70	25	☐	☐
1916	**1241**	25p multicoloured	90	30	☐	☐
1917	**1242**	30p multicoloured	1·00	1·25	☐	☐
1918	**1243**	35p multicoloured	1·10	1·50	☐	☐
1919	**1244**	41p multicoloured	1·50	1·60	☐	☐
		Set of 5	4·75	4·50	☐	☐
		First Day Cover		5·25		☐
		Presentation Pack	5·25		☐	
		PHQ Cards (set of 5)	6·00	9·00	☐	☐
		Set of 5 Gutter Pairs	10·50		☐	

1245 The Odeon, Harrogate

1246 Laurence Olivier and Vivien Leigh in *Lady Hamilton* (film)

1247 Old Cinema Ticket

1248 Pathé News Still

1249 Cinema Sign, The Odeon, Manchester

Centenary of Cinema

1996 (16 APR.) *One phosphor band* (19p) *or two phosphor bands* (others). *Perf* 14 × 14½

1920	**1245**	19p multicoloured	50	25	☐	☐
1921	**1246**	25p multicoloured	70	30	☐	☐
1922	**1247**	30p multicoloured	90	1·10	☐	☐
1923	**1248**	35p black, red and silver	1·25	1·25	☐	☐
1924	**1249**	41p multicoloured	1·60	1·60	☐	☐
		Set of 5	4·50	4·00	☐	☐
		First Day Cover		5·00		☐
		Presentation Pack	5·00		☐	
		PHQ Cards (set of 5)	6·00	9·00	☐	☐
		Set of 5 Gutter Pairs	10·00		☐	

1250 Dixie Dean

1251 Bobby Moore

1252 Duncan Edwards

1253 Billy Wright

1254   Danny Blanchflower

European Football Championship

1996 (14 MAY) *One phosphor band* (19p) *or two phosphor bands* (*others*). *Perf* 14½ × 14

1925	**1250**	19p multicoloured	40	20	☐	☐
1926	**1251**	25p multicoloured	70	20	☐	☐
1927	**1252**	35p multicoloured	1·25	1·60	☐	☐
1928	**1253**	41p multicoloured	1·40	1·60	☐	☐
1929	**1254**	60p multicoloured	1·75	1·90	☐	☐
		Set of 5	5·00	5·00	☐	☐
		First Day Cover		5·50		☐
		Presentation Pack	5·50		☐	
		PHQ Cards (set of 5)	6·00	9·00	☐	☐
		Set of 5 Gutter Pairs	11·00		☐	

1255   Athlete on Starting Blocks

1256   Throwing the Javelin

1257   Basketball

1258   Swimming

1259   Athlete celebrating and Olympic Rings

T **1255/9** were printed together, *se-tenant*, in horizontal strips of 5 throughout the sheet.

Olympic and Paralympic Games, Atlanta

1996 (9 JULY) *Two phosphor bands. Perf* 14½ × 14

1930	**1255**	26p multicoloured	1·10	1·00	☐	☐
		a. Horiz strip of 5. Nos. 1930/4	5·00	5·50	☐	☐
1931	**1256**	26p multicoloured	1·10	1·00	☐	☐
1932	**1257**	26p multicoloured	1·10	1·00	☐	☐
1933	**1258**	26p multicoloured	1·10	1·00	☐	☐
1934	**1259**	26p multicoloured	1·10	1·00	☐	☐
		Set of 5	5·00	4·50	☐	☐
		First Day Cover		5·75		☐
		Presentation Pack	5·50		☐	
		PHQ Cards (set of 5)	6·00	9·00	☐	☐
		Gutter Strip of 10	11·00		☐	

1260   Prof. Dorothy Hodgkin (scientist)

1261   Dame Margot Fonteyn (ballerina)

1262   Dame Elisabeth Frink (sculptress)

1263   Dame Daphne du Maurier (novelist)

1264   Dame Marea Hartman (sports administrator)

Europa. Famous Women

1996 (6 AUG.) *One phosphor band* (20p) *or two phosphor bands* (*others*). *Perf* 14½

1935	**1260**	20p dull blue-green, brownish grey and black	60	25	☐	☐
1936	**1261**	26p dull mauve, brownish grey and black . . .	75	25	☐	☐
1937	**1262**	31p bronze, brownish grey and black . . .	95	1·10	☐	☐

1938	**1263**	37p silver, brownish grey				
		and black	1·25	1·40	☐	☐
1939	**1264**	43p gold, brownish grey				
		and black	1·40	1·50	☐	☐
		Set of 5	4·50	4·50	☐	☐
		First Day Cover		5·75		☐
		Presentation Pack	5·25		☐	
		PHQ Cards (set of 5)	6·00	9·00	☐	☐
		Set of 5 Gutter Pairs	9·00		☐	

Nos. 1936/7 include the 'EUROPA' emblem.

1265 *Muffin the Mule*

1266 *Sooty*

1267 *Stingray*

1268 *The Clangers*

1269 *Dangermouse*

50th Anniversary of Children's Television

1996 (3 SEPT.)–**97** *One phosphor band (20p) or two phosphor bands (others). Perf 14½ × 14*

1940	**1265**	20p multicoloured	55	20	☐	☐
		a. Perf 15 × 14 (23.9.97)	2·00	2·00	☐	☐
1941	**1266**	26p multicoloured	80	20	☐	☐
1942	**1267**	31p multicoloured	1·00	1·50	☐	☐
1943	**1268**	37p multicoloured	1·40	1·60	☐	☐
1944	**1269**	43p multicoloured	1·60	1·75	☐	☐
		Set of 5	4·75	4·75	☐	☐
		First Day Cover		5·50		☐
		Presentation Pack	5·25		☐	
		PHQ Cards (set of 5)	6·00	9·00	☐	☐
		Set of 5 Gutter Pairs	10·50		☐	

No. 1940a comes from stamp booklets.

1270 Triumph TR3

1271 MG TD

1272 Austin-Healey 100

1273 Jaguar XK120

1274 Morgan Plus 4

Classic Sports Cars

1996 (1 OCT.) *One phosphor band (20p) or two phosphor bands (others). Perf 14½*

1945	**1270**	20p multicoloured	55	20	☐	☐
1946	**1271**	26p multicoloured	80	20	☐	☐
1947	**1272**	37p multicoloured	1·40	1·50	☐	☐
1948	**1273**	43p multicoloured	1·40	1·50	☐	☐
1949	**1274**	63p multicoloured	1·75	1·50	☐	☐
		Set of 5	5·25	4·50	☐	☐
		First Day Cover		6·00		☐
		Presentation Pack	5·50		☐	
		PHQ Cards (set of 5)	6·00	9·00	☐	☐
		Set of 5 Gutter Pairs	11·00		☐	

1275 The Three Kings

1276 The Annunciation

1277 The Journey to Bethlehem

1278 The Nativity

1279 The Shepherds

Christmas

1996 (28 Oct.) *One phosphor band* (2nd) *or two phosphor bands* (others)

1950	**1275**	(2nd) multicoloured	...	75	20	□ □
1951	**1276**	(1st) multicoloured	...	1·00	35	□ □
1952	**1277**	31p multicoloured	...	1·10	1·50	□ □
1953	**1278**	43p multicoloured	...	1·25	1·50	□ □
1954	**1279**	63p multicoloured	...	1·60	1·75	□ □
		Set of 5	....	5·25	4·75	□ □
		First Day Cover	....		5·75	□
		Presentation Pack	....	5·75		□
		PHQ Cards (set of 5)	......	6·00	9·00	□ □
		Set of 5 Gutter Pairs	......	11·00		□

Collectors Pack 1996

1996 (28 Oct.) *Comprises Nos. 1901/4 and 1915/54*

Collectors Pack .... 55·00 □

Post Office Yearbook

1996 (28 Oct.) *Comprises Nos. 1901/4 and 1915/54 in hardback book with slip case*

Yearbook .... 65·00 □

1280 Gentiana acaulis
(Georg Ehret)

1281 Magnolia grandiflora
(Ehret)

1282 Camellia japonica
(Alfred Chandler)

1283 Tulipa
(Ehret)

1284 Fuchsia 'Princess of Wales' (Augusta Withers)

1285 Tulipa gesneriana
(Ehret)

1286 Guzmania splendens
(Charlotte Sowerby)

1287 Iris latifolia
(Ehret)

1288 Hippeastrum rutilum
(Pierre-Joseph Redoute)

1289 Passiflora coerulea
(Ehret)

T **1280/9** were printed together, *se-tenant*, in booklet panes of 10 stamps and 20 half stamp-size labels.

Greeting Stamps. 19th-century Flower Paintings

1997 (6 Jan.) *Two phosphor bands. Perf* $14\frac{1}{2} \times 14$ (*with one elliptical hole on each vertical side*)

1955	**1280**	(1st) multicoloured	....	85	90	□ □
		a. Booklet pane. Nos.				
		1955/64	....	9·00		□
1956	**1281**	(1st) multicoloured	....	85	90	□ □
1957	**1282**	(1st) multicoloured	....	85	90	□ □
1958	**1283**	(1st) multicoloured	....	85	90	□ □
1959	**1284**	(1st) multicoloured	....	85	90	□ □
1960	**1285**	(1st) multicoloured	....	85	90	□ □
1961	**1286**	(1st) multicoloured	....	85	90	□ □
1962	**1287**	(1st) multicoloured	....	85	90	□ □

1963	**1288**	(1st) multicoloured	. . . .	85	90	□	□
1964	**1289**	(1st) multicoloured	. . . .	85	90	□	□
		Set of 10	. . . .	9·00	8·00	□	□
		First Day Cover	. . . .		10·00		□
		Presentation Pack	. . . .	10·00		□	
		PHQ Cards (set of 10)	. . . . . .	10·00	18·00	□	□

Nos. 1955/64 were re-issued on 21 January 2003 in *se-tenant* sheets of 20, each accompanied by a label showing flowers or personal photograph. Such sheets are perforated without elliptical holes.

1290 'King Henry VIII'

1291 'Catherine of Aragon'   **1292** 'Anne Boleyn'

1293 'Jane Seymour'   **1294** 'Anne of Cleves'

1295 'Catherine Howard'   **1296** 'Catherine Parr'

T **1290/6** were printed together, *se-tenant,* in horizontal strips of 6 throughout the sheet.

450th Death Anniversary of King Henry VIII

1997 (21 Jan.) *Two phosphor bands. Perf 15 (No. 1965) or 14 × 15 (others)*

1965	**1290**	26p multicoloured	. . . .	1·00	90	□	□
1966	**1291**	26p multicoloured	. . . .	1·25	1·00	□	□
		a. Horiz strip of 6. Nos.					
		1966/71	. . . .	7·50	8·50	□	□
1967	**1292**	26p multicoloured	. . . .	1·25	1·00	□	□
1968	**1293**	26p multicoloured	. . . .	1·25	1·00	□	□
1969	**1294**	26p multicoloured	. . . .	1·25	1·00	□	□
1970	**1295**	26p multicoloured	. . . .	1·25	1·00	□	□
1971	**1296**	26p multicoloured	. . . .	1·25	1·00	□	□
		Set of 7	. . . .	7·75	6·25	□	□
		First Day Cover	. . . `.		9·00		□
		Presentation Pack	. . . .	10·00		□	
		PHQ Cards (set of 7)	. . . . . .	10·00	14·00	□	□
		Gutter Pair and Gutter Block of 12	17·00		□	

1297 St Columba in Boat   **1298** St Columba on Iona

1299 St Augustine with King Ethelbert   **1300** St Augustine with Model of Cathedral

Religious Anniversaries

1997 (11 Mar.) *Two phosphor bands. Perf 14½*

1972	**1297**	26p multicoloured	. . . .	75	35	□	□
1973	**1298**	37p multicoloured	. . . .	1·10	1·50	□	□
1974	**1299**	43p multicoloured	. . . .	1·50	1·50	□	□
1975	**1300**	63p multicoloured	. . . .	2·00	2·10	□	□
		Set of 4	. . . .	4·75	5·00	□	□
		First Day Cover	. . . .		6·00		□
		Presentation Pack	. . . .	5·25		□	
		PHQ Cards (set of 4)	. . . . . .	5·00	8·00	□	□
		Set of 4 Gutter Pairs	. . . . . .	10·50		□	

Nos. 1972/3 commemorate the 1400th death anniversary of St Columba and Nos. 1974/5 the 1400th anniversary of the arrival of St Augustine of Canterbury in Kent.

1301 **1302**

Self-adhesive Coil Stamps

1997 (18 Mar.) *Photo Enschedé. One centre phosphor band (2nd) or two phosphor bands (1st). Perf* 14 × 15 *die-cut (with one elliptical hole on each vertical side)*

1976	1301	(2nd) bright blue	2·00	2·50	☐	☐
1977	1302	(1st) bright orange-red .	2·00	2·75	☐	☐
		Set of 2	4·00	5·25	☐	☐
		First Day Cover		5·50		☐
		Presentation Pack	4·00		☐	

Nos. 1976/7, which were priced at 20p and 26p, were each sold in rolls of 100 with the stamps separate on the backing paper.

Machin stamps printed in gold were issued on 21 April 1997 for the Royal Golden Wedding. These are listed as definitives under Nos. 1664*b* (1st) and Y1683*b* 26p.

Dracula

1303 *Dracula*

Frankenstein

1304 *Frankenstein*

Dr Jekyll and Mr Hyde

1305 *Dr Jekyll and Mr Hyde*

The Hound of the Baskervilles

1306 *The Hound of the Baskervilles*

Minimum Price. The minimum price quoted is 10p. This represents a handling charge rather than a basis for valuing common stamps. Where the actual value of a stamp is less than 10p this may be apparent when set prices are shown, particularly for sets containing a number of 10p stamps. It therefore follows that in valuing common stamps the 10p catalogue price should not be reckoned automatically since it covers a variation in real scarcity.

Europa. Tales and Legends. Horror Stories

1997 (13 May) *Two phosphor bands. Perf* 14 × 15

1980	1303	26p multicoloured	90	40	☐	☐
1981	1304	31p multicoloured	1·00	1·40	☐	☐
1982	1305	37p multicoloured	1·25	1·50	☐	☐
1983	1306	43p multicoloured	1·50	1·60	☐	☐
		Set of 4	4·25	4·50	☐	☐
		First Day Cover		6·00		☐
		Presentation Pack	5·50		☐	
		PHQ Cards (set of 4)	5·00	8·00	☐	☐
		Set of 4 Gutter Pairs	9·50		☐	

Nos. 1980/3 commemorate the birth bicentenary of Mary Shelley (creator of Frankenstein) with the 26p and 31p values incorporating the 'EUROPA' emblem.

1307 Reginald Mitchell and Supermarine Spitfire MkIIA

1308 Roy Chadwick and Avro Lancaster MkI

1309 Ronald Bishop and De Havilland Mosquito B MkXVI

1310 George Carter and Gloster Meteor T Mk7

1311 Sir Sidney Camm and Hawker Hunter FGA Mk9

British Aircraft Designers

1997 (10 June) *One phosphor band* (20p) *or two phosphor bands (others)*

1984	1307	20p multicoloured	55	40	☐	☐
1985	1308	26p multicoloured	95	1·10	☐	☐
1986	1309	37p multicoloured	1·25	1·10	☐	☐
1987	1310	43p multicoloured	1·40	1·40	☐	☐
1988	1311	63p multicoloured	1·90	1·90	☐	☐
		Set of 5	5·50	5·25	☐	☐
		First Day Cover		6·50		☐
		Presentation Pack	6·25		☐	
		PHQ Cards	6·00	10·00	☐	☐
		Set of 5 Gutter Pairs	12·00		☐	

1312 Carriage Horse and Coachman

1313 Lifeguards Horse and Trooper

1314 Household Cavalry Drum Horse and Drummer

1315 Duke of Edinburgh's Horse and Groom

'All The Queen's Horses'. 50th Anniv of the British Horse Society

1997 (8 JULY) *One phosphor band* (20p) *or two phosphor bands* (*others*). *Perf* 14½

1989	1312	20p multicoloured	. . . .	75	45	☐	☐
1990	1313	26p multicoloured	. . . .	1·10	1·40	☐	☐
1991	1314	43p multicoloured	. . . .	1·40	1·50	☐	☐
1992	1315	63p multicoloured	. . . .	1·90	2·00	☐	☐
		Set of 4	. . . .	4·75	4·75	☐	☐
		First Day Cover	. . . .		5·75	☐	
		Presentation Pack	. . . .	5·50		☐	
		PHQ Cards (set of 4)	. . . . . .	5·00	8·00	☐	☐
		Set of 4 Gutter Pairs	. . . . .	10·50		☐	

CASTLE

Harrison printing (Nos. 1611/14)

CASTLE

Enschedé printing (Nos. 1993/6)

Differences between Harrison and Enschedé printings:
Harrison – 'C' has top serif and tail of letter points to right. 'A' has flat top. 'S' has top and bottom serifs.
Enschedé – 'C' has no top serif and tail of letter points upwards. 'A' has pointed top. 'S' has no serifs.

1997 (29 JULY) *Designs as Nos. 1612/14 with Queen's head in silhouette as T* **1044**, *but re-engraved as above. Perf* 15 × 14 (*with one elliptical hole on each vertical side*).

1993	880	£1·50 deep claret and gold†	7·50	4·00	☐	☐
1994	881	£2 indigo and gold†	. . .	8·50	2·25	☐	☐

1995	1044	£3 violet and gold†	. . .	20·00	3·50	☐	☐
1996	882	£5 deep brown and gold†		20·00	10·00	☐	☐
		Set of 4	. . . .	50·00	18·00	☐	☐
		Set of 4 Gutter Pairs	. . . . . .	£100		☐	
		Presentation Pack (P.O Pack No. 40)	. . . .	60·00		☐	

† The Queen's head on these stamps is printed in optically variable ink which changes colour from gold to green when viewed from different angles.

1316 Haroldswick, Shetland

1317 Painswick, Gloucestershire

1318 Beddgelert, Gwynedd

1319 Ballyroney, County Down

Sub-Post Offices

1997 (12 AUG.) *One phosphor band* (20p) *or two phosphor bands* (*others*). *Perf* 14½

1997	1316	20p multicoloured	. . . .	65	50	☐	☐
1998	1317	26p multicoloured	. . . .	85	60	☐	☐
1999	1318	43p multicoloured	. . . .	1·40	1·50	☐	☐
2000	1319	63p multicoloured	. . . .	1·90	2·10	☐	☐
		Set of 4	. . . .	4·25	4·25	☐	☐
		First Day Cover	. . . .		5·75	☐	
		Presentation Pack	. . . .	5·00		☐	
		PHQ Cards (set of 4)	. . . . .	5·00	8·00	☐	☐
		Set of 4 Gutter Pairs	. . . . .	9·50		☐	

Nos. 1997/2000 also mark the centenary of the National Federation of Sub-Postmasters.

Enid Blyton's *Noddy*

Enid Blyton's *Famous Five*

1320 Noddy

1321 Famous Five

Enid Blyton's *Secret Seven*

1322 Secret Seven

Enid Blyton's *Faraway Tree*

1323 Faraway Tree

Enid Blyton's *Malory Towers*

1324 Malory Towers

Birth Centenary of Enid Blyton (children's author)

1997 (9 SEPT.) *One phosphor band* (20p) *or two phosphor bands* (*others*). *Perf* 14 × 14½

2001	**1320**	20p multicoloured	. . . .	60	45 ☐	☐
2002	**1321**	26p multicoloured	. . . .	1·00	1·25 ☐	☐
2003	**1322**	37p multicoloured	. . . .	1·25	1·25 ☐	☐
2004	**1323**	43p multicoloured	. . . .	1·50	1·50 ☐	☐
2005	**1324**	63p multicoloured	. . . .	2·00	2·00 ☐	☐
		Set of 5	. . . .	5·75	5·75 ☐	☐
		First Day Cover	. . . .		6·50	☐
		Presentation Pack	. . . .	6·00		☐
		PHQ Cards (set of 5)	. . . . . .	6·00	10·00 ☐	☐
		Set of 5 Gutter Pairs	. . . . . .	12·00		☐

1325 Children and Father Christmas pulling Cracker

1326 Father Christmas with Traditional Cracker

1327 Father Christmas riding Cracker

1328 Father Christmas on Snowball

1329 Father Christmas and Chimney

Christmas. 150th Anniversary of the Christmas Cracker

1997 (27 OCT.) *One phosphor band* (2nd) *or two phosphor bands* (*others*)

2006	**1325**	(2nd) multicoloured	. . . .	75	20 ☐	☐
2007	**1326**	(1st) multicoloured	. . . .	90	30 ☐	☐
2008	**1327**	31p multicoloured	. . . .	1·00	1·60 ☐	☐
2009	**1328**	43p multicoloured	. . . .	1·25	1·75 ☐	☐
2010	**1329**	63p multicoloured	. . . .	1·60	1·90 ☐	☐
		Set of 5	. . . .	5·00	5·00 ☐	☐
		First Day Cover	. . . .		6·00	☐
		Presentation Pack	. . . .	5·75		☐
		PHQ Cards (set of 5)	. . . . . .	6·00	9·00 ☐	☐
		Set of 5 Gutter Pairs	. . . . . .	11·00		☐

The 1st value was re-issued on 3 October 2000, in sheets of 10 in photogravure, each stamp with a *se-tenant* label, in connection with 'customised' service available from the Philatelic Bureau. On 1 October 2002 in sheet size of 20 in lithography the 1st value was again issued but perforated 14½ × 14. The labels show either Christmas greetings or a personal photograph.

1330 Wedding Photograph, 1947

1331 Queen Elizabeth II and Prince Philip, 1997

Royal Golden Wedding

1997 (13 NOV.) *One phosphor band* (20p) *or two phosphor bands* (*others*). *Perf* 15

2011	**1330**	20p gold, yellow-brown and grey-black	. . .	85	45 ☐	☐
2012	**1331**	26p multicoloured	. . . .	1·10	70 ☐	☐
2013	**1330**	43p gold, bluish green and grey-black	. . .	1·90	2·25 ☐	☐
2014	**1331**	63p multicoloured	. . . .	2·50	3·00 ☐	☐
		Set of 4	. . . .	5·75	5·75 ☐	☐
		First Day Cover	. . . .		6·50	☐
		Presentation Pack	. . . .	6·25		☐
		Souvenir Book (contains Nos. 1979, 1989/92 and 2011/14)	. .	18·00		☐
		PHQ Cards (set of 4)	. . . . .	5·00	8·00 ☐	☐
		Set of 4 Gutter Pairs	. . . . . .	12·00		☐

Collectors Pack 1997

1997 (13 Nov.) *Comprises Nos. 1965/75, 1980/92 and 1997/2014*
  Collectors Pack . . . . 60·00   □

Post Office Yearbook

1997 (13 Nov.) *Comprises Nos. 1965/75, 1980/92 and 1997/2014 in hardback book with slip case*
  Yearbook . . . . 60·00   □

20 **ENDANGERED SPECIES**
Common dormouse
Muscardinus avellanarius

1332 Common Doormouse

26 **ENDANGERED SPECIES**
Lady's slipper orchid
Cypripedium calceolus

1333 Lady's Slipper Orchid

31 **ENDANGERED SPECIES**
Song thrush
Turdus philomelos

1334 Song Thrush

37 **ENDANGERED SPECIES**
Shining ram's-horn snail
Segmentina nitida

1335 Shining Ram's-horn Snail

43 **ENDANGERED SPECIES**
Mole cricket
Gryllotalpa gryllotalpa

1336 Mole Cricket

63 **ENDANGERED SPECIES**
Devil's bolete
Boletus satanas

1337 Devil's Bolete

Endangered Species

1998 (20 Jan.) *One side phosphor band* (20p) *or two phosphor bands* (others). *Perf* 14 × 14½

2015	**1332**	20p multicoloured	60	40	□	□
2016	**1333**	26p multicoloured	75	40	□	□
2017	**1334**	31p multicoloured	1·00	1·00	□	□
2018	**1335**	37p multicoloured	1·25	1·10	□	□

2019	**1336**	43p multicoloured	1·40	1·25	□	□
2020	**1337**	63p multicoloured	1·90	1·75	□	□
		Set of 6	6·25	5·25	□	□
		First Day Cover		5·75		□
		Presentation Pack	6·75			□
		PHQ Cards (Set of 6)	8·00	10·00	□	□
		Set of 6 Gutter Pairs	13·50			□

1338 Diana, Princess of Wales (photo by Lord Snowdon)

1339 At British Lung Foundation Function, April 1997 (photo by John Stillwell)

1340 Wearing Tiara, 1991 (photo by Lord Snowdon)

1341 On Visit to Birmingham, October 1995 (photo by Tim Graham)

1342 In Evening Dress, 1987 (photo by Terence Donovan)

T **1338/42** were printed together, *se-tenant*, in horizontal strips of 5 throughout the sheet.

Diana, Princess of Wales Commemoration

1998 (3 Feb.) *Two phosphor bands*

2021	**1338**	26p multicoloured	90	90	□	□
		a. Horiz strip of 5. Nos. 2021/5	4·00	4·50	□	□
2022	**1339**	26p multicoloured	90	90	□	□
2023	**1340**	26p multicoloured	90	90	□	□

2024	**1341**	26p multicoloured	90	90	☐	☐
2025	**1342**	26p multicoloured	90	90	☐	☐
		Set of 5	4·00	4·00	☐	☐
		First Day Cover		6·00		☐
		Presentation Pack	15·00		☐	
		Presentation Pack (Welsh) . . .	£150		☐	
		Gutter Strip of 10	9·00		☐	

1343 Lion of England and Griffin of Edward III

1344 Falcon of Plantagenet and Bull of Clarence

1345 Lion of Mortimer and Yale of Beaufort

1346 Greyhound of Richmond and Dragon of Wales

1347 Unicorn of Scotland and Horse of Hanover

T **1343/7** were printed together, *se-tenant,* in horizontal strips of 5 throughout the sheet.

650th Anniversary of the Order of the Garter. The Queen's Beasts

1998 (24 FEB.) *Two phosphor bands*

2026	**1343**	26p multicoloured	90	90	☐	☐
		a. Horiz strip of 5. *Nos.*				
		2026/30	4·00	4·50	☐	☐
2027	**1344**	26p multicoloured	90	90	☐	☐
2028	**1345**	26p multicoloured	90	90	☐	☐
2029	**1346**	26p multicoloured	90	90	☐	☐
2030	**1347**	26p multicoloured	90	90	☐	☐
		Set of 5	4·00	4·00	☐	☐
		First Day Cover		5·25		☐
		Presentation Pack	5·00		☐	
		PHQ Cards (set of 5)	6·00	9·00	☐	☐
		Gutter Block of 10	9·00		☐	

The phosphor bands on Nos. 2026/30 are only half the height of the stamps and do not cover the silver parts of the designs.

1348

Booklet Stamps

1998 (10 MAR.) *Design as T* **157** *(issued 1952–54), but with face values in decimal currency as T* **1348**. *One side phosphor band* (20p) *or two phosphor bands* (others). *Perf* 14 (with one elliptical hole on each vertical side)

2031	**1348**	20p light green	70	75	☐	☐
2032		26p red-brown	90	95	☐	☐
2033		37p light purple	2·75	2·75	☐	☐
		Set of 3	4·00	4·00	☐	☐

For further Wilding designs see Nos. 2258/9, **MS**2326, **MS**2367 and 2378/80.

1349 St John's Point Lighthouse, County Down

1350 Smalls Lighthouse, Pembrokeshire

1351 Needles Rock Lighthouse, Isle of Wight, *c* 1900

1352 Bell Rock Lighthouse, Arbroath, mid-19th-century

1353 Eddystone Lighthouse, Plymouth, 1698

Lighthouses

1998 (24 MAR.) *One side phosphor band (20p) or two phosphor bands (others). Perf 14½ × 14*

2034	**1349**	20p multicoloured	50	40 □ □
2035	**1350**	26p multicoloured	75	50 □ □
2036	**1351**	37p multicoloured	1·10	1·25 □ □
2037	**1352**	43p multicoloured	1·50	1·50 □ □
2038	**1353**	63p multicoloured	2·10	2·10 □ □
		Set of 5	5·50	5·25 □ □
		First Day Cover		5·75 □
		Presentation Pack	6·00	□
		PHQ Cards (set of 5)	7·00	10·00 □ □
		Set of 5 Gutter Pairs	12·00	□

Nos. 2034/8 commemorate the 300th anniversary of the first Eddystone Lighthouse and the final year of manned light-houses.

Self-adhesive stamps

1998 (6 APR.) *Photo Enschedé, Questa or Walsall. Designs as T 913/14. One centre phosphor band (2nd) or two phosphor bands (1st). Perf 15 × 14 die-cut (with one elliptical hole on each vertical side)*

2039	(2nd) bright blue	30	35 □ □
	b. Perf 14½ × 14 die-cut	£125	□ □
2040	(1st) bright orange-red	40	45 □ □
	b. Perf 14½ × 14 die-cut	£125	□ □
	Set of 2	70	80 □ □

Nos. 2039/40 were initially priced at 20p and 26p, and were available in coils of 200 (Enschedé), sheets of 100 (Enschedé, Questa or Walsall) or self-adhesive booklets (Questa or Walsall). See also Nos. 2295/8.

1354 Tommy Cooper

1355 Eric Morecambe

1356 Joyce Grenfell

1357 Les Dawson

1358 Peter Cook

Comedians

1998 (23 APR.) *One phosphor band (20p) or two phosphor bands (others). Perf 14½ × 14*

2041	**1354**	20p multicoloured	50	50 □ □
2042	**1355**	26p multicoloured	90	85 □ □
2043	**1356**	37p multicoloured	1·25	1·25 □ □
2044	**1357**	43p multicoloured	1·50	1·50 □ □
2045	**1358**	63p multicoloured	2·10	2·10 □ □
		Set of 5	5·75	5·50 □ □
		First Day Cover		6·50 □
		Presentation Pack	6·00	□
		PHQ Cards (set of 5)	6·50	10·00 □ □
		Set of 5 Gutter Pairs	12·50	□

1359 Hands forming Heart

1360 Adult and Child holding Hands

1361 Hands forming Cradle

1362 Hands taking Pulse

50th Anniversary of National Health Service

1998 (23 JUNE) *One side phosphor band (20p) or two phosphor bands (others). Perf 14 × 14½*

2046	**1359**	20p multicoloured	50	50 □ □
2047	**1360**	26p multicoloured	90	90 □ □
2048	**1361**	43p multicoloured	1·50	1·50 □ □
2049	**1362**	63p multicoloured	2·10	2·10 □ □
		Set of 4	4·50	4·50 □ □
		First Day Cover		5·00 □
		Presentation Pack	4·75	□
		PHQ Cards (set of 4)	5·00	8·00 □ □
		Set of 4 Gutter Pairs	10·00	□

For full information on all future British issues, collectors should write to Royal Mail, Freepost EH3647, 21 South Gyle Crescent, Edinburgh EH12 9PE.

1363 *The Hobbit*
(J. R. R. Tolkien)

1364 *The Lion, The Witch and the Wardrobe*
(C. S. Lewis)

1365 *The Phoenix and the Carpet* (E. Nesbit)

1366 *The Borrowers*
(Mary Norton)

1367 *Through the Looking Glass* (Lewis Carroll)

Famous Children's Fantasy Novels

1998 (21 JULY) *One phosphor band* (20p) *or two phosphor bands* (others)

2050	**1363**	20p multicoloured	50	45	☐	☐
2051	**1364**	26p multicoloured	85	55	☐	☐
2052	**1365**	37p multicoloured	1·25	1·50	☐	☐
2053	**1366**	43p multicoloured	1·40	1·50	☐	☐
2054	**1367**	63p multicoloured	2·10	2·00	☐	☐
		Set of 5	5·50	5·50	☐	☐
		First Day Cover		6·25		☐
		Presentation Pack	6·00		☐	
		PHQ Cards (set of 5)	6·00	10·00	☐	☐
		Set of 5 Gutter Pairs	12·00		☐	

Nos. 2050/4 commemorate the birth centenary of C. S. Lewis and the death centenary of Lewis Carroll.

1368 Woman in Yellow Feathered Costume

1369 Woman in Blue Costume and Headdress

1370 Group of Children in White and Gold Robes

1371 Child in 'Tree' Costume

Europa. Festivals. Notting Hill Carnival

1998 (25 AUG.) *One centre phosphor band* (20p) *or two phosphor bands* (others). Perf 14 × 14½

2055	**1368**	20p multicoloured	75	45	☐	☐
2056	**1369**	26p multicoloured	95	55	☐	☐
2057	**1370**	43p multicoloured	1·50	1·60	☐	☐
2058	**1371**	63p multicoloured	2·00	2·10	☐	☐
		Set of 4	4·75	4·25	☐	☐
		First Day Cover		5·00		☐
		Presentation Pack	5·25		☐	
		PHQ Cards (set of 4)	5·00	9·00	☐	☐
		Set of 4 Gutter Pairs	10·50		☐	

Nos. 2055/6 include the 'EUROPA' emblem.

1372 Sir Malcolm Campbell's *Bluebird*, 1925

1373 Sir Henry Segrave's *Sunbeam*, 1926

1374 John G. Parry Thomas's *Babs*, 1926

1375 John R. Cobb's *Railton Mobil Special*, 1947

1376 Donald Campbell's *Bluebird CN7*, 1964

British Land Speed Record Holders

1998 (29 Sept.–13 Oct.) *One phosphor band* (20p) *or two phosphor bands* (others). *Perf* 15 × 14

2059	**1372**	20p multicoloured (centre band)	70	25	□	□
		a. Perf 14½ × 13½ (side band) (13 Oct.) . . .	1·00	1·00	□	□
2060	**1373**	26p multicoloured	85	30	□	□
2061	**1374**	30p multicoloured	1·25	1·50	□	□
2062	**1375**	43p multicoloured	1·50	1·60	□	□
2063	**1376**	63p multicoloured	2·25	2·40	□	□
		Set of 5	6·00	5·50	□	□
		First Day Cover		6·50		□
		Presentation Pack	6·50		□	
		PHQ Cards (set of 5)	7·00	9·00	□	□
		Set of 5 Gutter Pairs	13·00		□	

No. 2059a, which occurs with the phosphor band at the left or right of the stamp, comes from stamp booklets. There are minor differences of design between No. 2059 and No. 2059a, which also omits the copyright symbol and date.

Nos. 2059/63 commemorate the 50th death anniversary of Sir Malcolm Campbell.

1377 Angel with Hands raised in Blessing	**1378** Angel praying

1379 Angel playing Flute	**1380** Angel playing Lute

1381 Angel praying

Christmas. Angels

1998 (2 Nov.) *One phosphor band* (20p) *or two phosphor bands* (others)

2064	**1377**	20p multicoloured	70	50	□	□
2065	**1378**	26p multicoloured	85	60	□	□
2066	**1379**	30p multicoloured	1·25	1·50	□	□

2067	**1380**	43p multicoloured	1·40	1·60	□	□
2068	**1381**	63p multicoloured	2·00	2·25	□	□
		Set of 5	5·50	5·75	□	□
		First Day Cover		6·00		□
		Presentation Pack	6·00		□	
		PHQ Cards (set of 5)	6·00	9·00	□	□
		Set of 5 Gutter Pairs	12·00		□	

Collectors Pack 1998

1998 (2 Nov.) *Comprises Nos.* 2015/30, 2034/8 *and* 2041/68

	Collectors Pack	55·00	□

Post Office Yearbook

1998 (2 Nov.) *Comprises Nos.* 2015/30, 2034/8 *and* 2041/68 *in hardback book with slip case*

	Yearbook	60·00	□

1382 Greenwich Meridian and Clock (John Harrison's chronometer)	**1383** Industrial Worker and Blast Furnace (James Watt's discovery of steam power)

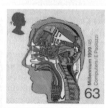

1384 Early Photos of Leaves (Henry Fox-Talbot's photographic experiments)	**1385** Computer inside Human Head (Alan Turing's work on computers)

Millennium Series. The Inventors' Tale

1999 (12 Jan.–21 Sept.) *One centre phosphor band* (20p) *or two phosphor bands* (others). *Perf* 14 × 14½

2069	**1382**	20p multicoloured	75	70	□	□
2070	**1383**	26p multicoloured	95	1·00	□	□
2071	**1384**	43p multicoloured	1·50	1·60	□	□
2072	**1385**	63p multicoloured	2·25	2·40	□	□
		a. Perf 13½ × 14 (21 Sept.)	3·00	3·00	□	□
		Set of 4	5·00	5·25	□	□
		First Day Cover		6·50		□
		Presentation Pack	5·50		□	
		PHQ Cards (set of 4)	5·00	10·00	□	□
		Set of 4 Gutter Pairs	10·00		□	

No. 2072a comes from stamp booklets.

1386 Airliner hugging Globe (International air travel)

1387 Woman on Bicycle (Development of the bicycle)

1388 Victorian Railway Station (Growth of public transport)

1389 Captain Cook and Maori (Captain James Cook's voyages)

Millennium Series. The Travellers' Tale

1999 (2 Feb.) *One centre phosphor band* (20p) *or two phosphor bands* (others). *Perf* 14 × 14½

2073	1386	20p multicoloured	75	70	□	□
2074	1387	26p multicoloured	95	1·00	□	□
2075	1388	43p grey-black, stone and bronze	1·50	1·60	□	□
2076	1389	63p multicoloured	2·25	2·40	□	□
		Set of 4	5·00	5·25	□	□
		First Day Cover		6·00		□
		Presentation Pack	5·50		□	
		PHQ Cards (set of 4)	5·00	10·00	□	□
		Set of 4 Gutter Pairs	10·00		□	

1390

1999 (16 Feb.) (a) *Embossed and litho Walsall. Self-adhesive. Die-cut perf* 14 × 15

2077	1390	(1st) grey (face value) (Queen's head in colourless relief) (phosphor background around head)	2·25	2·25	□	□

(b) Recess Enschedé. Perf 14 × 14½

2078	1390	(1st) grey-black (2 phosphor bands)	2·25	2·25	□	□

(c) Typo Harrison. Perf 14 × 15

2079	1390	(1st) black (2 phosphor bands)	2·25	2·25	□	□
		Set of 3	6·00	6·00	□	□

Nos. 2077/9 were only issued in £7·54 stamp booklets.

1391 Vaccinating Child (pattern in cow markings) (Jenner's development of smallpox vaccine)

1392 Patient on Trolley (nursing care)

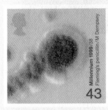

1393 Penicillin Mould (Fleming's discovery of penicillin)

1394 Sculpture of Test-tube Baby (development of in vitro fertilization)

Millennium Series. The Patients' Tale

1999 (2 Mar.) *One centre phosphor band* (20p) *or two phosphor bands* (others). *Perf* 13½ × 14

2080	1391	20p multicoloured	75	70	□	□
2081	1392	26p multicoloured	95	1·00	□	□
2082	1393	43p multicoloured	1·50	1·60	□	□
2083	1394	63p multicoloured	2·25	2·40	□	□
		Set of 4	5·00	5·25	□	□
		First Day Cover		6·00		□
		Presentation Pack	5·50		□	
		PHQ Cards (set of 4)	5·00	10·00	□	□
		Set of 4 Gutter Pairs	10·00		□	

Minimum Price. The minimum price quoted is 10p. This represents a handling charge rather than a basis for valuing common stamps. Where the actual value of a stamp is less than 10p this may be apparent when set prices are shown, particularly for sets including a number of 10p stamps. It therefore follows that in valuing common stamps the 10p catalogue price should not be reckoned automatically since it covers a variation in real scarcity.

1395 Dove and Norman Settler (medieval migration to Scotland)

1396 Pilgrim Fathers and Red Indian (17th-century migration to America)

1397 Sailing Ship and Aspects of Settlement (19th-century migration to Australia)

1398 Hummingbird and Superimposed Stylised Face (20th-century migration to Great Britain)

Millennium Series. The Settlers' Tale

1999 (6 APR.) *One centre phosphor band* (20p) *or two phosphor bands* (*others*). *Perf* 14 × 14½

2084	**1395**	20p multicoloured	. . . .	75	70	☐	☐
2085	**1396**	26p multicoloured	. . . .	95	1·00	☐	☐
2086	**1397**	43p multicoloured	. . . .	1·50	1·60	☐	☐
2087	**1398**	63p multicoloured	. . . .	2·25	2·40	☐	☐
		Set of 4	. . . .	5·00	5·25	☐	☐
		First Day Cover	. . . .		6·00		☐
		Presentation Pack	. . . .	5·50		☐	
		PHQ Cards (set of 4)	. . . . . .	5·00	10·00	☐	☐
		Set of 4 Gutter Pairs	. . . . . .	10·00		☐	

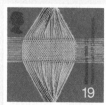

1399 Woven Threads (woollen industry)

1400 Salts Mill, Saltaire (worsted cloth industry)

1401 Hull on Slipway (shipbuilding)

1402 Lloyd's Building (City of London finance centre)

Millennium Series. The Workers' Tale

1999 (4 MAY) *One centre phosphor band* (19p) *or two phosphor bands* (*others*). *Perf* 14 × 14½

2088	**1399**	19p multicoloured	. . . .	75	70	☐	☐
2089	**1400**	26p multicoloured	. . . .	95	1·00	☐	☐
2090	**1401**	44p multicoloured	. . . .	1·50	1·60	☐	☐
2091	**1402**	64p multicoloured	. . . .	2·25	2·40	☐	☐
		Set of 4	. . . .	5·00	5·25	☐	☐
		First Day Cover	. . . .		6·00		☐
		Presentation Pack	. . . .	5·50		☐	
		PHQ Cards (set of 4)	. . . . .	5·00	10·00	☐	☐
		Set of 4 Gutter Pairs	. . . . . .	10·00		☐	

1403 Freddie Mercury (lead singer of Queen) ('Popular Music')

1404 Bobby Moore with World Cup, 1966 ('Sport')

1405 Dalek from *Dr Who* (science-fiction series) ('Television')

1406 Charlie Chaplin (film star) ('Cinema')

Millennium Series. The Entertainers' Tale

1999 (1 JUNE) *One centre phosphor band* (19p) *or two phosphor bands* (*others*). *Perf* 14 × 14½

2092	**1403**	19p multicoloured	. . . .	75	70	☐	☐
2093	**1404**	26p multicoloured	. . . .	95	1·00	☐	☐

2094	**1405**	44p multicoloured	1·50	1·60	☐	☐
2095	**1406**	64p multicoloured	2·25	2·40	☐	☐
		Set of 4	5·00	5·25	☐	☐
		First Day Cover		6·00		☐
		Presentation Pack	5·50		☐	
		PHQ Cards (set of 4)	5·00	10·00	☐	☐
		Set of 4 Gutter Pairs	10·00		☐	

1407 Prince Edward and Miss Sophie Rhys-Jones **1408**
(from photos by John Swannell)

Royal Wedding

1999 (15 JUNE) Two phosphor bands

2096	**1407**	26p multicoloured	85	85	☐	☐
2097	**1408**	64p multicoloured	1·90	1·90	☐	☐
		Set of 2	2·75	2·75	☐	☐
		First Day Cover		4·25		☐
		Presentation Pack	3·25		☐	
		PHQ Cards (set of 2)	4·00	6·00	☐	☐
		Set of 2 Gutter Pairs	6·75		☐	

1409 Suffragette behind Prison Window ('Equal Rights for Women') **1410** Water Tap ('Right to Health')

1411 Generations of School Children ('Right to Education') **1412** 'MAGNA CARTA' ('Human Rights')

Millennium Series. The Citizens' Tale

1999 (6 JULY) One centre phosphor band (19p) or two phosphor bands (others). Perf 14 × 14½

2098	**1409**	19p multicoloured	75	70	☐	☐
2099	**1410**	26p multicoloured	95	1·00	☐	☐

2100	**1411**	44p multicoloured	1·50	1·60	☐	☐
2101	**1412**	64p multicoloured	2·25	2·40	☐	☐
		Set of 4	5·00	5·25	☐	☐
		First Day Cover		6·00		☐
		Presentation Pack	5·50		☐	
		PHQ Cards (set of 4)	5·00	10·00	☐	☐
		Set of 4 Gutter Pairs	10·00		☐	

1413 Molecular Structures ('DNA decoding') **1414** Galapagos Finch and Fossilized Skeleton ('Darwin's theory of evolution')

1415 Rotation of Polarized Light by Magnetism (Faraday's work on electricity) **1416** Saturn (development of astronomical telescopes)

Millennium Series. The Scientists' Tale

1999 (3 AUG.–21 SEPT.) One centre phosphor band (19p) or two phosphor bands (others). Perf 13½ × 14 (19p, 64p) or 14 × 14½ (26p, 44p)

2102	**1413**	19p multicoloured	75	70	☐	☐
2103	**1414**	26p multicoloured	95	1·00	☐	☐
		b. Perf 14½ × 14 (21 Sept.)	3·00	3·00	☐	☐
2104	**1415**	44p multicoloured	1·50	1·60	☐	☐
		a. Perf 14½ × 14 (21 Sept.)	3·00	3·00	☐	☐
2105	**1416**	64p multicoloured	2·25	2·40	☐	☐
		Set of 4	5·00	5·25	☐	☐
		First Day Cover		6·00		☐
		Presentation Pack	5·50		☐	
		PHQ Cards (set of 4)	5·00	10·00	☐	☐
		Set of 4 Gutter Pairs	10·00		☐	

Nos. 2103*b* and 2104*a* come from stamp booklets.

For full information on all future British issues, collectors should write to Royal Mail, Freepost EH3647, 21 South Gyle Crescent, Edinburgh EH12 9PE.

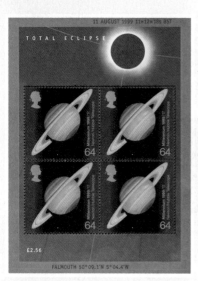

1416a

Solar Eclipse

1999 (11 Aug.) *Sheet* 89 × 121 *mm. Two phosphor bands. Perf*
14 × 14½

MS2106	**1416a**	64p × 4 multicoloured	18·00	18·00	□	□
	First Day Cover			19·00		□

1417 Upland Landscape (Strip farming)

1418 Horse-drawn Rotary Seed Drill (Mechanical farming)

1419 Man peeling Potato (Food imports)

1420 Aerial View of Combine Harvester (Satellite agriculture)

Millennium Series. The Farmers' Tale

1999 (7 Sept.) *One centre phosphor band* (19p) *or two
phosphor bands* (*others*)*. Perf* 14 × 14½

2107	**1417**	19p multicoloured	75	70	□	□
2108	**1418**	26p multicoloured	95	1·00	□	□
2109	**1419**	44p multicoloured	1·50	1·60	□	□
2110	**1420**	64p multicoloured	2·25	2·40	□	□
	Set of 4		5·00	5·25	□	□
	First Day Cover			6·00		□
	Presentation Pack		5·50		□	
	PHQ Cards (*set of 4*)		5·00	10·00	□	□
	Set of 4 Gutter Pairs		10·00		□	

No. 2107 includes the 'EUROPA' emblem.

1421 Robert the Bruce (Battle of Bannockburn, 1314)

1422 Cavalier and Horse (English Civil War)

1423 War Graves Cemetery, The Somme (World Wars)

1424 Soldiers with Boy (Peace-keeping)

Millennium Series. The Soldiers' Tale

1999 (5 Oct.) *One centre phosphor band* (19p) *or two phosphor
bands* (*others*)*. Perf* 14 × 14½

2111	**1421**	19p black, stone and silver	75	70	□	□
2112	**1422**	26p multicoloured	95	1·00	□	□
2113	**1423**	44p grey-black, black and silver	1·50	1·60	□	□
2114	**1424**	64p multicoloured	2·25	2·40	□	□
	Set of 4		5·00	5·25	□	□
	First Day Cover			6·00		□
	Presentation Pack		5·50		□	
	PHQ Cards (*set of 4*)		5·00	10·00	□	□
	Set of 4 Gutter Pairs		10·00		□	

For full information on all future British issues, collectors
should write to Royal Mail, Freepost EH3647, 21 South Gyle
Crescent, Edinburgh EH12 9PE.

1425 'Hark the herald angels sing', and Hymnbook (John Wesley)

1426 King James I and Bible (Authorised Version of Bible)

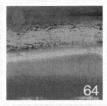

1431 'World of Literature' (Lisa Milroy)

1432 'New Worlds' (Sir Howard Hodgkin)

Millennium Series. The Artists' Tale

1999 (7 DEC.) *One centre phosphor band* (19p) *or two phosphor bands* (others). *Perf* 14 × 14½

2119	1429	19p multicoloured	75	70	☐	☐
2120	1430	26p multicoloured	95	1·00	☐	☐
2121	1431	44p multicoloured	1·50	1·60	☐	☐
2122	1432	64p multicoloured	2·25	2·40	☐	☐
		Set of 4	5·00	5·25	☐	☐
		First Day Cover		6·00		☐
		Presentation Pack	5·50		☐	
		PHQ Cards (set of 4)	5·00	10·00	☐	☐
		Set of 4 Gutter Pairs	10·00		☐	

1427 St Andrews Cathedral, Fife ('Pilgrimage')

1428 Nativity ('First Christmas')

Millennium Series. The Christians' Tale

1999 (2 NOV.) *One centre phosphor band* (19p) *or two phosphor bands* (others). *Perf* 14 × 14½

2115	1425	19p multicoloured	75	70	☐	☐
2116	1426	26p multicoloured	95	1·00	☐	☐
2117	1427	44p multicoloured	1·50	1·60	☐	☐
2118	1428	64p multicoloured	2·25	2·40	☐	☐
		Set of 4	5·00	5·25	☐	☐
		First Day Cover		6·00		☐
		Presentation Pack	5·50		☐	
		PHQ Cards (set of 4)	5·00	10·00	☐	☐
		Set of 4 Gutter Pairs	10·00		☐	

Collectors Pack 1999

1999 (7 DEC.) *Comprises Nos.* 2069/76, 2080/105 *and* 2107/22

	Collectors Pack	55·00	☐

Post Office Yearbook

1999 (7 DEC.) *Comprises Nos.* 2069/76, 2080/105 *and* 2107/22 *in hardback book with slip case*

	Yearbook	60·00	☐

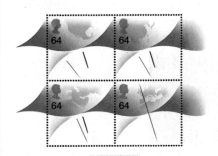

1433a

1429 'World of the Stage' (Allen Jones)

1430 'World of Music' (Bridget Riley)

Millennium Series. 'Millennium Timekeeper'

1999 (14 Dec.) *Sheet* 120 × 89 *mm. Multicoloured. Two phosphor bands. Perf* 14 × 14½

MS2123 **1433***a* 64p Clock face and map
of North America; 64p Clock face
and map of Asia; 64p Clock face
and map of Middle East; 64p Clock
face and map of Europe . . . . . 17·00 17·00 □ □
First Day Cover . . . . 18·00 □
Presentation Pack . . . . 24·00 □
PHQ Cards (set of 5) . . . . . 8·00 22·00 □ □

No. **MS2123** also exists overprinted 'EARLS COURT, LONDON 22–28 MAY 2000 THE STAMP SHOW 2000' from Exhibition Premium Passes, costing £10, available from 1 March 2000.

1437   Queen Elizabeth II

New Millennium

2000 (6 Jan.) *Photo De La Rue, Questa or Walsall (No. 2124); Questa or Walsall (No. 2124d). Two phosphor bands. Perf* 15 × 14 *(with one elliptical hole on each vertical side)*

2124 **1437** (1st) olive-brown . . . . 80 90 □ □
      d. Perf 14 . . . . 80 90 □ □
First Day Cover . . . . 3·00 □
Presentation Pack . . . . 3·25 □
PHQ Card (23 May) . . . . . . 5·00 16·00 □ □

No. 2124 comes from sheets or stamp booklets and No. 2124*d* from booklets only.

1438 Barn Owl (World Owl Trust, Muncaster)

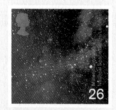

1439 Night Sky (National Space Science Centre, Leicester)

1440 River Goyt and Textile Mills (Torrs Walkway, New Mills)

1441 Cape Gannets (Seabird Centre, North Berwick)

Millennium Projects (1st series). 'Above and Beyond'

2000 (18 Jan.–26 May) *One centre phosphor band* (19p) *or two phosphor bands* (others). *Perf* 14 × 14½ (1st, 44p) *or* 13½ × 14 (others)

2125 **1438** 19p multicoloured . . 75 70 □ □
2126 **1439** 26p multicoloured . . 95 1·00 □ □
2126*a*   (1st) multicoloured
            (26 May) . . . . . 3·50 3·50 □ □
2127 **1440** 44p multicoloured . . 1·50 1·60 □ □
2128 **1441** 64p multicoloured . . 2·25 2·40 □ □
      Set of 4 (ex No. 2126a) . . . . 5·00 5·25 □ □
      First Day Cover . . . .   6·00 □
      Presentation Pack . . . . 5·50 □
      PHQ Cards (set of 4) . . . . . 5·00 10·00 □ □
      Set of 4 Gutter Pairs . . . . . 10·00 □

No. 2126*a* was only issued in stamp booklets.

1442 Millennium Beacon (Beacons across the Land)

1443 Garratt Steam Locomotive No. 143 pulling Train (Rheilffordd Eryri, Welsh Highland Railway)

1444 Lightning (Dynamic Earth Centre, Edinburgh)

1445 Multicoloured Lights (Lighting Croydon's Skyline)

Millennium Projects (2nd series). 'Fire and Light'

2000 (1 Feb.) *One centre phosphor band* (19p) *or two phosphor bands* (others). *Perf* 14 × 14½

2129 **1442** 19p multicoloured . . . . 75 70 □ □
2130 **1443** 26p multicoloured . . . . 95 1·00 □ □
2131 **1444** 44p multicoloured . . . . 1·50 1·60 □ □
2132 **1445** 64p multicoloured . . . . 2·25 2·40 □ □
      Set of 4 . . . . 5·00 5·25 □ □
      First Day Cover . . . .   6·00 □
      Presentation Pack . . . . 5·50 □
      PHQ Cards (set of 4) . . . . . 5·00 10·00 □ □
      Set of 4 Gutter Pairs . . . . . . 10·00 □

1446 Queen Victoria and Queen Elizabeth II

2000 (15 FEB.) *Design T* **929**, *but redrawn with '1st' face value as* *T* **1446**. *Two phosphor bands. Perf 14* (*with one elliptical hole on each vertical side*)

| 2133 | **1446** | (1st) brownish black and cream | . . . . | 1·10 | 1·25 □ □ |

No. 2133 was only issued in stamp booklets.

1451 Reed Beds, River Braid (ECOS, Ballymena)   **1452** South American Leaf-cutter Ants ('Web of Life' Exhibition, London Zoo)

1447 Beach Pebbles (Turning the Tide, Durham Coast)   **1448** Frog's Legs and Water Lilies (National Pondlife Centre, Merseyside)

1453 Solar Sensors (Earth Centre, Doncaster)   **1454** Hydroponic Leaves (Project SUZY, Teesside)

Millennium Projects (4th series). 'Life and Earth'

2000 (4 APR.) *One centre phosphor band* (2nd) *or two phosphor bands* (*others*). *Perf 14 × 14½*

2138	**1451**	(2nd) multicoloured	. . .	75	70 □ □
2139	**1452**	(1st) multicoloured	. . .	95	1·00 □ □
2140	**1453**	44p multicoloured	. . .	1·50	1·60 □ □
2141	**1454**	64p multicoloured	. . .	2·25	2·40 □ □
	Set of 4	. . . .		5·00	5·25 □ □
	First Day Cover	. . . .			6·00 □
	Presentation Pack	. . . .		5·50	□
	PHQ Cards (set of 4)	. . . . . .		5·00	10·00 □ □
	Set of 4 Gutter Pairs	. . . . . .		10·00	□

1449 Cliff Boardwalk (Parc Arfordirol, Llanelli Coast)   **1450** Reflections in Water (Portsmouth Harbour Development)

Millennium Projects (3rd series). 'Water and Coast'

2000 (7 MAR.) *One centre phosphor band* (19p) *or two phosphor bands* (*others*). *Perf 14 × 14½*

2134	**1447**	19p multicoloured	. . . .	75	70 □ □
2135	**1448**	26p multicoloured	. . . .	95	1·00 □ □
2136	**1449**	44p black, grey and silver		1·50	1·60 □ □
2137	**1450**	64p multicoloured	. . . .	2·25	2·40 □ □
	Set of 4	. . . .		5·00	5·25 □ □
	First Day Cover	. . . .			6·00 □
	Presentation Pack	. . . .		5·50	□
	PHQ Cards (set of 4)	. . . . . .		5·00	10·00 □
	Set of 4 Gutter Pairs	. . . . . .		10·00	□

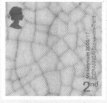

1455 Pottery Glaze (Ceramica Museum, Stoke-on-Trent)   **1456** Bankside Galleries (Tate Modern, London)

1457 Road Marking (Cycle Network Artworks)

1458 People of Salford (Lowry Centre, Salford)

Millennium Projects (5th series). 'Art and Craft'

2000 (2 MAY) *One centre phosphor band* (2nd) *or two phosphor bands* (others). *Perf 14 × 14½*

2142	**1455**	(2nd) multicoloured . . .	75	70	☐	☐
2143	**1456**	(1st) multicoloured . . .	95	1·00	☐	☐
2144	**1457**	45p multicoloured . . .	1·50	1·60	☐	☐
2145	**1458**	65p multicoloured . . .	2·25	2·40	☐	☐
	Set of 4	. . . .	5·00	5·25	☐	
	First Day Cover	. . . .		6·00	☐	
	Presentation Pack	. . . .	5·50		☐	
	PHQ Cards (set of 4)	. . . . .	5·00	10·00	☐	☐
	Set of 4 Gutter Pairs	. . . . .	10·00		☐	

'Stamp Show 2000' International Stamp Exhibition, London. Jeffrey Matthews Colour Palette

2000 (22 MAY) *Sheet, 124 × 70 mm, containing stamps as T* **367** *with two labels. Phosphorised paper. Perf 15 × 14 (with one elliptical hole on each vertical side)*

MS2146   4p new blue; 5p dull red-brown; 6p yellow-olive; 10p dull orange; 31p dp mauve; 39p brt magenta; 64p turq-green; £1 bluish violet   13·00   12·00 ☐ ☐

First Day Cover . . . .   12·00 ☐

Exhibition Card (wallet, sold at £4.99, containing one mint sheet and one cancelled on postcard) . . . .   20·00   ☐

The £1 value is printed in Iriodin ink which gives a shiny effect to the solid part of the background behind the Queen's head.

1459

'Stamp Show 2000' International Stamp Exhibition, London. 'Her Majesty's Stamps'

2000 (23 MAY) *Sheet 121 × 89 mm. Phosphorised paper. Perf 15 × 14 (with one elliptical hole on each vertical side of stamps as T* **1437**)

MS2147 **1459** (1st) olive-brown (Type **1437**) × 4; £1 slate-green (as Type **163**) . . . .   18·00   12·00 ☐ ☐

First Day Cover . . . .   14·00   ☐

Presentation Pack . . . .   70·00   ☐

PHQ Cards (set of 2) . . . .   12·00   25·00 ☐ ☐

The £1 value is an adaptation of the 1953 Coronation 1s. 3d. stamp. It is shown on one of the PHQ cards with the other depicting the complete miniature sheet.

See also No. 2380 for *T* **163** from £7·46 stamp booklet.

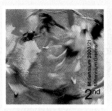   

1460 Children playing (Millennium Greens Project)

1461 Millennium Bridge, Gateshead

1462 Daisies (Mile End Park, London)

1463 African Hut and Thatched Cottage ('On the Meridian Line' Project)

Millennium Projects (6th series). 'People and Places'

2000 (6 JUNE) *One centre phosphor band* (2nd) *or two phosphor bands* (others). *Perf 14 × 14½*

2148	**1460**	(2nd) multicoloured . . .	75	70	☐	☐
2149	**1461**	(1st) multicoloured . . .	95	1·00	☐	☐
2150	**1462**	45p multicoloured . . .	1·50	1·60	☐	☐
2151	**1463**	65p multicoloured . . .	2·25	2·40	☐	☐
	Set of 4	. . . .	5·00	5·25	☐	
	First Day Cover	. . . .		6·00	☐	
	Presentation Pack	. . . .	5·50		☐	
	PHQ Cards (set of 4)	. . . . .	5·00	10·00	☐	☐
	Set of 4 Gutter Pairs	. . . . .	10·00		☐	

1464   Raising the Stone
(Strangford Stone,
Killyleagh)

1465   Horse's Hooves
(Trans Pennine Trail,
Derbyshire)

1466   Cyclist (Kingdom of
Fife Cycle Ways,
Scotland)

1467   Bluebell Wood
(Groundwork's
'Changing Places'
Project)

Millennium Projects (7th series). 'Stone and Soil'

2000 (4 JULY) *One centre phosphor band* (2nd) *or two phosphor bands* (others). Perf 14 × 14½

2152	**1464**	(2nd) brownish black, grey-black and silver	75	70	□	□
2153	**1465**	(1st) multicoloured . . .	95	1·00	□	□
2154	**1466**	45p multicoloured . . .	1·50	1·60	□	□
2155	**1467**	65p multicoloured . . .	2·25	2·40	□	□
		Set of 4	5·00	5·25	□	□
		First Day Cover		6·00		□
		Presentation Pack	5·50		□	
		PHQ *Cards* (*set of* 4)	5·00	10·00	□	□
		Set of 4 *Gutter Pairs*	10·00		□	

1468   Tree Roots ('Yews for
the Millennium'
Project)

1469   Sunflower ('Eden'
Project, St. Austell)

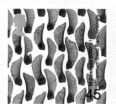

1470   Sycamore Seeds
(Millennium Seed
Bank, Wakehurst
Place, Surrey)

1471   Forest, Doire Dach
('Forest for Scotland')

Millennium Projects (8th series). 'Tree and Leaf'

2000 (1 AUG.) *One centre phosphor band* (2nd) *or two phosphor bands* (others). Perf 14 × 14½

2156	**1468**	(2nd) multicoloured . . .	75	70	□	□
2157	**1469**	(1st) multicoloured . . .	95	1·00	□	□
2158	**1470**	45p multicoloured . . .	1·50	1·60	□	□
2159	**1471**	65p multicoloured . . .	2·25	2·40	□	□
		Set of 4	5·00	5·25	□	□
		First Day Cover		6·00		□
		Presentation Pack	5·50		□	
		PHQ *Cards* (*set of* 4)	5·00	10·00	□	□
		Set of 4 *Gutter Pairs*	10·00		□	

1472   Queen Elizabeth
the Queen Mother

1472a   Royal Family on Queen Mother's 99th Birthday
(from photo by J. Swannell)

Queen Elizabeth the Queen Mother's 100th Birthday

2000 (4 Aug.) *Phosphorised paper plus two phosphor bands.*
Perf 14½

2160	**1472**	27p multicoloured . . .	2·50	2·50	☐	☐

MS2161 121 × 89 mm. **1472a** 27p
Queen Elizabeth II; 27p Prince
William; 27p Queen Elizabeth the
Queen Mother; 27p Prince Charles 10·00 10·00 ☐ ☐

First Day Cover (**MS**2161)		12·00	☐
Presentation Pack (**MS**2161) . .	15·00		☐
PHQ Cards (set of 5)	6·00	18·00	☐ ☐

No. 2160 was only issued in stamp booklets and in No.
MS2161.

The complete miniature sheet is shown on one of the PHQ
cards with the others depicting individual stamps.

1473 Head of *Gigantiops destructor* (Ant) (Wildscreen at Bristol)

1474 Gathering Water Lilies on Broads (Norfolk and Norwich Project)

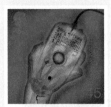

1475 X-ray of Hand holding Computer Mouse (Millennium Point, Birmingham)

1476 Tartan Wool Holder (Scottish Cultural Resources Access Network)

Millennium Projects (9th series). 'Mind and Matter'

2000 (5 Sept.) *One centre phosphor band* (2nd) *or two phosphor bands (others). Perf 14 × 14½*

2162	**1473**	(2nd) multicoloured . . .	75	70	☐	☐
2163	**1474**	(1st) multicoloured . . .	95	1·00	☐	☐
2164	**1475**	45p multicoloured . . .	1·50	1·60	☐	☐
2165	**1476**	65p multicoloured . . .	2·25	2·40	☐	☐
		Set of 4	5·00	5·25	☐	☐
		First Day Cover		6·50		☐
		Presentation Pack	5·50			☐
		PHQ Cards (set of 4)	5·00	10·00	☐	☐
		Set of 4 Gutter Pairs	10·00			☐

1477 Acrobatic Performers (Millennium Dome)

1478 Football Players (Hampden Park, Glasgow)

1479 Bather (Bath Spa Project)

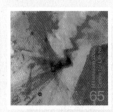

1480 Hen's Egg under Magnification (Centre for Life, Newcastle)

Millennium Projects (10th series). 'Body and Bone'

2000 (3 Oct.) *One centre phosphor band* (2nd) *or two phosphor bands (others). Perf 14 × 14½* (2nd) *or 13½ × 14 (others)*

2166	**1477**	(2nd) black, slate-blue and silver	75	70	☐	☐
2167	**1478**	(1st) multicoloured . . .	95	1·00	☐	☐
2168	**1479**	45p multicoloured . . .	1·50	1·60	☐	☐
2169	**1480**	65p multicoloured . . .	2·25	2·40	☐	☐
		Set of 4	5·00	5·25	☐	☐
		First Day Cover		6·50		☐
		Presentation Pack	5·50			☐
		PHQ Cards (set of 4)	5·00	10·00	☐	☐
		Set of 4 Gutter Pairs	10·00			☐

1481 Virgin and Child Stained Glass Window, St. Edmundsbury Cathedral (Suffolk Cathedral Millennium Project)

1482 Floodlit Church of St. Peter and St. Paul, Overstowey (Church Floodlighting Trust)

1483 12th-cent. Latin Gradual (St. Patrick Centre, Downpatrick)

1484 Chapter House Ceiling, York Minster (York Millennium Mystery Plays)

Millennium Projects (11th series). 'Spirit and Faith'

2000 (7 Nov.) One centre phosphor band (2nd) or two phosphor bands (others). Perf 14 × 14½

2170	**1481**	(2nd) multicoloured . . .	75	70	□	□
2171	**1482**	(1st) multicoloured	95	1·00	□	□
2172	**1483**	45p multicoloured	1·50	1·60	□	□
2173	**1484**	65p multicoloured	2·25	2·40	□	□
	Set of 4	. . . .	5·00	5·25	□	□
	First Day Cover	. . . .		6·25		□
	Presentation Pack	. . . .	5·50		□	
	PHQ Cards (set of 4)	. . . . . .	5·00	10·00	□	□
	Set of 4 Gutter Pairs	. . . . . .	10·00		□	

Post Office Yearbook

2000 (7 Nov.) Comprises Nos. **MS**2125/6, 2127/32, 2134/45, 2148/59 and **MS**2161/81 in hardback book with slip case

	Yearbook	75·00	□

The last two issues in the Millennium Projects Series were supplied for insertion into the above at a later date.

1485 Church Bells (Ringing in the Millennium)

1486 Eye (Year of the Artist)

1487 Top of Harp (Canolfan Mileniwm, Cardiff)

1488 Figure within Latticework (TS2K Creative Enterprise Centres, London)

Millennium Projects (12th series). 'Sound and Vision'

2000 (5 Dec.) One centre phosphor band (2nd) or two phosphor bands (others). Perf 14 × 14½

2174	**1485**	(2nd) multicoloured . . .	75	70	□	□
2175	**1486**	(1st) multicoloured . . .	95	1·00	□	□
2176	**1487**	45p multicoloured . . .	1·50	1·60	□	□
2177	**1488**	65p multicoloured . . .	2·25	2·40	□	□
	Set of 4	. . . .	5·00	5·25	□	□
	First Day Cover	. . . .		6·25		□
	Presentation Pack	. . . .	5·50		□	
	PHQ Cards (set of 4)	. . . . .	5·00	10·00	□	□
	Set of 4 Gutter Pairs	. . . . .	10·00		□	

Collectors Pack 2000

2000 (5 Dec.) Comprises Nos. **MS**2125/6, 2127/32, 2134/45, 2148/59 and **MS**2161/81

	Collectors Pack	65·00	□

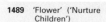

1489 'Flower' ('Nurture Children')

1490 'Tiger' ('Listen to Children')

1491 'Owl' ('Teach Children')

1492 'Butterfly' ('Ensure Children's Freedom')

New Millennium. Rights of the Child. Face Paintings

2001 (16 Jan.) One centre phosphor band (2nd) or two phosphor bands (others). Perf 14 × 14½

2178	**1489**	(2nd) multicoloured . . .	75	75	□	□
2179	**1490**	(1st) multicoloured . . .	1·00	1·10	□	□
2180	**1491**	45p multicoloured . . .	1·60	1·75	□	□
2181	**1492**	65p multicoloured . . .	2·40	2·50	□	□
	Set of 4	. . . .	5·25	5·50	□	□
	First Day Cover	. . . .		6·25		□
	Presentation Pack	. . . .	6·25		□	
	PHQ Cards (set of 4)	. . . . . .	5·00	10·00	□	□
	Set of 4 Gutter Pairs	. . . . . .	11·00		□	

1493 'Love'

1494 'THANKS'

1495 'abc' (New Baby)

1496 'WELCOME'

1497 'Cheers'

1500 Boxer at Dog Show

1501 Cat in Handbag

1502 Cat on Gate

1503 Dog in Car

1504 Cat at Window

1505 Dog behind Fence

1506 Cat watching Bird

1507 Cat in Washbasin

T **1498/1507** were printed together in sheetlets of 10 (5 × 2), with the surplus self-adhesive paper around each stamp retained.

'Occasions' Greetings Stamps

2001 (6 FEB.) *Two phosphor bands. Perf* $14\frac{1}{2} \times 14$

2182	**1493**	(1st) multicoloured	. . . .	90	90 □	□
2183	**1494**	(1st) multicoloured	. . . .	90	90 □	□
2184	**1495**	(1st) multicoloured	. . . .	90	90 □	□
2185	**1496**	(1st) multicoloured	. . . .	90	90 □	□
2186	**1497**	(1st) multicoloured	. . . .	90	90 □	□
		Set of 5	. . . .	4·00	4·00 □	□
		First Day Cover	. . . .		4·75	□
		Presentation Pack (13 Feb.)	. . .	4·50		□
		PHQ Cards (set of 5)	. . . . . .	6·00	10·00 □	□
		Set of 5 Gutter Pairs	. . . . . .	8·00		□

The silver-grey backgrounds are printed in Iriodin ink which gives a shiny effect.

Nos. 2182/6 were printed in photogravure. They were subsequently re-issued on 1 May, as sheets of 20, including a *se-tenant* format, printed in lithography with each stamp accompanied by a half stamp-size label showing either postal symbols or a personal photograph.

1498 Dog and Owner on Bench

1499 Dog in Bath

Cats and Dogs

2001 (13 FEB.) *Self-adhesive. Two phosphor bands. Die-cut perf* 15 × 14

2187	**1498**	(1st) black, grey and silver	1·25	1·00 □	□
		a. Sheetlet. Nos. 2187/96	11·00		□
2188	**1499**	(1st) black, grey and silver	1·25	1·00 □	□
2189	**1500**	(1st) black, grey and silver	1·25	1·00 □	□
2190	**1501**	(1st) black, grey and silver	1·25	1·00 □	□
2191	**1502**	(1st) black, grey and silver	1·25	1·00 □	□
2192	**1503**	(1st) black, grey and silver	1·25	1·00 □	□
2193	**1504**	(1st) black, grey and silver	1·25	1·00 □	□
2194	**1505**	(1st) black, grey and silver	1·25	1·00 □	□
2195	**1506**	(1st) black, grey and silver	1·25	1·00 □	□
2196	**1507**	(1st) black, grey and silver	1·25	1·00 □	□
		Set of 10	. . . .	11·00	9·00 □	□
		First Day Cover	. . . .		12·00	□
		Presentation Pack	. . . .	12·00		□
		PHQ Cards (set of 10)	. . . . . .	8·00	20·00 □	□

1508 'RAIN'

1509 'FAIR'

1510 'STORMY'

1511 'VERY DRY'

Nos. 2197/200 show the four quadrants of a barometer dial which are combined on the miniature sheet.

The Weather

2001 (13 MAR.) *One side phosphor band* (19p) *or two phosphor bands* (others). *Perf* 14½

2197	**1508**	19p multicoloured	70	75 □ □	
2198	**1509**	27p multicoloured	85	90 □ □	
2199	**1510**	45p multicoloured	1·50	1·60 □ □	
2200	**1511**	65p multicoloured	2·40	2·50 □ □	
		Set of 4	5·00	5·25 □ □	
		First Day Cover		6·25 □	
		Presentation Pack	6·25	□	
		Set of 4 Gutter Pairs	11·00	□	
MS2201		105 × 105 mm. Nos. 2197/200	11·50	9·00 □ □	
		First Day Cover		10·00 □	
		PHQ Cards (set of 5)	7·00	12·00 □ □	

The reddish violet on both the 27p and the miniature sheet is printed in thermochromic ink which changes from reddish violet to light blue when exposed to heat.

The PHQ cards depict the four values and the miniature sheet.

1512 *Vanguard* Class Submarine, 1992

1513 *Swiftsure* Class Submarine, 1973

1514 *Unity* Class Submarine, 1939

1515 'Holland' Type Submarine, 1901

1516 White Ensign

1517 Union Jack

1518 Jolly Roger flown by H.M.S. *Proteus* (submarine)

1519 Flag of Chief of Defence Staff

Centenary of Royal Navy Submarine Service

2001 (10 APR.–22 OCT.) *One centre phosphor band* (2nd) *or two phosphor bands* (others). (a) *Submarines. PVA gum.* Perf 15 × 14

2202	**1512**	(2nd) multicoloured	70	75 □ □	
		a. Perf 15½ × 15 (22 Oct.)	3·00	3·00 □ □	
2203	**1513**	(1st) multicoloured	85	90 □ □	
		a. Perf 15½ × 15 (22 Oct.)	3·00	3·00 □ □	
2204	**1514**	45p multicoloured	1·50	1·60 □ □	
		a. Perf 15½ × 15 (22 Oct.)	3·00	3·00 □ □	
2205	**1515**	65p multicoloured	2·40	2·50 □ □	
		a. Perf 15½ × 15 (22 Oct.)	3·00	3·00 □ □	
		Set of 4	5·00	5·25 □ □	
		First Day Cover		6·00 □	
		Presentation Pack	5·00	□	
		PHQ Cards (set of 4)	6·00	10·00 □ □	
		Set of 4 Gutter Pairs	11·00	□	

(b) *Flags. Sheet* 92 × 97 mm. *PVA gum. Perf* 14½

MS2206	**1516** (1st) multicoloured; **1517** (1st) multicoloured; **1518** (1st) multicoloured; **1519** (1st) multicoloured (22 Oct.)	7·50 6·00 □ □
	First Day Cover	9·00 □
	Presentation Pack	9·00 □
	PHQ Cards (set of 5)	5·00 12·00 □ □

(c) Self-adhesive. Die-cut perf 15½ × 14 (No. 2207) or 14½ (others)

2207	**1513**	(1st) multicoloured (17 Apr.)	25·00	20·00	☐	☐
2208	**1516**	(1st) multicoloured (22 Oct.)	8·50	7·50	☐	☐
2209	**1518**	(1st) multicoloured (22 Oct.)	8·50	7·50	☐	☐

Nos. 2202*a*/5*a* only come from stamp booklets.

The five PHQ cards depict the four designs and the complete miniature sheet.

Nos. 2207/9 only come from two different £1.62 booklets.

1520 Leyland X2 Open-top, London General B Type, Leyland Titan TD1 and AEC Regent 1

1521 AEC Regent 1, Daimler COG5, Utility Guy Arab Mk II and AEC Regent III RT Type

1522 AEC Regent III RT Type, Bristol KSW5G Open-top, AEC Routemaster and Bristol Lodekka FSF6G

1523 Bristol Lodekka FSF6G, Leyland Titan PD3/4, Leyland Atlantean PDR1/1 and Daimler Fleetline CRG6LX-33

1524 Daimler Fleetline CRG6LX-33, MCW Metrobus DR102/43, Leyland Olympian ONLXB/1R and Dennis Trident

T **1520**/4 were printed together, *se-tenant*, in horizontal strips of 5 throughout the sheet. The illustrations of the first bus on No. 2210 and the last bus on No. 2214 continue onto the sheet margins.

150th Anniversary of First Double-decker Bus

2001 (15 May) *'All-over' phosphor. Perf* 14½ × 14

2210	**1520**	(1st) multicoloured ...	1·10	1·10	☐	☐
		a. Horiz strip of 5. Nos. 2210/14	5·00	5·75	☐	☐
2211	**1521**	(1st) multicoloured ...	1·10	1·10	☐	☐
2212	**1522**	(1st) multicoloured ...	1·10	1·10	☐	☐
2213	**1523**	(1st) multicoloured ...	1·10	1·10	☐	☐
2214	**1524**	(1st) multicoloured ...	1·10	1·10	☐	☐
		Set of 5	5·00	5·00	☐	☐
		First Day Cover		6·00		☐
		Presentation Pack	6·00			☐
		PHQ Cards (set of 5)	7·00	14·00	☐	☐
		Gutter Strip of 10	11·00			☐
MS2215		120 × 105 mm. Nos. 2210/14	8·25	7·50	☐	☐
		First Day Cover		8·50		☐

In No. **MS**2215 the illustrations of the AEC Regent III RT Type and the Daimler Fleetline CRG6LX-33 appear twice.

1525 Toque Hat by Pip Hackett

1526 Butterfly Hat by Dai Rees

1527 Top Hat by Stephen Jones

1528 Spiral Hat by Philip Treacy

Fashion Hats

2001 (19 June) *'All-over' phosphor. Perf* 14½

2216	**1525**	(1st) multicoloured ...	85	90	☐	☐
2217	**1526**	(E) multicoloured ...	1·10	1·25	☐	☐
2218	**1527**	45p multicoloured ...	1·50	1·60	☐	☐
2219	**1528**	65p multicoloured ...	2·40	2·50	☐	☐
		Set of 4	5·25	5·50	☐	☐
		First Day Cover		5·75		☐
		Presentation Pack	5·50			☐
		PHQ Cards (set of 4)	5·00	10·00	☐	☐
		Set of 4 Gutter Pairs	11·00			☐

1529 Common Frog

1530 Great Diving Beetle

1535 Mr. Punch

1536 Judy

1531 Three-spined
      Stickleback

1532 Southern Hawker
      Dragonfly

1537 Beadle

1538 Crocodile

Europa. Pond Life

2001 (10 JULY) *Two phosphor bands*

2220	**1529**	(1st) multicoloured . . .	75	85	☐	☐
2221	**1530**	(E) multicoloured . . .	95	1·00	☐	☐
2222	**1531**	45p multicoloured . . .	1·25	1·40	☐	☐
2223	**1532**	65p multicoloured . . .	2·00	2·10	☐	☐
	Set of 4		4·50	4·75	☐	☐
	First Day Cover			6·00		☐
	Presentation Pack		5·00		☐	
	PHQ Cards (*set of* 4)		5·00	10·00	☐	☐
	Set of 4 *Gutter Pairs*		10·00		☐	

The 1st and E values incorporate the 'EUROPA' emblem.
The bluish silver on all four values is in Iriodin ink and was used as a background for those parts of the design below the water line.

Nos. 2224/9 were printed together, *se-tenant*, in horizontal strips of 6 throughout the sheet.

Punch and Judy Show Puppets

2001 (4 SEPT.) *Two phosphor bands.* (*a*) *PVA gum. Perf* 14 × 15

2224	**1533**	(1st) multicoloured . . .	80	75	☐	☐
		a. Horiz strip of 6.				
		Nos. 2224/9	4·50	4·75	☐	☐
2225	**1534**	(1st) multicoloured . . .	80	75	☐	☐
2226	**1535**	(1st) multicoloured . . .	80	75	☐	☐
2227	**1536**	(1st) multicoloured . . .	80	75	☐	☐
2228	**1537**	(1st) multicoloured . . .	80	75	☐	☐
2229	**1538**	(1st) multicoloured . . .	80	75	☐	☐
	Set of 6		4·50	4·00	☐	☐
	First Day Cover			5·00		☐
	Presentation Pack		5·00		☐	
	PHQ Cards (*set of* 6)		8·00	12·00	☐	☐
	Gutter Block of 12		10·00		☐	

(*b*) *Self-adhesive. Die-cut perf* 14 × 15½

2230	**1535**	(1st) multicoloured . . .	7·50	7·50	☐	☐
2231	**1536**	(1st) multicoloured . . .	7·50	7·50	☐	☐

Nos. 2230/1 were only issued in £1.62 stamp booklets.

533 Policeman

1534 Clown

For full information on all future British issues, collectors should write to Royal Mail, Freepost EH3647, 21 South Gyle Crescent, Edinburgh EH12 9PE.

2nd

CHEMISTRY
Nobel Prize 100th Anniversary

1539 Carbon 60 Molecule (Chemistry)

1st

ECONOMIC SCIENCES
Nobel Prize 100th Anniversary

1540 Globe (Economic Sciences)

E

PEACE
Nobel Prize 100th Anniversary

1541 Embossed Dove (Peace)

40

PHYSIOLOGY OR MEDICINE
Nobel Prize 100th Anniversary

1542 Crosses (Physiology or Medicine)

45

LITERATURE
Nobel Prize 100th Anniversary

1543 Poem 'The Addressing of Cats' by T. S. Eliot in Open Book (Literature)

65

PHYSICS
Nobel Prize 100th Anniversary

1544 Hologram of Boron Molecule (Physics)

Centenary of Nobel Prizes

2001 (2 Oct.) *One side phosphor band* (2nd) *or phosphor frame* (others). *Perf* 14½

2232	**1539**	(2nd) black, silver and grey-black	60	65	☐	☐
2233	**1540**	(1st) multicoloured . . .	80	90	☐	☐
2234	**1541**	(E) black, silver and bright green	1·00	1·10	☐	☐
2235	**1542**	40p multicoloured . . .	1·00	1·10	☐	☐
2236	**1543**	45p multicoloured . . .	1·40	1·50	☐	☐
2237	**1544**	65p black and silver . .	2·10	2·25	☐	☐
	Set of 6	. . . .	6·25	6·75	☐	☐
	First Day Cover	. . . .		7·50	☐	
	Presentation Pack	. . . .	6·75		☐	
	PHQ Cards (set of 6)	. . . .	8·00	12·00	☐	☐
	Set of 6 Gutter Pairs	. . . . .	12·50		☐	

The grey-black on No. 2232 is printed in thermochromic ink which temporarily changes to pale grey when exposed to heat.

The centre of No. 2235 is coated with a eucalyptus scent.

2nd

1545 Robins with Snowman

1st

1546 Robins on Bird Table

E

1547 Robins skating on Bird Bath

45

1548 Robins with Christmas Pudding

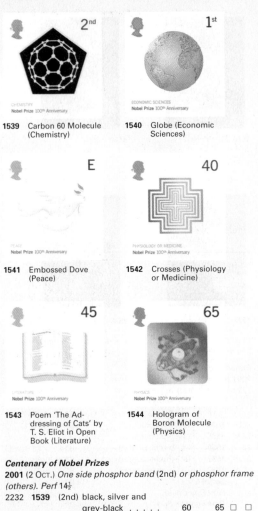

65

1549 Robins in Paper Chain Nest

Christmas. Robins

2001 (6 Nov.) *Self-adhesive. One centre phosphor band* (2nd) *or two phosphor bands* (others). *Die-cut perf* 14½

2238	**1545**	(2nd) multicoloured . . .	75	70	☐	☐
2239	**1546**	(1st) multicoloured . . .	95	1·00	☐	☐
2240	**1547**	(E) multicoloured . . .	1·00	1·10	☐	☐
2241	**1548**	45p multicoloured . . .	1·40	1·50	☐	☐
2242	**1549**	65p multicoloured . . .	2·10	2·25	☐	☐
	Set of 5	. . . .	5·50	6·00	☐	☐
	First Day Cover	. . . .		7·00		☐
	Presentation Pack	. . . .	6·00		☐	
	PHQ Cards (set of 5)	. . . .	6·00	10·00	☐	☐

The 1st value was re-issued on 30 September 2003, in sheets each stamp *se-tenant* in lithography with a Christmas label o a personal photograph. The sheet contained die-cut perforated stamps and labels.

Collectors Pack 2001

2001 (6 Nov.) *Comprises Nos.* 2178/2200, 2202/**MS**2206 2210/14, 2216/29 *and* 2232/42

	Collectors Pack	. . . . 55·00	☐

Post Office Yearbook

2001 (6 Nov.) *Comprises Nos.* 2178/96, **MS**2201/6, **MS**2215/2 *and* 2232/42 *in hardback book with slip case*

	Yearbook	. . . . 60·00	☐

1550 'How the Whale got his Throat'

1551 'How the Camel got his Hump'

1552 'How the Rhinoceros got his Skin'

1553 'How the Leopard got his Spots'

1554 'The Elephant's Child'

1555 'The Sing-Song of Old Man Kangaroo'

1556 'The Beginning of the Armadillos'

1557 'The Crab that played with the Sea'

1558 'The Cat that walked by Himself'

1559 'The Butterfly that stamped'

T **1550/9** were printed together in sheetlets of 10 (5×2), with the surplus self-adhesive paper around each stamp retained.

Centenary of Publication of Rudyard Kipling's Just So Stories

2002 (15 JAN.) *Self-adhesive. Two phosphor bands. Die-cut perf 15 × 14*

2243	1550	(1st) multicoloured	95	85	☐	☐
		a. Sheetlet. Nos. 2243/				
		52	9·00		☐	
2244	1551	(1st) multicoloured	95	85	☐	☐
2245	1552	(1st) multicoloured	95	85	☐	☐
2246	1553	(1st) multicoloured	95	85	☐	☐
2247	1554	(1st) multicoloured	95	85	☐	☐
2248	1555	(1st) multicoloured	95	85	☐	☐
2249	1556	(1st) multicoloured	95	85	☐	☐
2250	1557	(1st) multicoloured	95	85	☐	☐
2251	1558	(1st) multicoloured	95	85	☐	☐
2252	1559	(1st) multicoloured	95	85	☐	☐
		Set of 10	9·00	7·75	☐	☐
		First Day Cover		8·00		☐
		Presentation Pack	10·00		☐	
		PHQ Cards (set of 10)	7·00	15·00	☐	☐

1560 Queen Elizabeth II, 1952 (Dorothy Wilding)

1561 Queen Elizabeth II, 1968 (Cecil Beaton)

1562 Queen Elizabeth II, 1978 (Lord Snowdon)

1563 Queen Elizabeth II, 1984 (Yousef Karsh)

1564 Queen Elizabeth II, 1996 (Tim Graham)

1565

Golden Jubilee. Studio portraits of Queen Elizabeth II by photographers named

2002 (6 FEB.) *One centre phosphor band* (2nd) *or two phosphor bands* (others). *W* **1565**. *Perf* 14½ × 14

2253	**1560**	(2nd) multicoloured	. . . .	55	55 □ □
2254	**1561**	(1st) multicoloured	. . . .	80	80 □ □
2255	**1562**	(E) multicoloured	. . . .	1·00	1·00 □ □
2256	**1563**	45p multicoloured	. . . .	1·40	1·40 □ □
2257	**1564**	65p multicoloured	. . . .	2·10	2·00 □ □
		Set of 5	. . . .	5·25	5·25 □ □
		First Day Cover	. . . .		6·00 □
		Presentation Pack	. . . .	5·75	□
		PHQ Cards (set of 5)	. . . . . .	4·00	9·00 □ □
		Set of 5 Gutter Pairs		10·50	□

Stamps from sheets had the watermark sideways: those from stamp booklets had the watermark upright.

1566

Booklet Stamps

2002 (6 FEB.) *Designs as* 1952-54 *issue, but with service indicator as T* **1566**. *One centre phosphor band* (2nd) *or two phosphor bands* (1st). *W* **1565**. *Uncoated paper. Perf* 15 × 14 (*with one elliptical hole on each vertical side*)

2258	**1566**	(2nd) carmine-red	. . . . .	1·00	1·00 □ □
2259	**154**	(1st) green	. . . .	1·25	1·25 □ □
		Set of 2	. . . .	2·25	2·25 □ □

Nos. 2258/9 were only issued in £7.29 stamp booklets.
See also Nos. 2031/3, **MS**2326, **MS**2367 and 2378/80.

1567 Rabbits ('a new baby')

1568 'LOVE'

1569 Aircraft Sky-writing 'hello'

1570 Bear pulling Potted Topiary Tree (Moving Home)

1571 Flowers ('best wishes')

'Occasions' Greetings Stamps

2002 (5 MAR.) 03 *Two phosphor bands.* (a) *Litho. PVA gum. Perf* 15 × 14

2260	**1567**	(1st) multicoloured	. . . .	80	90 □ □
2261	**1568**	(1st) multicoloured	. . . .	80	90 □ □
2262	**1569**	(1st) multicoloured	. . .	80	90 □ □
2263	**1570**	(1st) multicoloured	. . . .	80	90 □ □
2264	**1571**	(1st) multicoloured	. . . .	80	90 □ □
		Set of 5	. . . .	3·50	4·00 □ □
		First Day Cover	. . . .		5·00 □
		Presentation Pack	. . . .	4·50	□
		PHQ Cards (set of 5)	. . . . .	3·25	9·00 □ □
		Set of 5 Gutter Pairs	. . . . . .	8·00	□

(b) *Photo. Self-adhesive. Die-cut perf* 15 × 14

2264a	**1569**	(1st) multicoloured (4.3.03)	65 ·	65

Nos. 2260/4 were subsequently available in sheets of 20 perforated 14½ × 14, either of one design or *se-tenant*, with each stamp accompanied by a half stamp-size label showing either greetings or a personal photograph.

No. 2264*a* was only issued in £1·62 stamp booklets in which the surplus self-adhesive paper around each stamp was removed.

1572 Studland Bay, Dorset

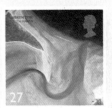

1573 Luskentyre, South Harris

1574 Cliffs, Dover, Kent

1575 Padstow Harbour, Cornwall

1576 Broadstairs, Kent

1577 St. Abb's Head, Scottish Borders

1578 Dunster Beach, Somerset

1579 Newquay Beach, Cornwall

1580 Portrush, County Antrim

1581 Sand-spit, Conwy

T **1572/81** were printed together, *se-tenant*, in blocks of 10 (5 × 2) throughout the sheet.

British Coastlines

2002 (19 MAR.) *Two phosphor bands. Perf* 14½

2265	**1572**	27p multicoloured	75	80	□	□
		a. Block of 10.				
		Nos. 2265/74	7·00		□	
2266	**1573**	27p multicoloured	75	80	□	□
2267	**1574**	27p multicoloured	75	80	□	□
2268	**1575**	27p multicoloured	75	80	□	□
2269	**1576**	27p multicoloured	75	80	□	□
2270	**1577**	27p multicoloured	75	80	□	□
2271	**1578**	27p multicoloured	75	80	□	□
2272	**1579**	27p multicoloured	75	80	□	□
2273	**1580**	27p multicoloured	75	80	□	□
2274	**1581**	27p multicoloured	75	80	□	□
	Set of 10		7·00	7·25	□	□
	First Day Cover			8·50		□
	Presentation Pack		7·50		□	
	PHQ Cards (set of 10)		7·00	15·00	□	□
	Gutter Block of 20		15·00		□	

1582 Slack Wire Act

1583 Lion Tamer

1584 Trick Tri-cyclists

1585 Krazy Kar

1586 Equestrienne

Europa. Circus

2002 (10 APR.) *One centre phosphor band* (2nd) *or two phosphor bands* (others). *Perf* 14½

2275	**1582**	(2nd) multicoloured	50	55	□	□	
2276	**1583**	(1st) multicoloured	70	80	□	□	
2277	**1584**	(E) multicoloured	90	1·00	□	□	
2278	**1585**	45p multicoloured	1·25	1·40	□	□	
2279	**1586**	65p multicoloured	1·90	2·00	□	□	
	Set of 5		4·75	5·25	□	□	
	First Day Cover			6·00		□	
	Presentation Pack		5·75		□		
	PHQ Cards (set of 5)		4·00	9·00	□	□	
	Set of 5 Gutter Pairs		10·50		□		

The 1st and E values incorporate the "EUROPA" emblem.

Due to the funeral of the Queen Mother, the actual issue of Nos. 2275/9 was delayed from 9 April which is the date that appears on first day covers.

1587 Queen Elizabeth the Queen Mother

Queen Elizabeth the Queen Mother Commemoration

2002 (25 APR.) *Vert designs as T 955/8 with changed face values and showing both the Queen's head and frame in black as in T 1587. Two phosphor bands. Perf 14 × 15*

2280	**1587**	(1st) multicoloured	70	80	□	□
2281	**956**	(E) black and indigo . .	90	1·00	□	□
2282	**957**	45p multicoloured	1·25	1·40	□	□
2283	**958**	65p black, stone and sepia	1·90	2·00	□	□
	Set of 4		4·25	4·75	□	□
	First Day Cover			6·00		□
	Presentation Pack		4·75			□
	Set of 4 Gutter Pairs		9·50			□

50th Anniversary of Passenger Jet Aviation. Airliners

2002 (2 MAY) *One centre phosphor band (2nd) or two phosphor bands (others). Perf 14½.* (a) *Photo De La Rue. PVA gum*

2284	**1588**	(2nd) multicoloured	50	55	□	□
2285	**1589**	(1st) multicoloured	70	80	□	□
2286	**1590**	(E) multicoloured	90	1·00	□	□
2287	**1591**	45p multicoloured	1·25	1·40	□	□
2288	**1592**	65p multicoloured	1·90	2·00	□	□
	Set of 5		4·75	5·25	□	□
	First Day Cover			6·00		□
	Presentation Pack		5·25			□
	Set of 5 Gutter Pairs		9·50			□
MS2289	120 × 105 mm. Nos. 2284/8 .		5·00	5·25	□	□
	First Day Cover			6·00		□
	PHQ Cards (set of 6)		5·00	7·00	□	□

(b) *Photo Questa. Self-adhesive*

2290	**1589**	(1st) multicoloured	1·60	1·60	□	□

The complete miniature sheet is shown on one of the PHQ cards with the others depicting individual stamps.

No. 2290 was only issued in £1.62 stamp booklets.

1588 Airbus A340-600 (2002)

1589 Concorde (1976)

1593 Crowned Lion with Shield of St. George

1590 Trident (1964)

1591 VC 10 (1964)

1594 Top Left Quarter of English Flag, and Football

1595 Top Right Quarter of English Flag, and Football

1592 Comet (1952)

1596 Bottom Left Quarter of English Flag, and Football

1597 Bottom Right Quarter of English Flag, and Football

World Cup Football Championship, Japan and Korea

2002 (21 MAY) *Two phosphor bands. Perf* 14½ *(a) PVA gum*

2291	**1593**	(1st) deep turquoise-blue, scarlet-vermilion and silver	1·50	1·25	☐	☐
MS2292	145 × 74 mm. No. 2291; **1594** (1st) multicoloured; **1595** (1st) multicoloured; **1596** (1st) multicoloured; **1597** (1st) multicoloured		3·50	4·00	☐	☐
	First Day Cover (**MS**2292)			4·50		☐
	Presentation Pack (**MS**2292)		4·50		☐	
	PHQ Cards (set of 6)		5·00	9·00	☐	☐
	Gutter Pair (No. 2291)		1·50		☐	

(b) Self-adhesive. Die-cut perf 15 × 14

2293	**1594**	(1st) multicoloured	1·50	1·50	☐	☐
2294	**1595**	(1st) multicoloured	1·50	1·50	☐	☐

The complete miniature sheet is shown on one of the PHQ cards with the others depicting individual stamps from **MS**2292 and No. 2291.

Nos. 2293/4 were only issued in £1.62 stamp booklets.

Stamps as Type **1597** were also issued in sheets of 20, *se-tenant* with half stamp-sized labels, printed by lithography and perforated 14½ × 14. The labels show either match scenes or personal photographs.

Booklet Stamps

2002 (5 JUNE–4 JULY) *Self-adhesive. Photo Questa, Walsall or Enschedé (No. 2295) or Walsall (others). Two phosphor bands. Perf* 15 × 14 *die-cut (with one elliptical hole on each vertical side)*

2295	**914**	(1st) gold	45	50	☐	☐
2296	**1093a**	(E) deep blue (4 July)	60	65	☐	☐
2297	**367a**	42p deep olive-grey (4 July)	65	70	☐	☐
2298		68p grey-brown (4 July)	1·10	1·25	☐	☐
	Set of 4		2·75	3·00	☐	☐

A further printing of No. 2295 in sheets of 100 appeared on 4 July 2002 produced by Enschedé.

1598 Swimming

1599 Running

1600 Cycling

1601 Long Jumping

1602 Wheelchair Racing

17th Commonwealth Games, Manchester

2002 (16 JULY) *One side phosphor band (2nd) or two phosphor bands (others). Perf* 14½

2299	**1598**	(2nd) multicoloured	50	55	☐	☐
2300	**1599**	(1st) multicoloured	70	80	☐	☐
2301	**1600**	(E) multicoloured	90	1·00	☐	☐
2302	**1601**	47p multicoloured	1·25	1·40	☐	☐
2303	**1602**	68p multicoloured	1·90	2·00	☐	☐
	Set of 5		4·75	5·25	☐	☐
	First Day Cover			6·00		☐
	Presentation Pack		5·25		☐	
	PHQ Cards (set of 5)		4·00	8·00	☐	☐
	Set of 5 Gutter Pairs		9·50		☐	

1603 Tinkerbell

1604 Wendy, John and Michael Darling in front of Big Ben

1605 Crocodile and Alarm Clock

1606 Captain Hook

1607 Peter Pan

150th Anniversary of Great Ormond Street Children's Hospital. Peter Pan *by Sir James Barrie*

2002 (20 Aug.) *One centre phosphor band* (2nd) *or two phosphor bands* (*others*). *Perf* 15×14

2304	**1603**	(2nd) multicoloured	50	55	□	□
2305	**1604**	(1st) multicoloured	70	80	□	□
2306	**1605**	(E) multicoloured	90	1·00	□	□
2307	**1606**	47p multicoloured	1·25	1·40	□	□
2308	**1607**	68p multicoloured	1·90	2·00	□	□
	Set of 5		4·75	5·25	□	□
	First Day Cover			6·00	□
	Presentation Pack		5·25		□
	PHQ Cards (*set of* 5)		4·00	8·00	□	□
	Set of 5 Gutter Pairs		9·50		□

1608 Millennium Bridge, 2001

1609 Tower Bridge, 1894

1610 Westminster Bridge, 1864

1611 'Blackfriars Bridge, *c*1800' (William Marlow)

1612 'London Bridge, *c*1670' (Wenceslaus Hollar)

Bridges of London

2002 (10 Sept.) *One centre phosphor band* (2nd) *or two phosphor bands* (*others*). (*a*) *Litho. PVA gum. Perf* 15 × 14

2309	**1608**	(2nd) multicoloured	50	55	□	□
2310	**1609**	(1st) multicoloured	70	80	□	□
2311	**1610**	(E) multicoloured	90	1·00	□	□
2312	**1611**	47p multicoloured	1·25	1·40	□	□
2313	**1612**	68p multicoloured	1·90	2·00	□	□
	Set of 5		4·75	5·25	□	□
	First Day Cover			6·00	□
	Presentation Pack		5·25		□
	PHQ Cards (*set of* 5)		4·00	7·00	□	□
	Set of 5 Gutter Pairs		9·50		□

(*b*) *Photo. Self-adhesive. Die-cut perf* 14½ × 14

2314	**1609**	(1st) multicoloured	1·50	1·50	□	□

No. 2314 was only issued in £1.62 stamp booklets.

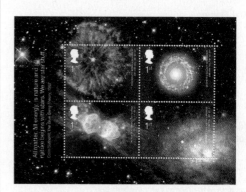

1613 Galaxies and Nebula

Astronomy

2002 (24 Sept.) *Sheet* 120 × 89 *mm. Multicoloured. Two phosphor bands. Perf* 14½ × 14

MS2315 **1613** (1st) Planetary nebula in Aquila; (1st) Seyfert 2 galaxy in Pegasus; (1st) Planetary nebula in Norma; (1st) Seyfert 2 galaxy in Circinus .... 2·75 3·00 □ □
First Day Cover .... 3·50 □
Presentation Pack .... 3·25 □
PHQ Cards (*set of* 5) ..... 4·00 6·00 □ □

The five PHQ cards depict the four designs and the complete miniature sheet.

1614 Green Pillar Box, 1857

1615 Horizontal Aperture Box, 1874

1616 Air Mail Box, 1934

1617 Double Aperture Box, 1939

1618 Modern Style Box, 1980

1619 Blue Spruce Star

1620 Holly

1621 Ivy

1622 Mistletoe

1623 Pine Cone

150th Anniversary of the First Pillar Box

2002 (8 Oct.) *One centre phosphor band* (2nd) *or two phosphor bands* (*others*)*. Perf* $14 \times 14\frac{1}{2}$

2316	**1614**	(2nd) multicoloured	. . . .	50	55	☐ ☐
2317	**1615**	(1st) multicoloured	. . . .	70	80	☐ ☐
2318	**1616**	(E) multicoloured	. . . .	90	1·00	☐ ☐
2319	**1617**	47p multicoloured	. . . .	1·25	1·40	☐ ☐
2320	**1618**	68p multicoloured	. . . .	1·90	2·00	☐ ☐
		Set of 5	. . . .	4·75	5·25	☐ ☐
		First Day Cover	. . . .		6·00	☐
		Presentation Pack	. . . .	5·25		☐
		PHQ Cards (set of 5)	. . . . . .	4·00	7·00	☐ ☐
		Set of 5 Gutter Pairs	. . . . . .	9·50		☐

Christmas

2002 (5 Nov.) *Self-adhesive. One centre phosphor band* (2nd) *or two phosphor bands* (*others*)*. Die-cut perf* $14\frac{1}{2} \times 14$

2321	**1619**	(2nd) multicoloured	. . . .	50	55	☐ ☐
2322	**1620**	(1st) multicoloured	. . . .	70	80	☐ ☐
2323	**1621**	(E) multicoloured	. . . .	90	1·00	☐ ☐
2324	**1622**	47p multicoloured	. . . .	1·25	1·40	☐ ☐
2325	**1623**	68p multicoloured	. . . .	1·90	2·00	☐ ☐
		Set of 5	. . . .	4·75	5·25	☐ ☐
		First Day Cover	. . . .		6·00	☐
		Presentation Pack	. . . .	5·25		☐
		PHQ Cards (set of 5)	. . . . . .	4·00	7·00	☐ ☐

Collectors Pack 2002

2002 (5 Nov.) *Comprises Nos. 2243/57, 2260/88, 2291/2, 2299/313 and* **MS**2315/25

	Collectors Pack	. . . . 40·00	☐

Post Office Yearbook

2002 (5 Nov.) *Comprises Nos. 2243/57, 2260/88, 2291//2, 2299/313 and* **MS**2315/25 *in hardback book with slip case*

	Yearbook	. . . . 48·00	☐

50th Anniversary of Wilding Definitives (1st issue)

2002 (5 Dec.) *Sheet, 124 × 70 mm, containing designs as T* **154/5** *and* **157/60** *(1952–54 issue), but with values in decimal currency as T* **1348** *or with service indicator as T* **1566**, *printed on pale cream. One centre phosphor band (2nd) or two phosphor bands (others). W* **1565**. *Perf 15 × 14 (with one elliptical hole on each vertical side)*

MS2326	1p orange-red; 2p ultramarine; 5p red-brown; (2nd) carmine-red; (1st) green; 33p brown; 37p magenta; 47p bistre-brown; 50p green and label showing national emblems	6·25	6·50	□	□
	First Day Cover		7·00		□
	Presentation Pack	£100			□
	PHQ Cards (set of 5)	3·00	12·00	□	□

The PHQ cards depict the (2nd), (1st), 33p, 37p and 47p stamps.

See also No. **MS**2367.

1624 Barn Owl landing

1625 Barn Owl with folded Wings and Legs down

1626 Barn Owl with extended Wings and Legs down

1627 Barn Owl in Flight with Wings lowered

1628 Barn Owl in Flight with Wings raised

1629 Kestrel with Wings folded

1630 Kestrel with Wings fully extended upwards

1631 Kestrel with Wings horizontal

1632 Kestrel with Wings partly extended downwards

1633 Kestrel with Wings fully extended downwards

T **1624/33** were printed together, *se-tenant*, in blocks of 10 (5 × 2) throughout the sheet.

Birds of Prey

2003 (14 Jan.) *Phosphor background. Perf 14½*

2327	**1624**	(1st) multicoloured	45	50	□	□
		a. Block of 10.				
		Nos. 2327/36	4·50		□	
2328	**1625**	(1st) multicoloured	45	50	□	□
2329	**1626**	(1st) multicoloured	45	50	□	□
2330	**1627**	(1st) multicoloured	45	50	□	□
2331	**1628**	(1st) multicoloured	45	50	□	□
2332	**1629**	(1st) multicoloured	45	50	□	□
2333	**1630**	(1st) multicoloured	45	50	□	□
2334	**1631**	(1st) multicoloured	45	50	□	□
2335	**1632**	(1st) multicoloured	45	50	□	□
2336	**1633**	(1st) multicoloured	45	50	□	□
		Set of 10	4·50	5·00	□	□
		First Day Cover		5·50		□
		Presentation Pack	4·50		□	
		PHQ Cards (set of 10)	3·75	8·00	□	□
		Gutter Block of 20	9·50		□	

1634 'Gold star, See me, Playtime'

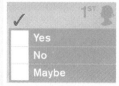

1635 '1♥U, XXXX, S.W.A.L.K.'

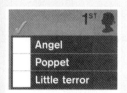

1636 'Angel, Poppet, Little terror'

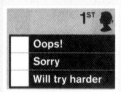

1637 'Yes, No, Maybe'

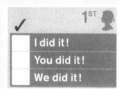

1638 'Oops!, Sorry, Will try harder'

1639 'I did it!, You did it!, We did it!'

T **2337/42** were printed together, *se-tenant*, in blocks of 6 (3 × 2) throughout the sheet.

'Occasions' Greetings Stamps
2003 (4 Feb.) Two phosphor bands. Perf $14\frac{1}{2}$ × 14

2337	**1634**	(1st) lemon and new blue	45		50 □	□
		a. Block of 6.				
		Nos. 2337/42	2·50			□
2338	**1635**	(1st) red and deep				
		ultramarine	45		50 □	□
2339	**1636**	(1st) purple and bright				
		yellow-green	45		50 □	□
2340	**1637**	(1st) bright yellow-green				
		and red	45		50 □	□
2341	**1638**	(1st) deep ultramarine and				
		lemon	45		50 □	□
2342	**1639**	(1st) new blue and purple	45		50 □	□
		Set of 6	2·50		3·00 □	□
		First Day Cover			3·50	□
		Presentation Pack	3·00			□
		PHQ Cards (set of 6)	2·25		4·75 □	□
		Gutter Block of 12	5·25			□

Nos. 2337/42 were also available in *se-tenant* sheets of 20 containing four examples of Nos. 2338 and 2340 and three of each of the others. The stamps are accompanied by half stamp-size printed labels or a personal photograph.

1640 Completing the Genome Jigsaw

1641 Ape with Moustache and Scientist

1642 DNA Snakes and Ladders

1643 'Animal Scientists'

1644 Genome Crystal Ball

50th Anniversary of Discovery of DNA
2003 (25 Feb.) One centre phosphor band (2nd) or two phosphor bands (others). Perf $14\frac{1}{2}$

2343	**1640**	(2nd) multicoloured	30		35 □	□
2344	**1641**	(1st) multicoloured	45		50 □	□
2345	**1642**	(E) multicoloured	60		65 □	□
2346	**1643**	47p multicoloured	75		80 □	□
2347	**1644**	68p multicoloured	1·10		1·25 □	□
		Set of 5	3·00		3·50 □	□
		First Day Cover			4·00	□
		Presentation Pack	3·50			□
		PHQ Cards (set of 5)	1·90		5·00 □	□
		Set of 5 Gutter Pairs	6·25			□

155

1645 Strawberry

1646 Potato

1647 Apple

1648 Red Pepper

1649 Pear

1650 Orange

1651 Tomato

1652 Lemon

1653 Cabbage

1654 Aubergine

T **1645/54** were printed together in sheets of 10 with the surplus self-adhesive paper around each stamp retained. The stamp pane is accompanied by a similar-sized pane of self-adhesive labels showing ears, eyes, mouths, hats etc which are intended for the adornment of fruit and vegetables depicted. This pane is separated from the stamps by a line of roulettes.

Fruit and Vegetables

2003 (25 Mar.) *Self-adhesive. Two phosphor bands. Perf 14½ × 14 die-cut (without teeth around protruding tops or bottoms of the designs)*

2348	**1645**	(1st) multicoloured	45	50	□	□
		a. Sheetlet. Nos. 2348/57				
		and pane of				
		decorative labels . .	4·50		□	
2349	**1646**	(1st) multicoloured	45	50	□	□
2350	**1647**	(1st) multicoloured	45	50	□	□
2351	**1648**	(1st) multicoloured	45	50	□	□
2352	**1649**	(1st) multicoloured	45	50	□	□
2353	**1650**	(1st) multicoloured	45	50	□	□
2354	**1651**	(1st) multicoloured	45	50	□	□
2355	**1652**	(1st) multicoloured	45	50	□	□
2356	**1653**	(1st) multicoloured	45	50	□	□
2357	**1654**	(1st) multicoloured	45	50	□	□
		Set of 10	4·50	5·00	□	□
		First Day Cover		5·50		□
		Presentation Pack	4·50		□	
		PHQ Cards (*set of* 10)	3·75	8·00	□	□

1655

Overseas Booklet Stamps

2003 (27 Mar.) *Self-adhesive. Two phosphor bands. Perf 15 × 14 die-cut with one elliptical hole on each vertical side*

2358	**1655**	(Europe) new blue and				
		rosine	80	85	□	□
2359		(Worldwide) rosine and				
		new blue	1·60	1·75	□	□
		First Day Cover		3·50		□
		Presentation Pack	3·00		□	
		PHQ Cards (*set of* 2)	1·00	4·00	□	□

Nos. 2358/9 were intended to pay postage on mail up to 40 grams to either Europe (52p) or to foreign destinations outside Europe (£1.12).

Operationally they were only available in separate booklets of 4, initially sold at £2.08 and £4.48, with the surplus self-adhesive paper around each stamp removed. Single examples of the stamps were available from philatelic outlets as sets of two or in presentation packs.

1656 Amy Johnson (pilot) and Biplane

1657 Members of 1953 British Team on Everest

1658 Freya Stark (traveller and writer) and Desert

1659 Ernest Shackleton (Antarctic explorer) and Wreck of *Endurance*

1660 Francis Chichester (yachtsman) and *Gipsy Moth IV*

1661 Robert Falcon Scott (Antarctic explorer) and Norwegian Expedition at the Pole

Extreme Endeavours (British Explorers)

2003 (29 APR.) *One centre phosphor band (2nd) or two phosphor bands (others). (a) Photo Questa. PVA gum. Perf 15 × 14½*

2360	**1656**	2nd) multicoloured	. . . .	30	35	□ □
2361	**1657**	(1st) multicoloured	. . . .	45	50	□ □
2362	**1658**	(E) multicoloured	. . . .	60	65	□ □
2363	**1659**	42p multicoloured	. . . .	65	70	□ □
2364	**1660**	47p multicoloured	. . . .	75	80	□ □
2365	**1661**	68p multicoloured	. . . .	1·10	1·25	□ □
		Set of 6	. . . .	3·75	4·25	□ □

First Day Cover	. . . .		5·00	□
Presentation Pack	. . . .	4·25		□
PHQ Cards (set of 6)	. . . . . .	2·25	6·25	□ □
Set of 6 Gutter Pairs	. . . . .	7·75		□

(b) Photo De La Rue. Self-adhesive. Die-cut perf 14½

2366	**1657**	(1st) multicoloured	. . . .	45	50	□ □

The phosphor bands on Nos. 2361/5 are at the centre and right of each stamp.

No. 2366 was only issued in £1.62 stamp booklets in which the surplus self-adhesive paper around each stamp was removed.

50th Anniversary of Wilding Definitives (2nd issue)

2003 (20 MAY) *Sheet, 124 × 70 mm, containing designs as T **155/8** and **160** (1952–54 issue), but with values in decimal currency as T **1348** or with service indicator as T **1566**, printed on pale cream. One centre phosphor band (20p) or two phosphor bands (others). W **1565**. P 15 × 14 (with one elliptical hole on each vertical side).*

MS2367	4p deep lilac; 8p ultramarine; 10p reddish purple; 20p bright green; 28p bronze-green; 34p brown-purple; (E) chestnut; 42p Prussian blue; 68p grey-blue and label showing national emblems	9·50	9·75	□ □
	First Day Cover		10·00	□
	Presentation Pack	10·00		□

1662 Guardsmen in Coronation Procession

1663 East End Children reading Coronation Party Poster

1664 Queen Elizabeth II in Coronation Chair with Bishops of Durham and Bath & Wells

1665 Children in Plymouth working on Royal Montage

1666 Queen Elizabeth II in Coronation Robes (photograph by Cecil Beaton)

1667 Children's Race at East End Street Party

1668 Coronation Coach passing through Marble Arch

1669 Children in Fancy Dress

1670 Coronation Coach outside Buckingham Palace

1671 Children eating at London Street Party

T **1662/71** were printed together, *se-tenant,* in blocks of 10 (5 × 2) throughout sheets of 60

50th Anniversary of Coronation
2003 (2 JUNE) W **1565**. Two phosphor bands. Perf 14½ × 14

2368	**1662**	(1st) multicoloured		45		50 □	□
		a. Block of 10.					
		Nos. 2368/77		4·50		□	
2369	**1663**	(1st) black and gold		45		50 □	□
2370	**1664**	(1st) multicoloured		45		50 □	□
2371	**1665**	(1st) black and gold		45		50 □	□
2372	**1666**	(1st) multicoloured		45		50 □	□
2373	**1667**	(1st) black and gold		45		50 □	□
2374	**1668**	(1st) multicoloured		45		50 □	□
2375	**1669**	(1st) black and gold		45		50 □	□
2376	**1670**	(1st) multicoloured		45		50 □	□
2377	**1671**	(1st) black and gold		45		50 □	□
		Set of 10		4·50		5·00 □	□
		First Day Cover				5·50	□
		Presentation Pack		4·75			□
		PHQ Cards (set of 10)		3·75		8·00 □	□
		Gutter Block of 20		9·25			□

No. 2372 does not show the Queen's head in gold as do the other nine designs.

50th Anniversary of Coronation. Booklet Stamps
2003 (2 JUNE) Designs as T **160** (Wilding definitive of 1952) and **163** (Coronation commemorative of 1953), but with values in decimal currency as T **1348**. W **1565**. Two phosphor bands. P 15 × 14 (with one elliptical hole on each vertical side for Nos. 2378/9)

2378	**160**	47p bistre-brown	75	80 □	□
2379		68p grey-blue	1·10	1·25 □	□
2380	**163**	£1 deep yellow-green .	1·50	1·60 □	□
		Set of 3	3·25	3·50 □	□

Nos. 2378/80 were only available in £7.46 stamp booklets. Stamps as Nos. 2378/9, but on pale cream, were also included in the Wilding miniature sheets, Nos. **MS**2326 or **MS**2367. A £1 design as No. 2380, but on phosphorised paper, was previously included in the "Stamp Show 2000" miniature sheet, No. **MS**2147.

1672 Prince William in September 2001 (Brendan Beirne)

1673 Prince William in September 2000 (Tim Graham)

1674 Prince William in September 2001 (Camera Press)

1675 Prince William in September 2001 (Tim Graham)

21st Birthday of Prince William of Wales
2003 (17 JUNE) Phosphor backgrounds. Perf 14½

2381	**1672**	28p multicoloured	45	50 □	□
2382	**1673**	(E) dull mauve, grey-black and light green . . .	60	65 □	□

2383	**1674**	47p multicoloured	75	80 □ □
2384	**1675**	68p sage-green, black and		
		bright green	1·10	1·25 □ □
		Set of 4	2·75	3·00 □ □
		First Day Cover		3·75 □
		Presentation Pack	3·25	□
		PHQ Cards (set of 4)	1·50	4·25 □ □
		Set of 4 Gutter Pairs	5·75	□

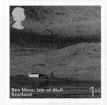

1676 Loch Assynt,
Sutherland

1677 Ben More, Isle of Mull

1678 Rothiemurchus,
Cairngorms

1679 Dalveen Pass, Lowther
Hills

1680 Glenfinnan Viaduct,
Lochaber

1681 Papa Little, Shetland
Islands

A British Journey: Scotland

2003 (15 JULY) *One phosphor band* (2nd) *or two phosphor bands* (others). *Perf* 14½. (*a*) *PVA gum*

2385	**1676**	(2nd) multicoloured	30	35 □ □
2386	**1677**	(1st) multicoloured	45	50 □ □
2387	**1678**	(E) multicoloured	60	65 □ □

2388	**1679**	42p multicoloured	65	70 □ □
2389	**1680**	47p multicoloured	75	80 □ □
2390	**1681**	68p multicoloured	1·10	1·25 □ □
		Set of 6	3·75	4·25 □ □
		First Day Cover		5·00 □
		Presentation Pack	4·25	□
		PHQ Cards (set of 6)	2·25	6·25 □ □
		Set of 6 Gutter Pairs	7·75	□

(*b*) *Self-adhesive. Die-cut perf* 14½

| 2391 | **1677** | (1st) multicoloured . . . | 45 | 50 □ □ |

No. 2391 was only issued in £1.68 stamp booklets in which the surplus self-adhesive paper around each stamp was removed.

1682 'The Station'
(Andrew Davidson)

1683 'Black Swan'
(Stanley Chew)

1684 'The Cross Keys'
(George Mackenney)

1685 'The Mayflower'
(Ralph Ellis)

1686 'The Barley Sheaf' (Joy Cooper)

British Pub Signs

2003 (12 AUG.) *Two phosphor bands. Perf* 14 × 14½

2392	**1682**	(1st) multicoloured	45	50 □ □
2393	**1683**	(E) multicoloured	60	65 □ □
2394	**1684**	42p multicoloured	65	70 □ □
2395	**1685**	47p multicoloured	75	80 □ □

2396	**1686**	68p multicoloured	. . . .	1·10	1·25	☐ ☐
		Set of 5	. . . .	3·50	3·75	☐ ☐
		First Day Cover	. . . .		4·50	☐
		Presentation Pack	. . . .		4·00	☐
		PHQ Cards (set of 5)	. . . . . .	1·90	5·50	☐ ☐
		Set of 5 Gutter Pairs	. . . . . .	7·25		☐

MECCANO
Constructor Biplane c 1931

WELLS-BRIMTOY
Clockwork Double-decker Omnibus c 1938

1687 Meccano Constructor Biplane, *c.* 1931   **1688** Wells-Brimtoy Clockwork Double-decker Omnibus, *c.* 1938

HORNBY
M1 Clockwork Locomotive and Tender c 1948

DINKY TOYS
Ford Zephyr c 1956

1689 Hornby M1 Clockwork Locomotive and Tender, *c.* 1948   **1690** Dinky Toys Ford Zephyr, *c.* 1956

METTOY
Friction Drive
Space Ship Eagle c 1960

1691 Mettoy Friction Drive Space Ship Eagle, *c.* 1960

Classic Transport Toys

2003 (18 SEPT.) *Two phosphor bands.* (*a*) *Photo Enschedé. PVA gum. Perf* 14½ × 14

2397	**1687**	(1st) multicoloured	. . . .	45	50	☐ ☐
2398	**1688**	(E) multicoloured	. . . .	60	65	☐ ☐
2399	**1689**	42p multicoloured	. . . .	65	70	☐ ☐
2400	**1690**	47p multicoloured	. . . .	75	80	☐ ☐
2401	**1691**	68p multicoloured	. . . .	1·10	1·25	☐ ☐
		Set of 5	. . . .	3·50	3·75	☐ ☐
		First Day Cover	. . . .		4·50	☐
		Presentation Pack	. . . .		4·00	☐
		PHQ Cards (set of 6)	. . . . . .	2·75	6·25	☐ ☐
		Set of 5 Gutter Pairs	. . . . . .	7·25		☐
MS2402		115 × 105 mm. Nos. 2397/401		3·50	3·75	☐ ☐
		First Day Cover	. . . .		4·50	☐

(*b*) *Photo DLR. Self-adhesive. Die-cut perf* 14½ × 14

| 2403 | **1687** | (1st) multicoloured | | 45 | 50 | ☐ ☐ |

The complete miniature sheet is shown on one of the PHQ cards with the others depicting individual stamps.

No. 2403 was only issued in £1.68 stamp booklets in which the surplus self-adhesive paper around each stamp was removed.

1692 Coffin of Denytenamun, Egyptian, *c.* 900BC   **1693** Alexander the Great, Greek, *c.* 200BC

1694 Sutton Hoo Helmet, Anglo-Saxon, *c.* AD600   **1695** Sculpture of Parvati, South Indian, *c.* AD1550

1696 Mask of Xiuhtecuhtli, Mixtec-Aztec, *c.* AD1500   **1697** Hoa Hakananai'a, Easter Island, *c.* AD1000

250th Anniversary of the British Museum

2003 (7 Oct.) *One side phosphor band* (2nd), *two phosphor bands* ((1st), (E), 47p) *or phosphor background at left and band at right* (42p, 68p). *Perf* 14 × 14½

2404	**1692**	(2nd) multicoloured	. . . .	30	35 ☐ ☐	
2405	**1693**	(1st) multicoloured	. . . .	45	50 ☐ ☐	
2406	**1694**	(E) multicoloured	. . . .	60	65 ☐ ☐	
2407	**1695**	42p multicoloured	. . . .	65	70 ☐ ☐	
2408	**1696**	47p multicoloured	. . . .	75	80 ☐ ☐	
2409	**1697**	68p multicoloured	. . . .	1·10	1·25 ☐ ☐	
		Set of 6	. . . .	3·75	4·25 ☐ ☐	
		First Day Cover	. . . .		4·75	
		Presentation Pack	. . . .	4·25	☐	
		PHQ Cards (set of 6)	. . . . . .	2·75	6·50 ☐ ☐	
		Set of 6 Gutter Pairs	. . . . . .	7·75	☐	

Christmas. Ice Sculptures by Andy Goldsworthy

2003 (4 Nov.) *Self-adhesive. One side phosphor band* (2nd), *'all-over' phosphor* (1st) *or two bands* (others). *Die-cut perf* 14½ × 14

2410	**1698**	(2nd) multicoloured	. . .	30	35 ☐ ☐
2411	**1699**	(1st) multicoloured	. . . .	45	50 ☐ ☐
2412	**1700**	(E) multicoloured	. . . .	60	65 ☐ ☐
2413	**1701**	53p multicoloured	. . . .	80	85 ☐ ☐
2414	**1702**	68p multicoloured	. . . .	1·10	1·25 ☐ ☐
2415	**1703**	£1.12 multicoloured	. . . .	1·60	1·75 ☐ ☐
		Set of 6	. . . .	4·75	5·25 ☐ ☐
		First Day Cover	. . . .		6·25
		Presentation Pack	. . . .	5·25	☐
		PHQ Cards (set of 6)	. . . . . .	2·75	☐

The 2nd and 1st class were also issued in separate sheets of 20, each stamp accompanied by a half stamp-size *se-tenant* label showing either animals, ice sculptures or a personal photograph.

Collectors Pack 2003

2003 (4 Nov.) *Comprises Nos.* 2327/57, 2360/5, 2368/77, 2381/90, 2392/401 *and* 2404/15
	Collectors Pack	. . . .	45·00	☐

Post Office Yearbook

2003 (4 Nov.) *Comprises Nos.* 2327/57, 2360/5, 2368/77, 2381/90, 2392/401 *and* 2404/15
	Yearbook	. . . .	50·00	☐

1698 Ice Spiral

1699 Icicle Star

1700 Wall of Ice Blocks

1701 Ice Ball

1702 Ice Hole

1703 Snow Pyramids

REGIONAL ISSUES

PERFORATION AND WATERMARK. All the following Regional stamps are perforated 15 × 14, unless otherwise stated.

For listing of First Day Covers see pages 173/5.

1 England

EN **1**   Three Lions

EN **2**   Crowned Lion
with Shield of
St. George

EN **3**   Oak Tree

EN **4**   Tudor Rose

2001 (23 Apr.)–**02** *Printed in photogravure by De La Rue or Questa (Nos. EN1/2), De La Rue (others). One centre phosphor band (2nd) or two phosphor bands (others). Perf 15 × 14 (with one elliptical hole on each vertical side)*

EN1	EN **1** (2nd) slate-green and silver	30		35	☐	☐
EN2	EN **2** (1st) lake-brown and silver	45		50	☐	☐
EN3	EN **3** (E) olive-green and silver	60		65	☐	☐
EN4	EN **4** 65p deep reddish lilac and silver	1·60		1·75	☐	☐
EN5	68p deep reddish lilac and silver	1·10		1·25	☐	☐
	Presentation Pack (P.O. Pack No. 54) (Nos. EN1/4)	2·75			☐	
	PHQ Cards (set of 4) (Nos. EN1/4)	1·50		10·00	☐	☐

Nos. EN1/3 were initially sold at 19p, 27p and 36p, the latter representing the basic European airmail rate.

Combined Presentation Packs for England, Northern Ireland, Scotland and Wales

Presentation Pack (P.O. Pack No. 59) (contains 68p from England, Northern Ireland, Scotland and Wales (Nos. EN5, NI93, S99, W88)) . . . . . .   4·50   ☐

2003 (14 Oct.) *As Nos. EN1/3 and EN5 but with white borders. Printed in photogravure by De La Rue. One centre phosphor band (2nd) or two phosphor bands (others). Perf 15×14 (with one elliptical hole on each vertical side).*

EN6	EN **1** (2nd) slate-green and silver	30		35	☐	☐
EN7	EN **2** (1st) lake-brown and silver	45		50	☐	☐
EN8	EN **3** (E) olive-green and silver	60		65	☐	☐
EN9	EN **4** 68p deep reddish lilac and silver	1·10		1·25	☐	☐
	Presentation Pack (P.O. Pack No. 63)	2·75			☐	
	PHQ Cards (set of 4)	1·75		4·00	☐	☐

Nos. EN6/8 were initially sold at 20p, 28p and 38p, the latter representing the basic European airmail rate.

2 Northern Ireland

N **1** 　　　　N **2** 　　　　N **3** 　　　　N **4**

1958–67 *Wmk* 179

NI1	N **1**	3d lilac	15	10	☐	☐
		p. One centre phosphor band	15	15	☐	☐
NI2		4d blue	15	15	☐	☐
		p. Two phosphor bands	15	15	☐	☐
NI3	N **2**	6d purple	20	25	☐	☐
NI4		9d bronze-green (2 phosphor bands) . .	30	70	☐	☐
NI5	N **3**	1s 3d green	30	70	☐	☐
NI6		1s 6d blue (2 phosphor bands)	30	70	☐	☐

1968–69 *One centre phosphor band* (*Nos.* NI8/9) *or two phosphor bands* (*others*). *No wmk*

NI7	N **1**	4d blue	15	15	☐	☐
NI8		4d sepia	15	15	☐	☐
NI9		4d vermilion	20	20	☐	☐
NI10		5d blue	20	20	☐	☐
NI11	N **3**	1s 6d blue	2·25	2·50	☐	☐
		Presentation Pack (comprises Nos. NI1p, NI4/6, NI8/10) . . .	3·25		☐	

Decimal Currency
1971–91 *Type* N **4**. *No wmk*
(a) Printed in photogravure with phosphor bands

NI12	2½p magenta (1 centre band) .	70	45	☐	☐
NI13	3p ultramarine (2 bands) . . .	25	25	☐	☐
NI14	3p ultramarine (1 centre band)	20	15	☐	☐
NI15	3½p olive-grey (2 bands)	20	25	☐	☐
NI16	3½p olive-grey (1 centre band)	20	25	☐	☐
NI17	4½p grey-blue (2 bands) . . .	30	25	☐	☐
NI18	5p violet (2 bands)	1·25	1·25	☐	☐
NI19	5½p violet (2 bands)	20	20	☐	☐
NI20	5½p violet (1 centre band) . .	20	25	☐	☐
NI21	6½p blue (1 centre band) . . .	20	20	☐	☐
NI22	7p brown (1 centre band) . .	35	25	☐	☐
NI23	7½p chestnut (2 bands) . . .	1·75	1·75	☐	☐
NI24	8p rosine (2 bands)	35	35	☐	☐
NI25	8½p yellow-green (2 bands) . .	35	40	☐	☐
NI26	9p violet (2 bands)	40	40	☐	☐
NI27	10p orange-brown (2 bands) .	40	50	☐	☐
NI28	10p orange-brown (1 centre band)	50	50	☐	☐
NI29	10½p blue (2 bands)	40	50	☐	☐
NI30	11p scarlet (2 bands)	50	50	☐	☐

(b) Printed in photogravure on phosphorised paper

NI31	12p yellowish green	50	50	☐	☐
NI32	13½p purple-brown	60	70	☐	☐
NI33	15p ultramarine	60	70	☐	☐

(c) Printed in lithography. Perf 14 (11½p, 12½p, 14p (No. NI38), 15½p, 16p, 18p, (No. NI45), 19½p, 20½p, 22p (No. NI53), 26p (No. NI60), 28p (No. NI62)) or 15 × 14 (others)

NI34	11½p drab (1 side band)	85	85	☐	☐
NI35	12p bright emerald (1 side band)	70	80	☐	☐
NI36	12½p light emerald (1 side band)	60	60	☐	☐
	a. Perf 15 × 14	4·25	4·00	☐	☐
NI37	13p pale chestnut (1 side band)	80	50	☐	☐
NI38	14p grey-blue (phosphorised paper)	75	75	☐	☐
NI39	14p deep blue (1 centre band)	75	60	☐	☐
NI40	15p bright blue (1 centre band)	90	60	☐	☐
NI41	15½p pale violet (phosphorised paper)	80	80	☐	☐
NI42	16p drab (phosphorised paper)	1·00	1·00	☐	☐
	a. Perf 15 × 14	7·50	7·50	☐	☐
NI43	17p grey-blue (phosphorised paper)	90	95	☐	☐
NI44	17p deep blue (1 centre band)	1·00	80	☐	☐
NI45	18p deep violet (phosphorised paper)	1·00	1·00	☐	☐
NI46	18p olive-grey (phosphorised paper)	1·00	90	☐	☐
NI47	18p bright green (1 centre band)	1·00	95	☐	☐
	a. Perf 14	1·90	1·60	☐	☐
NI48	18p bright green (1 side band)	2·25	2·25	☐	☐
NI49	19p bright orange-red (phosphorised paper) . . .	1·00	1·00	☐	☐
NI50	19½p olive-grey (phosphorised paper)	1·90	1·90	☐	☐
NI51	20p brownish black (phosphorised paper) . . .	1·00	80	☐	☐
NI52	20½p ultramarine (phosphorised paper)	3·00	3·50	☐	☐
NI53	22p blue (phosphorised paper)	1·10	1·10	☐	☐
NI54	22p yellow-green (phosphorised paper)	1·10	1·10	☐	☐
NI55	22p bright orange-red (phosphorised paper) . . .	1·25	90	☐	☐
NI56	23p bright green (phosphorised paper)	1·25	1·10	☐	☐
NI57	24p Indian red (phosphorised paper)	1·50	1·00	☐	☐
NI58	24p chestnut (phosphorised paper)	1·10	90	☐	☐
NI59	24p chestnut (2 bands)	2·50	2·25	☐	☐
NI60	26p rosine (phosphorised paper)	1·25	1·25	☐	☐
	a. Perf 15 × 14	4·00	3·50	☐	☐
NI61	26p drab (phosphorised paper)	1·50	1·25	☐	☐
NI62	28p deep violet-blue (phosphorised paper) . . .	1·40	1·25	☐	☐
	a. Perf 15 × 14	1·50	1·25	☐	☐

NI63	28p deep bluish grey (phosphorised paper) ...	1·60	1·40	□	□
NI64	31p bright purple (phosphorised paper) ...	1·60	1·60	□	□
NI65	32p greenish blue (phosphorised paper) ...	1·75	1·75	□	□
NI66	34p deep bluish grey (phosphorised paper) ...	1·90	1·90	□	□
NI67	37p rosine (phosphorised paper)	1·90	1·90	□	□
NI68	39p bright mauve (phosphorised paper) ...	1·90	1·90	□	□

Nos. NI48 and NI59 were only issued in stamp booklets.

Presentation Pack (*P.O. Pack No. 29*) (*contains* 2½p (NI12), 3p (NI13), 5p (NI18), 7½p (NI23)) .... 4·25 □

Presentation Pack (*P.O. Pack No. 61*) (*contains* 3p (NI14), 3½p (NI15), 5½p (NI19), 8p (NI24) *later with* 4½p (NI17) *added*) . 2·75 □

Presentation Pack (*P.O. Pack No. 84*) (*contains* 6½p (NI21), 8½p (NI25), 10p (NI27), 11p (NI30)) 2·00 □

Presentation Pack (*P.O. Pack No. 129d*) (*contains* 7p (NI22), 9p (NI26), 10½p (NI29), 11½p (NI34), 12p (NI31), 13½p (NI32), 14p (NI38), 15p (NI33), 18p (NI45), 22p (NI53)) ...... 9·00 □

Presentation Pack (*P.O. Pack No. 4*) (*contains* 10p (NI28), 12½p (NI36), 16p (NI42), 20½p (NI52), 26p (NI60), 28p (NI62)) ... 12·00 □

Presentation Pack (*P.O. Pack No. 8*) (*contains* 10p (NI28), 13p (NI37), 16p (NI42a), 17p (NI43), 22p (NI54), 26p (NI60), 28p (NI62), 31p (NI64)) .... 17·00 □

Presentation Pack (*P.O. Pack No. 12*) (*contains* 12p (NI35), 13p (NI37), 17p (NI43), 18p (NI46), 22p (NI54), 26p (NI60a), 28p (NI62a), 31p (NI64)) ..... 15·00 □

Combined Presentation Packs for Northern Ireland, Scotland and Wales

Presentation Pack (*P.O. Pack No. 17*) (*contains* 14p, 19p, 23p, 32p *from Northern Ireland, Scotland and Wales* (*Nos.* NI39, NI49, NI56, NI65, S54, S62, S67, S77, W40, W50,

W57, W66)) .... 16·00 □

Presentation Pack (*P.O. Pack No. 20*) (*contains* 15p, 20p, 24p, 34p *from Northern Ireland, Scotland and Wales* (*Nos.* NI40, NI51, NI57, NI66, S56, S64, S69, S78, W41, W52, W58, W67)) .... 18·00 □

Presentation Pack (*P.O. Pack No. 23*) (*contains* 17p, 22p, 26p, 37p *from Northern Ireland, Scotland and Wales* (*Nos.* NI44, NI55, NI61, NI67, S58, S66, S73, S79, W45, W56, W62, W68)) .... 18·00 □

Presentation Pack (*P.O. Pack No. 26*) (*contains* 18p, 24p, 28p, 39p *from Northern Ireland, Scotland and Wales* (*Nos.* NI47, NI58, NI63, NI68, S60, S70, S75, S80, W48, W59, W64, W69)) .... 18·00 □

1993 (7 Dec.)–**2000** (*a*) *Printed in lithography by Questa. Perf* 15 × 14 (*with one elliptical hole on each vertical side*)

NI69	N 4	19p bistre (1 centre band)	90	80	□	□
NI70		19p bistre (1 side band) ..	1·50	1·75	□	□
NI71		20p bright green (1 centre band)	1·50	1·25	□	□
NI72		25p red (2 bands)	75	75	□	□
NI73		26p red-brown (2 bands) .	1·40	1·40	□	□
NI74		30p deep olive-grey (2 bands)	1·50	1·40	□	□
NI75		37p bright mauve (2 bands)	2·25	2·25	□	
NI76		41p grey-brown (2 bands)	1·50	1·50	□	□
NI77		63p light emerald (2 bands)	3·50	3·50	□	□

(*b*) *Printed in photogravure by Walsall* (19*p*, 20*p*, 26*p* (*No.* NI81b), 38*p*, 40*p*, 63*p*, 64*p*, 65*p*), *Harrison or Walsall* (26*p* (*No.* NI81), 37*p*). *Perf* 14 (*No.* NI80) *or* 15 × 14 (*others*) (*both with one elliptical hole on each vertical side*)

NI78	N 4	19p bistre (1 centre band)	1·25	70	□	□
NI79		20p bright green (1 centre band)	75	70	□	□
NI80		20p bright green (1 side band)	1·75	1·90	□	□
NI81		26p chestnut (2 bands) ..	1·25	1·00	□	□
		b. Perf 14	2·25	1·75	□	□
NI82		37p bright mauve (2 bands)	1·50	1·25	□	□
NI83		38p ultramarine (2 bands)	2·10	2·10	□	□
NI84		40p deep azure (2 bands)	1·10	1·10	□	□
NI85		63p light emerald (2 bands)	2·40	2·25	□	□
NI86		64p turquoise-green (2 bands)	2·25	2·10	□	□
NI87		65p greenish blue (2 bands)	2·00	2·00	□	□

Nos. NI70, NI80 and NI81*b* were only issued in stamp booklets. No. NI70 exists with the phosphor band at the left or right of the stamp.

Presentation Pack (*P.O. Pack No. 47*) (*contains* 19p, 26p, 38p, 64p (*Nos.* NI78, NI81, NI83 NI86)) . . . . 4·50 □

Presentation Pack (*P.O. Pack No. 52*) (*contains* 1st, 40p, 65p) (*Nos.* NI84, NI87, NI88*b*) . . 4·00 □

Combined Presentation Packs for Northern Ireland, Scotland and Wales

Presentation Pack (*P.O. Pack No. 31*) (*contains* 19p, 25p, 30p, 41p *from Northern Ireland, Scotland and Wales* (*Nos.* NI69, NI72, NI74, NI76, S81, S84, S86, S88, W70, W73, W75, W77)) . . . . 18·00 □

Presentation Pack (*P.O. Pack No. 36*) (*contains* 20p, 26p, 37p, 63p *from Northern Ireland, Scotland and Wales* (*Nos.* NI71, NI73, NI75, NI77, S83, S85, S87, S89, W72, W74 W76, W78)) . . . . 22·00 □

Presentation Pack (*P.O. Pack No. 42*) (*contains* 20p (1 *centre band*), 26p, 37p, 63p *from Northern Ireland, Scotland and Wales* (*Nos.* NI79, NI81/2, NI85, S90/3, W79/82)) 12·00 □

N 5

2000 (15 FEB.–25 APR.) *Type* N **4** *redrawn with* '1st' *face value as Type* N **5**. *Two phosphor bands. Perf* 14 (*with one elliptical hole on each vertical side*)

NI88 N **5** (1st) bright orange-red . . 1·90 1·90 □ □
  b. Perf 15 ×14 (25 Apr.) 2·00 2·00 □ □

No. NI88 was only issued in stamp booklets. No. NI88*b* was issued in sheets on 25 April.

N **6** Basalt Columns, Giant's Causeway

N **7** Aerial View of Patchwork Fields

N **8** Linen Pattern

N **9** Vase Pattern from Belleck

2001 (6 MAR.)–02 *Printed in lithography by De La Rue* (68p), *De La Rue or Walsall* (E), *Walsall or Enschedé* (2nd) *or Walsall* (*others*). *One centre phosphor band* (2nd) *or two phosphor bands* (*others*). *Perf* 15 × 14 (*with one elliptical hole on each vertical side*)

NI89 N **6** (2nd) black, new blue, bright magenta and greenish yellow . . . 30 35 □ □
NI90 N **7** (1st) black, new blue and greenish yellow . . . 45 50 □ □
NI91 N **8** (E) black, new blue and pale orange . . . . . 60 70 □ □
NI92 N **9** 65p black, bright magenta and greenish yellow 1·60 1·75 □ □
NI93 68p black, bright magenta and greenish yellow 1·10 1·25 □ □
  Presentation Pack (*P.O. Pack No. 53*) (*Nos.* NI89/92) . . . . . 2·75 □
  PHQ Cards (*set of 4*) (*Nos.* NI89/92) . . . . 1·50 10·00 □ □

Nos. NI89, NI90 and NI91 were initially sold at 19p, 27p and 36p, the latter representing the basic European airmail rate.

For combined presentation packs for all four Regions, see under England.

2003 (14 OCT.) *As Nos.* NI89/91 *and* NI93 *but with white borders. Printed in lithography by De La Rue. One centre phosphor band* (2nd) *or two phosphor bands* (*others*). *Perf* 15 × 14 (*with one elliptical hole on each vertical side*).

NI94 N **6** (2nd) black, new blue, bright magenta and greenish yellow . . . . 30 35 □ □
NI95 N **7** (1st) black, new blue and greenish yellow . . . 45 50 □ □
NI96 N **8** (E) black and new blue . 60 65 □ □
NI97 N **9** 68p black, bright magenta and greenish yellow 1·10 1·25 □ □
  Presentation Pack (*P.O. Pack No. 66*) 2·75 □
  PHQ Cards (*set of* 4) . . . . . 1·75 4·00 □ □

Nos. NI94/6 were initially sold at 20p, 28p and 38p, the latter representing the basic European airmail rate.

3 Scotland

S **1**    S **2**    S **3**    S **4**

1958–67 *Wmk* **179**

S1	S **1**	3d lilac	15	15	□	□
		p. Two phosphor bands	16·00	2·00	□	□
		pa. One side band . . .	20	25	□	□
		pb. One centre band . .	15	15	□	□
S2		4d blue	15	15	□	□
		p. Two phosphor bands	15	15	□	□
S3	S **2**	6d purple	20	15	□	□
		p. Two phosphor bands	20	20	□	□
S4		9d bronze-green (2				
		phosphor bands) . .	35	40	□	□
S5	S **3**	1s 3d green	40	40	□	□
		p. Two phosphor bands	40	40	□	□
S6		1s 6d blue (2 phosphor				
		bands)	45	50	□	□

No. S1*pa* exists with the phosphor band at the left or right of the stamp.

1967–70 *One centre phosphor band* (*Nos.* S7, S9/10) *or two phosphor bands* (*others*). *No wmk*

S7	S **1**	3d lilac	10	15	□	□
S8		4d blue	10	15	□	□
S9		4d sepia	10	10	□	□
S10		4d vermilion	10	10	□	□
S11		5d blue	20	10	□	□
S12	S **2**	9d bronze-green	4·00	4·50	□	□
S13	S **3**	1s 6d blue	1·40	1·40	□	□
		Presentation Pack (*containing*				
		Nos. S3, S5p, S7, S9/13) . . .	10·00		□	

Decimal Currency

1971–93 *Type* S **4**. *No wmk*

(*a*) *Printed in photogravure by Harrison and Sons with phosphor bands. Perf* 15 × 14

S14	2½p magenta (1 centre band) .	25	20	□	□
S15	3p ultramarine (2 bands) . . .	35	15	□	□
S16	3p ultramarine (1 centre				
	band)	15	15	□	□
S17	3½p olive-grey (2 bands) . . .	20	25	□	□
S18	3½p olive-grey (1 centre band)	20	25	□	□
S19	4½p grey-blue (2 bands) . . .	30	25	□	□
S20	5p violet (2 bands)	85	1·00	□	□
S21	5½p violet (2 bands)	20	20	□	□
S22	5½p violet (1 centre band) . . .	20	25	□	□
S23	6½p blue (1 centre band) . . .	20	20	□	□
S24	7p brown (1 centre band) . .	30	30	□	□
S25	7½p chestnut (2 bands)	95	1·25	□	□
S26	8p rosine (2 bands)	45	40	□	□

S27	8½p yellow-green (2 bands) . .	40	40	□	□
S28	9p violet (2 bands)	40	40	□	□
S29	10p orange-brown (2 bands) .	45	50	□	□
S30	10p orange-brown (1 centre				
	band)	40	50	□	□
S31	10½p blue (2 bands)	45	50	□	□
S32	11p scarlet (2 bands)	50	50	□	□

(*b*) *Printed in photogravure by Harrison and Sons on phosphorised paper. Perf* 15 × 14

S33	12p yellowish green	50	50	□	□
S34	13½p purple-brown	70	80	□	□
S35	15p ultramarine	60	70	□	□

(*c*) *Printed in lithography by John Waddington. One side phosphor band* (11½p, 12p, 12½p, 13p) *or phosphorised paper* (*others*). *Perf* 14

S36	11½p drab	80	80	□	□
S37	12p bright emerald	2·00	1·60	□	□
S38	12½p light emerald	60	70	□	□
S39	13p pale chestnut	75	75	□	□
S40	14p grey-blue	75	75	□	□
S41	15½p pale violet	80	80	□	□
S42	16p drab	80	85	□	□
S43	17p grey-blue	3·00	2·25	□	□
S44	18p deep violet	80	80	□	□
S45	19½p olive-grey	1·50	1·50	□	□
S46	20½p ultramarine	3·75	3·75	□	□
S47	22p blue	1·10	1·10	□	□
S48	22p yellow-green	3·00	3·25	□	□
S49	26p rosine	1·25	1·25	□	□
S50	28p deep violet-blue	1·25	1·25	□	□
S51	31p bright purple	2·25	2·25	□	□

(*d*) *Printed in lithography by Questa. Perf* 15 × 14

S52	12p bright emerald (1 side				
	band)	2·00	2·00	□	□
S53	13p pale chestnut (1 side band)	70	75	□	□
S54	14p deep blue (1 centre band)	60	70	□	□
S55	14p deep blue (1 side band) . .	80	90	□	□
S56	15p bright blue (1 centre band)	70	70	□	□
S57	17p grey-blue (phosphorised				
	paper)	4·00	4·00	□	□
S58	17p deep blue (1 centre band)	1·00	1·10	□	□
S59	18p olive-grey (phosphorised				
	paper)	1·10	85	□	□
S60	18p bright green (1 centre				
	band)	1·25	90	□	□
	a. Perf 14	1·40	1·50	□	□
S61	18p bright green (1 side band)	2·25	2·25	□	□
S62	19p bright orange-red				
	(phosphorised paper) . . .	70	70	□	□
S63	19p bright orange-red (2				
	bands)	1·75	1·75	□	□
S64	20p brownish black				
	(phosphorised paper) . . .	95	95	□	□
S65	22p yellow-green (phosphorised				
	paper)	1·40	1·50	□	□
S66	22p bright orange-red				
	(phosphorised paper) . . .	1·25	90	□	□

S67	23p bright green (phosphorised				
	paper)	1·25	1·10	☐	☐
S68	23p bright green (2 bands) . .	12·00	12·00	☐	☐
S69	24p Indian red (phosphorised				
	paper)	1·50	1·00	☐	☐
S70	24p chestnut (phosphorised				
	paper)	1·40	1·25	☐	☐
	a. Perf 14	2·75	2·75	☐	☐
S71	24p chestnut (2 bands)	3·00	2·75	☐	☐
S72	26p rosine (phosphorised				
	paper)	3·25	3·00	☐	☐
S73	26p drab (phosphorised paper)	1·25	1·25	☐	☐
S74	28p deep violet-blue				
	(phosphorised paper) . . .	1·25	1·25	☐	☐
S75	28p deep bluish grey				
	(phosphorised paper) . . .	1·50	1·40	☐	☐
	a. Perf 14	5·50	4·50	☐	☐
S76	31p bright purple (phosphorised				
	paper)	2·00	1·90	☐	☐
S77	32p greenish blue				
	(phosphorised paper) . . .	1·75	1·60	☐	☐
S78	34p deep bluish grey				
	(phosphorised paper) . . .	1·90	1·90	☐	☐
S79	37p rosine (phosphorised				
	paper)	1·90	1·90	☐	☐
S80	39p bright mauve (phosphorised				
	paper)	2·00	1·90	☐	☐
	a. Perf 14	3·50	3·50	☐	☐

Nos. S55, S61, S63, S68 and S71 were only issued in stamp booklets.

Presentation Pack (P.O. Pack No.			
27) (contains 2½p (S14), 3p			
(S15), 5p (S20), 7½p (S25)) . .	4·25		☐
Presentation Pack (P.O. Pack No.			
62) (contains 3p (S16), 3½p			
(S17), 5½p (S21), 8p (S26),			
later with 4½p (S19) added) .	2·75		☐
Presentation Pack (P.O. Pack No.			
85) (contains 6½p (S23), 8½p			
(S27), 10p (S29), 11p (S32)) .	2·00		☐
Presentation Pack (P.O. Pack No.			
129b) (contains 7p (S24), 9p			
(S28), 10½p (S31), 11½p (S36),			
12p (S33), 13½p (S34), 14p			
(S40), 15p (S35), 18p (S44),			
22p (S47))	9·00		☐
Presentation Pack (P.O. Pack No.			
2) (contains 10p (S30), 12½p			
(S38), 16p (S42), 20½p (S46),			
26p (S49), 28p (S50)) . . .	12·00		☐
Presentation Pack (P.O. Pack No.			
6) (contains 10p (S30), 13p			
(S39), 16p (S42), 17p (S43),			
22p (S48), 26p (S49), 28p			
(S50), 31p (S51))	13·00		☐

Presentation Pack (P.O. Pack No.			
10) (contains 12p (S52), 13p			
(S53), 17p (S57), 18p (S59),			
22p (S65), 26p (S72), 28p (S74),			
31p (S76))	15·00		☐

For combined packs containing values from all three Regions see under Northern Ireland.

1993 (7 DEC.)–**98** (a) *Printed in lithography by Questa. Perf 15 × 14 (with one elliptical hole on each vertical side)*

S81	S 4	19p bistre (1 centre band)	80	70	☐	☐
S82		19p bistre (1 side band) .	2·40	2·40	☐	☐
S83		20p bright green (1 centre				
		band)	1·25	1·00	☐	☐
S84		25p red (2 bands)	1·10	1·00	☐	☐
S85		26p red-brown (2 bands)	1·50	1·50	☐	☐
S86		30p deep olive-grey (2				
		bands)	1·50	1·25	☐	☐
S87		37p bright mauve (2				
		bands)	2·50	2·25	☐	☐
S88		41p grey-brown (2 bands)	1·90	1·90	☐	☐
S89		63p light emerald (2				
		bands)	3·50	3·25	☐	☐

(b) *Printed in photogravure by Walsall (20p, 26p (No. S91a), 63p), Harrison or Walsall (26p (No. S91), 37p). Perf 14 (No. S90a) or 15 × 14 (others) (both with one elliptical hole on each vertical side)*

S90	S 4	20p bright green (1 centre				
		band)	60	60	☐	☐
S90a		20p bright green (1 side				
		band)	2·00	1·75	☐	☐
S91		26p chestnut (2 bands) .	1·00	1·00	☐	☐
		a. Perf 14	2·25	2·00	☐	☐
S92		37p bright mauve (2				
		bands)	1·25	90	☐	☐
S93		63p light emerald (2				
		bands)	2·25	2·00	☐	☐

Nos. S82, S90a and S91a were only issued in stamp booklets.
For combined presentation packs for all three Regions, see under Northern Ireland.

S 5 Scottish Flag

S 6 Scottish Lion

S 7 Thistle

S 8 Tartan

1999 (8 June)**–2002** *Printed in photogravure by De La Rue* (68p), *De La Rue, Questa or Walsall* (2nd, 1st) *or Walsall* (others). *One centre phosphor band* (2nd) *or two phosphor bands* (others). *Perf* 15 × 14 (*with one elliptical hole on each vertical side*)

S94	S 5	(2nd) new blue, blue and silver	30	35	□	□
S95	S 6	(1st) greenish yellow, deep rose-red, rose-red and silver	40	45	□	□
S96	S 7	(E) bright lilac, deep lilac and silver	60	70	□	□
S97	S 8	64p greenish yellow, bright magenta, new blue, grey-black and silver	3·00	2·25	□	□
S98		65p greenish yellow, bright magenta, new blue, grey-black and silver	1·60	1·75	□	□
S99		68p greenish yellow, bright magenta, new blue, grey-black and silver	1·10	1·25	□	□

Presentation Pack (*P.O. Pack No. 45*) (*contains 2nd, 1st, E, 64p*) (*Nos. S94/7*) . . . . . .   4·00   □

Presentation Pack (*P.O. Pack No. 50*) (*contains 65p*) (*No. S98*)   3·00   □

Presentation Pack (*P.O. Pack No. 55*) (*contains 2nd, 1st, E, 65p*) (*Nos. S94/6, S98*) . . . .   2·75   □

PHQ Cards (*Nos. S94/7*) . . . . .   1·50   10·00 □ □

Nos. S94, S95 and S96 were initially sold at 19p, 26p and 30p, the latter representing the basic European airmail rate.

For combined presentation packs for all four Regions, see under England.

S **9**

2000 (15 Feb.) *Type S* **4** *redrawn with '1st' face value as Type S* **9**. *Two phosphor bands. Perf* 14 (*with one elliptical hole on each vertical side*)

S108	S 9	(1st) bright orange-red . .	2·00	2·00	□	□

No. S108 was only issued in stamp booklets.

2003 (14 Oct.) *As Nos. S94/6 and S99 but with white borders. Printed in photogravure by De La Rue. One centre phosphor band* (2nd) *or two phosphor bands* (others). *Perf* 15 × 14 (*with one elliptical hole on each vertical side*).

S109	S 5	(2nd) new blue, blue and silver	30	35	□	□
S110	S 6	(1st) rose-red, greenish yellow, deep rose-red and silver	45	50	□	□
S111	S 7	(E) bright lilac, deep lilac and silver	60	65	□	□
S112	S 8	68p bright magenta, greenish yellow, new blue, grey-black and silver	1·10	1·25	□	□

Presentation Pack (*P.O. Pack No. 64*) 2·75   □

PHQ Cards (*set of 4*) . . . . . .   1·75   4·00 □ □

Nos. S109/11 were initially sold at 20p, 28p and 38p, the latter representing the basic European airmail rate.

4 Wales and Monmouthshire

W 1 W 2 W 3

1958–67 Wmk 179

W1	W 1	3d lilac	15	15	□	□
		p. One centre phosphor band	20	15	□	□
W2		4d blue	20	15	□	□
		p. Two phosphor bands	20	15	□	□
W3	W 2	6d purple	35	30	□	□
W4		9d bronze-green (2 phosphor bands)	40	35	□	□
W5	W 3	1s 3d green	40	40	□	□
W6		1s 6d blue (2 phosphor bands)	40	40	□	□

1967–69 One centre phosphor band (Nos. W7, W9/10) or two phosphor bands (others). No wmk

W7	W 1	3d lilac	10	15	□	□
W8		4d blue	10	15	□	□
W9		4d sepia	15	15	□	□
W10		4d vermilion	15	15	□	□
W11		5d blue	15	15	□	□
W12	W 3	1s 6d blue	3·50	3·50	□	
		Presentation Pack (comprises Nos. W4, W6/7, W9/11)	3·75		□	

W 4 With 'p' W 5 Without 'p'

Decimal Currency
1971–92 Type W 4. No wmk

(a) Printed in photogravure with phosphor bands

W13	2½p magenta (1 centre band)	20	20	□	□
W14	3p ultramarine (2 bands)	25	20	□	□
W15	3p ultramarine (1 centre band)	25	25	□	□
W16	3½p olive-grey (2 bands)	20	30	□	□
W17	3½p olive-grey (1 centre band)	20	30	□	□
W18	4½p grey-blue (2 bands)	30	30	□	□
W19	5p violet (2 bands)	1·00	1·10	□	□
W20	5½p violet (2 bands)	25	30	□	□
W21	5½p violet (1 centre band)	25	30	□	□
W22	6½p blue (1 centre band)	20	20	□	□
W23	7p brown (1 centre band)	25	25	□	□
W24	7½p chestnut (2 bands)	90	1·25	□	□
W25	8p rosine (2 bands)	30	35	□	□
W26	8½p yellow-green (2 bands)	30	35	□	□
W27	9p violet (2 bands)	40	40	□	□
W28	10p orange-brown (2 bands)	40	40	□	□
W29	10p orange-brown (1 centre band)	40	40	□	□
W30	10½p blue (2 bands)	40	45	□	□
W31	11p scarlet (2 bands)	40	45	□	□

(b) Printed in photogravure on phosphorised paper

W32	12p yellow-green	40	50	□	□
W33	13½p purple-brown	60	70	□	□
W34	15p ultramarine	60	70	□	□

(c) Printed in lithography. Perf 14 (11½p, 12½p, 14p (No. W39), 15½p, 16p, 18p (No. W46), 19½p, 20½p, 22p (No. W54), 26p (No. W61), 28p (No. W63)) or 15 × 14 (others)

W35	11½p drab (1 side band)	90	80	□	□
W36	12p bright emerald (1 side band)	1·50	1·25	□	□
W37	12½p light emerald (1 side band)	70	70	□	□
	a. Perf 15 × 14	4·50	5·00	□	□
W38	13p pale chestnut (1 side band)	60	60	□	□
W39	14p grey-blue (phosphorised paper)	70	70	□	□
W40	14p deep blue (1 centre band)	75	75	□	□
W41	15p bright blue (1 centre band)	80	75	□	□
W42	15½p pale violet (phosphorised paper)	75	75	□	□
W43	16p drab (phosphorised paper)	1·50	1·60	□	□
	a. Perf 15 × 14	1·75	1·90	□	□
W44	17p grey-blue (phosphorised paper)	70	80	□	□
W45	17p deep blue (1 centre band)	90	80	□	□
W46	18p deep violet (phosphorised paper)	1·00	95	□	□
W47	18p olive-grey (phosphorised paper)	95	90	□	□
W48	18p bright green (1 centre band)	75	75	□	□
	b. Perf 14	4·50	4·50	□	□
W49	18p bright green (1 side band)	2·25	2·25	□	□
W50	19p bright orange-red (phosphorised paper)	1·00	80	□	□
W51	19½p olive-grey (phosphorised paper)	1·50	1·50	□	□
W52	20p brownish black (phosphorised paper)	90	90	□	□
W53	20½p ultramarine (phosphorised paper)	3·25	3·25	□	□
W54	22p blue (phosphorised paper)	1·10	1·10	□	□
W55	22p yellow-green (phosphorised paper)	95	1·10	□	□
W56	22p bright orange-red (phosphorised paper)	1·00	1·10	□	□
W57	23p bright green (phosphorised paper)	1·00	1·10	□	□
W58	24p Indian red (phosphorised paper)	95	1·10	□	□

W59	24p chestnut (phosphorised paper)	75	75	☐	☐
	b. Perf 14	3·50	3·75	☐	☐
W60	24p chestnut (2 bands)	1·40	1·40	☐	☐
W61	26p rosine (phosphorised paper)	1·10	1·10	☐	☐
	a. Perf 15 × 14	5·50	5·00	☐	☐
W62	26p drap (phosphorised paper)	1·40	1·40	☐	☐
W63	28p deep violet-blue (phosphorised paper)	1·25	1·25	☐	☐
	a. Perf 15 × 14	1·40	1·40	☐	☐
W64	28p deep bluish grey (phosphorised paper)	1·50	1·40	☐	☐
W65	31p bright purple (phosphorised paper)	1·40	1·40	☐	☐
W66	32p greenish blue (phosphorised paper)	1·60	1·40	☐	☐
W67	34p deep bluish grey (phosphorised paper)	1·60	1·60	☐	☐
W68	37p rosine (phosphorised paper)	1·90	1·90	☐	☐
W69	39p bright mauve (phosphorised paper)	2·00	2·00	☐	☐

Nos. W49 and W60 were only issued in stamp booklets. The former exists with the phosphor band at the left or right of the stamp.

Presentation Pack (P.O. Pack No. 28) (contains 2½p (W13), 3p (W14), 5p (W19), 7½p (W24)) . 4·25 ☐

Presentation Pack (P.O. Pack No. 63) (contains 3p (W15), 3½p (W16), 5½p (W20), 8p (W25), later with 4½p (W18) added) . 2·75 ☐

Presentation Pack (P.O. Pack No. 86) (contains 6½p (W22), 8½p (W26), 10p (W28), 11p (W31)) 2·00 ☐

Presentation Pack (P.O. Pack No. 129c) (contains 7p (W23), 9p (W27), 10½p (W30), 11½p (W35), 12p (W32), 13½p (W33), 14p (W39), 15p (W34), 18p (W46), 22p (W53)) . . . . . . 9·00 ☐

Presentation Pack (P.O. Pack No. 3) (contains 10p (W29), 12½p (W37), 16p (W43), 20½p (W53), 26p (W61), 28p (W63)) . . . . 10·00 ☐

Presentation Pack (P.O. Pack No. 7) (contains 10p (W29), 13p (W38), 16p (W43a), 17p (W44), 22p (W55), 26p (W61), 28p (W63), 31p (W65)) . . . . 13·00 ☐

Presentation Pack (P.O. Pack No. 11) (contains 12p (W36), 13p (W38), 17p (W44), 18p (W47), 22p (W55), 26p (W61a), 28p (W63a), 31p (W65)) . . . . . . 15·00 ☐

For combined packs containing values from all three Regions see under Northern Ireland.

1993 (7 DEC.)–**96** Printed in lithography by Questa. Perf 15 × 14 (with one elliptical hole on each vertical side)

W70	W **4**	19p bistre (1 centre band)	80	70	☐	☐
W71		19p bistre (1 side band) .	3·25	3·00	☐	☐
W72		20p bright green (1 centre band)	1·25	1·40	☐	☐
W73		25p red (2 bands)	1·25	1·00	☐	☐
W74		26p red-brown (2 bands)	1·60	1·50	☐	☐
W75		30p deep olive-grey (2 bands)	1·10	1·25	☐	☐
W76		37p bright mauve (2 bands)	2·40	2·40	☐	☐
W77		41p grey-brown (2 bands)	1·75	1·90	☐	☐
W78		63p light emerald (2 bands)	3·75	3·75	☐	☐

No. W71 was only issued in stamp booklets.

For combined presentation packs for all three Regions see under Northern Ireland.

1997 (1 JULY)–**98** Printed in photogravure by Walsall (20p, 26p (No. W80a), 63p), Harrison or Walsall (26p (No. W80), 37p) Perf 14 (No. W79a) or 15 × 14 (both with one elliptical hole on each vertical side)

W79	W **5**	20p bright green (1 centre band)	80	80	☐	☐
W79a		20p bright green (1 side band)	2·25	2·00	☐	☐
W80		26p chestnut (2 bands) .	1·00	1·00	☐	☐
		a. Perf 14	2·00	2·00	☐	☐
W81		37p bright mauve (2 bands)	1·75	1·75	☐	☐
W82		63p light emerald (2 bands)	2·50	2·50	☐	☐

Presentation Pack (P.O. Pack No. 39) (Nos. W79 and W80/2) . . 6·50 ☐

Nos. W79a and W80a were only issued in stamp booklets.

W **6** Leek

W **7** Welsh Dragon

W **8** Daffodil

W **9** Prince of Wales Feathers

1999 (8 June)–**2002** *Printed in photogravure by De La Rue* (68p), *Walsall or De La Rue* (1st), (2nd), (No.W83) *or Walsall* (others). *One phosphor band* (2nd) *or two phosphor bands* (others). *Perf* 14 (*No.* W83a) *or* 15 × 14 (*others*) (*both with one elliptical hole on each vertical side*)

W83	W **6**	(2nd) orange-brown, yellow-orange and black (1 centre band) . . .	30	35	□	□
W83a		(2nd) orange-brown, yellow-orange and black (1 side band)	2·50	2·50	□	□
W84	W **7**	(1st) blue-green, greenish yellow, silver and black	40	45	□	□
W85	W **8**	(E) greenish blue, deep greenish blue and grey-black	60	70	□	□
W86	W **9**	64p violet, gold, silver and black	2·75	2·40	□	□
W87		65p violet, gold, silver and black	1·60	1·75	□	□
W88		68p violet, gold, silver and black	1·10	1·25	□	□
	Presentation Pack (*P.O. Pack No.* 46) (*contains* 2nd, 1st, E, 64p) (*Nos.* W83, W84/6))	4·50		□	
	Presentation Pack (*P.O. Pack No.* 51) (*contains* 65p) (*No.* W87))	3·00		□	
	Presentation Pack (*P.O. Pack No.* 56) (*contains* 2nd, 1st, E, 65p) (*Nos.* W83, W84/5, W87)) . . .	2·75		□	
	PHQ Cards (*Nos.* W83, W84/6) .	1·50	10·00	□	□

Nos. W83, W84 and W85 were initially sold at 19p, 26p and 30p, the latter representing the basic European airmail rate.

No. W83a was only issued in stamp booklets.

For combined presentation packs for all four Regions, see under England.

W **10**

2000 (15 Feb.) *Type* W **4** *redrawn with* '1af/st' *face value as Type* W **10**. *Two phosphor bands. Perf* 14 (*with one elliptical hole on each vertical side*)

W97	W **10**	(1st) bright orange-red	1·75	1·75	□	□

No. W97 was only issued in stamp booklets.

2003 (14 Oct.) *As Nos.* W83, W84/5 *and* W88, *but with white borders. Printed in photogravure by De La Rue. One centre phosphor band* (2nd) *or two phosphor bands* (others). *Perf* 15×14 (*with one elliptical hole on each vertical side*).

W98	W **6**	(2nd) yellow-orange, orange-brown and black . .	30	35	□	□
W99	W **7**	(1st) blue-green, greenish yellow, silver and black	45	50	□	□
W100	W **8**	(E) greenish blue, deep greenish blue and grey-black	60	65	□	□
W101	W **9**	68p violet, gold, silver and black	1·10	1·25	□	□
	Presentation Pack (*P.O. Pack No.* 65)	2·75		□		
	PHQ Cards (*set of 4*)	1·75	4·00	□	□

Nos. W98/100 were initially sold at 20p, 28p and 38p, the latter representing the basic European airmail rate.

ISLE OF MAN

Regional Issues

1

2

3

1958–67 *Wmk* **179**. *Perf* 15 × 14

1	1	2½d red	40	1·25 □ □
2	2	3d lilac	20	20 □ □
		p. One centre phosphor band	20	50 □ □
3		4d blue	1·40	1·40 □ □
		p. Two phosphor bands ..	20	30 □ □

1968–69 *One centre phosphor band (Nos. 5/6) or two phosphor bands (others). No wmk*

4	2	4d blue	25	30 □ □
5		4d sepia	25	40 □ □
6		4d vermilion	45	75 □ □
7		5d blue	45	75 □ □

Decimal Currency

1971 (7 JULY) *One centre phosphor band (2½p) or two phosphor bands (others). No wmk*

8	3	2½p magenta	20	15 □ □
9		3p ultramarine	20	15 □ □
10		5p violet	40	60 □ □
11		7½p chestnut	40	75 □ □
		Presentation Pack	2·75	□

For comprehensive listings of the Independent Administration issues of the Isle of Man, see Stanley Gibbons *Collect Channel Islands and Isle of Man Stamps*.

CHANNEL ISLANDS
1 General Issue

C 1 Gathering Vraic

C 2 Islanders gathering Vraic

Third Anniversary of Liberation

1948 (10 MAY) *Wmk Type* **127**. *Perf* 15 × 14

C1	C 1	1d red	25	30 □ □
C2	C 2	2½d blue	25	30 □ □
		First Day Cover		35·00 □

2 Guernsey

(a) War Occupation Issues

Stamps issued under British authority during the German Occupation.

1

2

3

1941–44 *Rouletted. (a) White paper. No wmk*

1d	1	½d green	3·00	1·75 □ □
2		1d red	2·00	90 □ □
3		2½d blue	3·25	4·00 □ □

(b) Bluish French bank-note paper. Wmk loops

4	1	½d green	20·00	18·00 □ □
5		1d red	10·00	16·00 □ □

(b) Regional Issues

1958–67 *Wmk* **179**. *Perf* 15 × 14

6	2	2½d red	35	40 □ □
7	3	3d lilac	30	30 □ □
		p. One centre phosphor band	15	20 □ □
8		4d blue	25	30 □ □
		p. Two phosphor bands ..	15	20 □ □

1968–69 *One centre phosphor band (Nos. 10/11) or two phosphor bands (others). No wmk*

9	3	4d blue	10	20 □ □
10		4d sepia	10	15 □ □
11		4d vermilion	20	25 □ □
12		5d blue	20	30 □ □

For comprehensive listings of the Independent Postal Administration issues of Guernsey, see Stanley Gibbons *Collect Channel Islands and Isle of Man Stamps*.

3 Jersey

(a) War Occupation Issues

Stamps issued under British authority during the German Occupation.

1

2 Old Jersey Farm

3 Portelet Bay

4   Corbière Lighthouse   5   Elizabeth Castle

6   Mont Orgueil Castle   7   Gathering Vraic
                                (seaweed)

1941–42 *White paper. No wmk Perf* 11

1	1	½d green	. . . .	4·00	3·25 ☐	☐
2		1d red	. . . .	4·50	2·50 ☐	☐

1943 *No wmk Perf* 13½

3	2	½d green	. . . .	7·50	5·50 ☐	☐
4	3	1d red	. . . .	2·00	75 ☐	☐
5	4	1½d brown	. . . .	3·50	3·25 ☐	☐
6	5	2d orange	. . . .	4·75	3·25 ☐	☐
7a	6	2½d blue	. . . .	2·00	1·00 ☐	☐
8	7	3d violet	. . . .	1·25	3·00 ☐	☐
		Set of 6	. . . .	18·00	15·00 ☐	☐

(b) Regional Issues

8   9

1958–67 *Wmk* 179. *Perf* 15 × 14

9	8	2½d red	. . . .	20	45 ☐	☐
10	9	3d lilac	. . . .	20	25 ☐	☐
		p. One centre phosphor band	. . . .	15	15 ☐	☐
11		4d blue	. . . .	25	30 ☐	☐
		p. Two phosphor bands	. .	15	25 ☐	☐

1968–69 *One centre phosphor band* (4d *values*) *or two phosphor bands* (5d). *No wmk*

12	9	4d sepia	. . . .	15	25 ☐	☐
13		4d vermilion	. . . .	15	25 ☐	☐
14		5d blue	. . . .	15	50 ☐	☐

For comprehensive listings of the Independent Postal Adminstration issues of Jersey, see Stanley Gibbons *Collect Channel Islands and Isle of Man Stamps.*

REGIONAL FIRST DAY COVERS

PRICES for First Day Covers listed below are for stamps, as indicated, used on illustrated envelopes and postmarked with operational cancellations (before 1964) or with special First Day of Issue cancellations (1964 onwards). First Day postmarks of 8 June 1964 and 7 February 1966 were of the machine cancellation 'envelope' type.

£sd Issues

18 Aug. 1958	Guernsey 3d (*No.* 7)	. . . . .	17·00 ☐
	Isle of Man 3d (*No.* 2)	. . . . .	32·00 ☐
	Jersey 3d (*No.* 10)	. . . . . .	17·00 ☐
	Northern Ireland 3d (*No.* NI1)	.	30·00 ☐
	Scotland 3d (*No.* S1)	. . . . . .	12·00 ☐
	Wales 3d (*No.* W1)	. . . .	12·00 ☐
29 Sept. 1958	Northern Ireland 6d, 1s 3d (*Nos.* NI3, NI5)	. . . .	35·00 ☐
	Scotland 6d, 1s 3d (*Nos.* S3, S5)	. . . .	25·00 ☐
	Wales 6d, 1s 3d (*Nos.* W3, W5)		25·00 ☐
8 June 1964	Guernsey 2½d (*No.* 6)	. . . . .	30·00 ☐
	Isle of Man 2½d (*No.* 1)	. . . .	45·00 ☐
	Jersey 2½d (*No.* 9)	. . . .	30·00 ☐
7 Feb. 1966	Guernsey 4d (*No.* 8)	. . . . . .	8·00 ☐
	Isle of Man 4d (*No.* 3)	. . . .	10·00 ☐
	Jersey 4d (*No.* 11)	. . . .	8·00 ☐
	Northern Ireland 4d (*No.* NI2)	.	7·00 ☐
	Scotland 4d (*No.* S2)	. . . . . .	7·00 ☐
	Wales 4d (*No.* W2)	. . . .	7·00 ☐
1 March 1967	Northern Ireland 9d, 1s 6d (*Nos.* NI4, NI6)	. . . .	4·00 ☐
	Scotland 9d, 1s 6d (*Nos.* S4, S6)	. . . .	4·00 ☐
	Wales 9d, 1s 6d (*Nos.* W4, W6)	. . . .	4·00 ☐
4 Sept. 1968	Guernsey 4d, 5d (*Nos.* 10, 12)		3·00 ☐
	Isle of Man 4d, 5d (*Nos.* 5, 7)	.	4·00 ☐
	Jersey 4d, 5d (*Nos.* 12, 14)	. .	3·00 ☐
	Northern Ireland 4d, 5d (*Nos.* NI8, NI10)	. . . .	3·00 ☐
	Scotland 4d, 5d (*Nos.* S9, S11)	.	3·00 ☐
	Wales 4d, 5d (*Nos.* W9, W11)	.	3·00 ☐
Decimal Issues		
7 July 1971	Isle of Man 2½p, 3p, 5p, 7½p (*Nos.* 8/11)	. . . .	3·00 ☐
	Northern Ireland 2½p, 3p, 5p, 7½p (*Nos.* NI12/13, NI18, NI23)	.	3·75 ☐
	Scotland 2½p, 3p, 5p, 7½p (*Nos.* S14/15, S20, S25)	. . . . . .	3·00 ☐
	Wales 2½p, 3p, 5p, 7½p (*Nos.* W13/14, W19, W24)	. . . . . .	3·00 ☐
23 Jan. 1974	Northern Ireland 3p, 3½p, 5½p, 8p (*Nos.* NI14/15, NI19, NI24)	.	2·00 ☐
	Scotland 3p, 3½p, 5½p, 8p (*Nos.* S16/17, S21, S26)	. . . . . .	2·00 ☐
	Wales 3p, 3½p, 5½p, 8p (*Nos.* W15/16, W20, W25)	. . . . . .	2·00 ☐

6 Nov. 1974	Northern Ireland 4½p (No. NI17)	1·50 ☐
	Scotland 4½p (No. S19)	1·50 ☐
	Wales 4½p (No. W18)	1·50 ☐
14 Jan. 1976	Northern Ireland 6½p, 8½p (Nos. NI21, NI25)	1·50 ☐
	Scotland 6½p, 8½p (Nos. S23, S27)	1·50 ☐
	Wales 6½p, 8½p (Nos. W22, W26)	1·50 ☐
20 Oct. 1976	Northern Ireland 10p, 11p (Nos. NI27, NI30)	1·50 ☐
	Scotland 10p, 11p (Nos. S29, S32)	1·50 ☐
	Wales 10p, 11p (Nos. W28, W31)	1·50 ☐
18 Jan. 1978	Northern Ireland 7p, 9p, 10½p (Nos. NI22, NI26, NI29)	1·75 ☐
	Scotland 7p, 9p, 10½p (Nos. S24, S28, S31	1·75 ☐
	Wales 7p, 9p, 10½p (Nos. W23, W27, W30)	1·75 ☐
23 July 1980	Northern Ireland 12p, 13½p, 15p (Nos. NI31/3)	2·25 ☐
	Scotland 12p, 13½p, 15p (Nos. S33/5)	2·25 ☐
	Wales 12p, 13½p, 15p (Nos. W32/4)	2·25 ☐
8 April 1981	Northern Ireland 11½p, 14p, 18p, 22p (Nos. NI34, NI38, NI45, NI53)	3·50 ☐
	Scotland 11½p, 14p, 18p, 22p (Nos. S36, S40, S44, S47) . . .	3·50 ☐
	Wales 11½p, 14p, 18p, 22p (Nos. W35, W39, W46, W54)	3·75 ☐
24 Feb. 1982	Northern Ireland 12½p, 15½p, 19½p, 26p (Nos. NI36, NI41, NI50, NI60)	5·00 ☐
	Scotland 12½p, 15½p, 19½p, 26p (Nos. S38, S41, S45, S49) . . .	4·50 ☐
	Wales 12½p, 15½p, 19½p, 26p (Nos. W37, W42, W51, W61) .	4·50 ☐
27 April 1983	Northern Ireland 16p, 20½p, 28p (Nos. NI42, NI52, NI62)	6·00 ☐
	Scotland 16p, 20½p, 28p (Nos. S42, S46, S50)	6·00 ☐
	Wales 16p, 20½p, 28p (Nos. W43, W53, W63)	6·50 ☐
23 Oct. 1984	Northern Ireland 13p, 17p, 22p, 31p (Nos. NI37, NI43, NI54, NI64)	4·75 ☐
	Scotland 13p, 17p, 22p, 31p (Nos. S39, S43, S48, S51) . . .	7·50 ☐
	Wales 13p, 17p, 22p, 31p (Nos. W38, W44, W55, W65)	4·25 ☐
7 Jan. 1986	Northern Ireland 12p (No. NI35)	1·50 ☐
	Scotland 12p (No. S37)	1·50 ☐
	Wales 12p (No. W36)	1·50 ☐
6 Jan. 1987	Northern Ireland 18p (No. NI46)	1·50 ☐
	Scotland 18p (No. S59)	1·50 ☐
	Wales 18p (No. W47)	1·50 ☐
8 Nov. 1988	Northern Ireland 14p, 19p, 23p, 32p (Nos. NI39, NI49, NI56, NI65)	4·00 ☐
	Scotland 14p, 19p, 23p, 32p (Nos. S54, S62, S67, S77) . . .	4·25 ☐
	Wales 14p, 19p, 23p, 32p (Nos. W40, W50, W57, W66)	4·50 ☐
28 Nov. 1989	Northern Ireland 15p, 20p, 24p, 34p (Nos. NI40, NI51, NI57, NI66)	4·50 ☐
	Scotland 15p, 20p, 24p, 34p (Nos. S56, S64, S69, S78) . . .	4·75 ☐
	Wales 15p, 20p, 24p, 34p (Nos. W41, W52, W58, W67)	4·75 ☐
4 Dec. 1990	Northern Ireland 17p, 22p, 26p, 37p (Nos. NI44, NI55, NI61, NI67)	4·75 ☐
	Scotland 17p, 22p, 26p, 37p (Nos. S58, S66, S73, S79) . . .	4·75 ☐
	Wales 17p, 22p, 26p, 37p (Nos. W45, W56. W62, W68)	4·75 ☐
3 Dec. 1991	Northern Ireland 18p, 24p, 28p, 39p (Nos. NI47, NI58, NI63, NI68)	5·50 ☐
	Scotland 18p, 24p, 28p, 39p (Nos. S60, S70, S75, S80) . . .	5·50 ☐
	Wales 18p, 24p, 28p, 39p (Nos. W48, W59, W64, W69)	5·50 ☐
7 Dec 1993	Northern Ireland 19p, 25p, 30p, 41p (Nos. NI69, NI72, NI74, NI76)	5·50 ☐
	Scotland 19p, 25p, 30p, 41p (Nos. S81, S84, S86, S88) . . .	5·50 ☐
	Wales 19p, 25p, 30p, 41p (Nos. W70, W73, W75, W77)	5·75 ☐
23 July 1996	Northern Ireland 20p (1 centre band), 26p, 37p, 63p (Nos. NI71, NI73, NI75, NI77)	8·75 ☐
	Scotland 20p (1 centre band), 26p, 37p, 63p (Nos. S83, S85, S87, S89)	8·75 ☐
	Wales 20p, 26p, 37p, 63p (Nos. W72, W74, W76, W78)	9·50 ☐
1 July 1997	Wales 20p (1 centre band), 26p, 37p, 63p (Nos. W79/82)	5·50 ☐
8 June 1999	Northern Ireland 38p, 64p (Nos. NI83, NI86)	4·00 ☐
	Scotland 2nd, 1st, E, 64p (Nos S94/7)	4·00 ☐
	Wales 2nd, 1st, E, 64p (Nos. W83, W84/6)	4·00 ☐

25 Apr 2000	Northern Ireland 1st, 40p, 65p (Nos. NI84, NI87, NI88b)	4·25	☐
	Scotland 65p (No. S98)	1·90	☐
	Wales 65p (No. W87)	1·90	☐
6 Mar 2001	Northern Ireland 2nd, 1st, E, 65p (Nos. NI89/92)	3·25	☐
23 Apr 2001	England 2nd, 1st, E, 65p (Nos. EN1/4)	3·25	☐
4 July 2002	England 68p (No. EN5)	1·75	☐
	Northern Ireland 68p (No. NI93)	1·75	☐
	Scotland 68p (No. S99)	1·75	☐
	Wales 68p (No. W88)	1·75	☐
14 Oct 2003	England 2nd, 1st, E, 68p (Nos. EN6/9)	3·25	☐
	Northern Ireland 2nd, 1st, E, 68p (Nos. NI94/7)	3·25	☐
	Scotland 2nd, 1st, E, 68p (Nos. S109/12)	3·25	☐
	Wales 2nd, 1st, E, 68p (Nos. W98/101)	3·25	☐

POSTAGE DUE STAMPS

PERFORATION. All postage due stamps to No. D101 are perf 14 × 15.

D 1   D 2

1914–22 *Wmk Type* **100** (*Royal Cypher* ('*Simple'*)) *sideways*

D1	D 1	½d green	50	25	□ □
D2		1d red	50	25	□ □
D3		1½d brown	48·00	20·00	□ □
D4		2d black	50	25	□ □
D5		3d violet	5·00	75	□ □
D6		4d green	18·00	5·00	□ □
D7		5d brown	6·00	3·50	□ □
D8		1s blue	40·00	4·75	□ □
	Set of 8		£110	32·00	□ □

1924–31 *Wmk Type* **111** (*Block* G v R) *sideways*

D10	D 1	½d green	1·25	75	□ □
D11		1d red	60	25	□ □
D12		1½d brown	45·00	18·00	□ □
D13		2d black	1·00	25	□ □
D14		3d violet	1·50	25	□ □
D15		4d green	15·00	3·00	□ □
D16		5d brown	32·00	28·00	□ □
D17		1s blue	10·00	1·00	□ □
D18	D 2	2s 6d purple/*yellow*	45·00	2·00	□ □
	Set of 9		£140	48·00	□ □

1936–37 *Wmk Type* **125** (E 8 R) *sideways*

D19	D 1	½d green	7·50	8·00	□ □
D20		1d red	1·50	2·00	□ □
D21		2d black	7·00	11·00	□ □
D22		3d violet	1·50	2·25	□ □
D23		4d green	23·00	35·00	□ □
D24*a*		5d brown	16·00	23·00	□ □
D25		1s blue	11·00	9·00	□ □
D26	D 2	2s 6d purple/*yellow*	£275	9·00	□ □
	Set of 8		£325	90·00	□ □

1937–38 *Wmk Type* **127** (G vi R) *sideways*

D27	D 1	½d green	9·00	5·00	□ □
D28		1d red	3·00	75	□ □
D29		2d black	2·50	75	□ □
D30		3d violet	12·00	1·00	□ □
D31		4d green	75·00	13·00	□ □
D32		5d brown	14·00	75	□ □
D33		1s blue	75·00	2·00	□ □
D34	D 2	2s 6d purple/*yellow*	75·00	2·50	□ □
	Set of 8		£250	23·00	□ □

1951–52 *Colours changed and new value* (1½d) *Wmk Type* **127** (G vi R) *sideways*

D35	D 1	½d orange	1·00	3·00	□ □
D36		1d blue	1·50	1·50	□ □
D37		1½d green	1·75	3·00	□ □
D38		4d blue	32·00	12·00	□ □
D39		1s brown	38·00	14·00	□ □
	Set of 5		65·00	30·00	□ □

1954–55 *Wmk Type* **153** (*Mult Tudor Crown and* E 2 R) *sideways*

D40	D 1	½d orange	4·50	8·00	□ □
D41		2d black	10·00	12·00	□ □
D42		3d violet	55·00	38·00	□ □
D43		4d blue	20·00	23·00	□ □
D44		5d brown	25·00	12·00	□ □
D45	D 2	2s 6d purple/*yellow*	£110	7·00	□ □
	Set of 6		£200	90·00	□ □

1955–57 *Wmk Type* **165** (*Mult St Edward's Crown and* E 2 R) *sideways*

D46	D 1	½d orange	2·00	4·00	□ □
D47		1d blue	5·50	1·75	□ □
D48		1½d green	6·00	5·00	□ □
D49		2d black	45·00	3·75	□ □
D50		3d violet	7·00	2·00	□ □
D51		4d blue	20·00	4·00	□ □
D52		5d brown	32·00	2·25	□ □
D53		1s brown	70·00	2·00	□ □
D54	D 2	2s 6d purple/*yellow*	£150	10·00	□ □
D55		5s red/*yellow*	80·00	26·00	□ □
	Set of 10		£375	55·00	□ □

1959–63 *Wmk Type* **179** (*Mult St Edward's Crown*) *sideways*

D56	D 1	½d orange	15	1·25	□ □
D57		1d blue	15	50	□ □
D58		1½d green	90	3·50	□ □
D59		2d black	1·10	50	□ □
D60		3d violet	30	30	□ □
D61		4d blue	30	30	□ □
D62		5d brown	45	60	□ □
D63		6d purple	50	30	□ □
D64		1s brown	90	30	□ □
D65	D 2	2s 6d purple/*yellow*	4·75	75	□ □
D66		5s red/*yellow*	6·50	1·00	□ □
D67		10s blue/*yellow*	10·00	5·50	□ □
D68		£1 black/*yellow*	40·00	7·50	□ □
	Set of 13		60·00	20·00	□ □

1968–69 *Design size* 22½ × 19 mm. *No wmk*

D69	D 1	2d black	25	75	□ □
D70		3d violet	30	75	□ □
D71		4d blue	40	75	□ □
D72		5d orange-brown	5·00	10·00	□ □
D73		6d purple	60	1·00	□ □
D74		1s brown	2·00	1·00	□ □
	Set of 6		7·50	13·00	□ □

1968–69 *Design size* 21½ × 17½ mm. *No wmk*

D75	D 1	4d blue	6·00	6·00	□ □
D76		8d red	1·25	1·00	□ □

D **3**　　　　　　　　　　D **4**

Decimal Currency
1970–77 *No wmk*

D77	D **3**	½p turquoise-blue . . .	15	50 □ □
D78		1p reddish purple	15	15 □ □
D79		2p myrtle-green	20	15 □ □
D80		3p ultramarine	20	15 □ □
D81		4p yellow-brown	25	15 □ □
D82		5p violet	25	15 □ □
D83		7p red-brown	35	80 □ □
D84	D **4**	10p red	30	30 □ □
D85		11p green	50	1·00 □ □
D86		20p brown	60	25 □ □
D87		50p ultramarine	1·75	25 □ □
D88		£1 black	3·25	50 □ □
D89		£5 orange-yellow and black	35·00	1·50 □ □
	Set of 13	38·00	5·25 □ □

Presentation Pack (*P.O. Pack No.*
36) (*Nos. D77/82, D84, D86/8*)　9·00　□

Presentation Pack (*P.O. Pack No.*
93) (*Nos. D77/88*) . . . .　9·00　□

D **5**　　　　　D **6**　　　　　D **7**

1982 *No wmk*

D90	D **5**	1p lake	10	30 □ □
D91		2p bright blue	30	30 □ □
D92		3p deep mauve	15	30 □ □
D93		4p deep blue	15	25 □ □
D94		5p sepia	20	25 □ □
D95	D **6**	10p light brown	30	40 □ □
D96		20p olive-green	50	60 □ □
D97		25p deep greenish blue .	80	90 □ □
D98		50p grey-black	1·50	1·10 □ □
D99		£1 red	3·00	1·25 □ □
D100		£2 turquoise-blue . . .	6·00	2·40 □ □
D101		£5 dull orange	14·00	2·00 □ □
	Set of 12	24·00	8·50 □ □
	Set of 12 *Gutter Pairs*	48·00	□
	Presentation Pack	26·00	□

For full information on all future British issues, collectors should write to Royal Mail, Freepost EH3647, 21 South Gyle Crescent, Edinburgh EH12 9PE.

1994 (15 FEB.) *Perf* 15 × 14 (*with one elliptical hole on each vertical side*)

D102	D **7**	1p red, yellow and black	10	50 □ □
D103		2p magenta, purple and black	10	50 □ □
D104		5p yellow, red-brown and black	15	35 □ □
D105		10p yellow, emerald and black	30	45 □ □
D106		20p blue-green, violet and black	50	70 □ □
D107		25p cerise, rosine and black	70	75 □ □
D108		£1 violet, magenta and black	3·00	2·50 □ □
D109		£1.20 greenish blue, blue-green and black	3·75	3·50 □ □
D110		£5 greenish black, blue-green and black	14·00	12·00 □ □
	Set of 9	20·00	19·00 □ □
	Presentation Pack	28·00	□

ROYAL MAIL POSTAGE LABELS

These imperforate labels were issued as an experiment by the Post Office. Special microprocessor-controlled machines were installed at post offices in Cambridge, London, Shirley (Southampton) and Windsor to provide an after-hours sales service to the public. The machines printed and dispensed the labels according to the coins inserted and the buttons operated by the customer. Values were initially available in $\frac{1}{2}$p steps to 16p and in addition, the labels were sold at philatelic counters in two packs containing either 3 values ($3\frac{1}{2}$, $12\frac{1}{2}$, 16p) or 32 values ($\frac{1}{2}$p to 16p).

From 28 August 1984 the machines were adjusted to provide values up to 17p. After 31 December 1984 labels including $\frac{1}{2}$p values were withdrawn. The machines were taken out of service on 30 April 1985.

Machine postage-paid impression in red on phosphorised paper with grey-green background design. No watermark. imperforate.

1984 (1 MAY–28 AUG.)

Set of 32 ($\frac{1}{2}$p to 16p)	13·00	22·00 ☐ ☐
Set of 3 ($3\frac{1}{2}$p, $12\frac{1}{2}$p, 16p)	2·50	3·00 ☐ ☐
Set of 3 on First Day Cover		
(1 May)		6·50 ☐
Set of 2 ($16\frac{1}{2}$p, 17p) (28 August)	4·00	3·00 ☐ ☐

OFFICIAL STAMPS

Various stamps of Queen Victoria and King Edward VII overprinted in Black.

I.R.	**I. R.**	**O.W.**
OFFICIAL	**OFFICIAL**	**OFFICIAL**
(O 1)	(O 2)	(O 3)
ARMY	**ARMY**	
		GOVᵗ
OFFICIAL	**OFFICIAL**	**PARCELS**
(O 4)	(O 5)	(O 7)

BOARD	**R.H.**	**ADMIRALTY**
OF		
EDUCATION	**OFFICIAL**	**OFFICIAL**
(O 8)	(O 9)	(O 10)

1 Inland Revenue

Overprinted with Types O 1 or O 2 (5s, 10s, £1)

1882–1901 *Queen Victoria*

O 1	52	$\frac{1}{2}$d green	50·00	20·00 ☐ ☐
O 5		$\frac{1}{2}$d blue	50·00	22·00 ☐ ☐
O13	67	$\frac{1}{2}$d vermilion	2·50	1·50 ☐ ☐
O17		$\frac{1}{2}$d green	6·00	4·50 ☐ ☐
O 3	57	1d lilac (Die II)	4·00	2·00 ☐ ☐
O 6	64	$2\frac{1}{2}$d lilac	£180	65·00 ☐ ☐
O14	70	$2\frac{1}{2}$d purple on blue	70·00	6·00 ☐ ☐
O 4	43	6d grey (Plate 18)	£190	50·00 ☐ ☐
O18	75	6d purple on red	£250	60·00 ☐ ☐
O 7	65	1s green	£3100	£650 ☐ ☐
O15	78	1s green	£240	£100 ☐ ☐
O19		1s green and red	£1100	£425 ☐ ☐
O 9	59	5s red	£1800	£500 ☐ ☐
O10	60	10s blue	£3750	£1000 ☐ ☐
O11	61	£1 brown (Wmk		
		Crowns)	£27000	£14000 ☐ ☐
O12		£1 brown (Wmk Orbs) . .	£35000	£16000 ☐ ☐
O16		£1 green	£4500	£750 ☐ ☐

1902–04 *King Edward VII*

O20	79	$\frac{1}{2}$d blue-green	22·00	3·00 ☐ ☐
O21		1d red	15·00	2·00 ☐ ☐
O22	82	$2\frac{1}{2}$d blue	£500	£125 ☐ ☐
O23	79	6d purple	£90000	£70000 ☐ ☐
O24	89	1s green and red	£850	£180 ☐ ☐
O25	91	5s red	£5750	£3500 ☐ ☐
O26	92	10s blue	£22000	£12000 ☐ ☐
O27	93	£1 green	£17000	£9500 ☐ ☐

2 Office of Works

Overprinted with Type O 3

1896–1902 *Queen Victoria*

O31	67	$\frac{1}{2}$d vermilion	£125	75·00 ☐ ☐
O32		$\frac{1}{2}$d green	£200	£100 ☐ ☐
O33	57	1d lilac (Die II)	£200	75·00 ☐ ☐
O34	74	5d dull purple and blue .	£1000	£250 ☐ ☐
O35	77	10d dull purple and red .	£1800	£400 ☐ ☐

1902–03 *King Edward VII*

O36	79	$\frac{1}{2}$d blue-green	£425	£110 ☐ ☐
O37		1d red	£425	£110 ☐ ☐
O38	81	2d green and red	£800	£250 ☐ ☐
O39	82	$2\frac{1}{2}$d blue	£850	£300 ☐ ☐
O40	88	10d purple and red	£10000	£3500 ☐ ☐

3 Army

Overprinted with Types O 4 ($\frac{1}{2}$d, 1d) or O 5 (2$\frac{1}{2}$d, 6d)

1896–1901 *Queen Victoria*

O41	67	$\frac{1}{2}$d vermilion	2·50	1·50 ☐ ☐
O42		$\frac{1}{2}$d green	2·50	4·50 ☐ ☐
O43	57	1d lilac (Die II)	2·50	1·50 ☐ ☐
O44	70	2$\frac{1}{2}$d purple on blue	6·00	3·50 ☐ ☐
O45	75	6d purple on red	22·00	24·00 ☐ ☐

Overprinted with Type O 4

1902 *King Edward VII*

O48	79	$\frac{1}{2}$d blue-green	3·00	1·50 ☐ ☐
O49		1d red	3·00	1·50 ☐ ☐
O50		6d purple	80·00	35·00 ☐ ☐

4 Government Parcels

Overprinted with Type O 7

1883–1900 *Queen Victoria*

O69	57	1d lilac (Die II)	30·00	9·00 ☐ ☐
O61	62	1$\frac{1}{2}$d lilac	£140	35·00 ☐ ☐
O65	68	1$\frac{1}{2}$d purple and green . . .	25·00	3·00 ☐ ☐
O70	69	2d green and red	50·00	8·00 ☐ ☐
O71	73	4$\frac{1}{2}$d green and red	£125	90·00 ☐ ☐
O62	63	6d green	£925	£350 ☐ ☐
O66	75	6d purple on red	60·00	18·00 ☐ ☐
O63	64	9d green	£700	£225 ☐ ☐
O67	76	9d purple and blue	70·00	20·00 ☐ ☐
O64	44	1s brown (Plate 13)	£500	90·00 ☐ ☐
O64c		1s brown (Plate 14)	£825	£140 ☐ ☐
O68	78	1s green	£150	80·00 ☐ ☐
O72		1s green and red	£190	65·00 ☐ ☐

1902 *King Edward VII*

O74	79	1d red	25·00	9·00 ☐ ☐
O75	81	2d green and red	70·00	18·00 ☐ ☐
O76	79	6d purple	£130	20·00 ☐ ☐
O77	87	9d purple and blue	£275	60·00 ☐ ☐
O78	89	1s green and red	£425	£100 ☐ ☐

5 Board of Education

Overprinted with Type O 8

1902 *Queen Victoria*

O81	74	5d dull purple and blue .	£600	£160 ☐ ☐
O82	78	1s green and red	£3000	£1800 ☐ ☐

1902–04 *King Edward VII*

O83	79	$\frac{1}{2}$d blue-green	90·00	30·00 ☐ ☐
O84		1d red	90·00	30·00 ☐ ☐
O85	82	2$\frac{1}{2}$d blue	£1000	90·00 ☐ ☐
O86	85	5d purple and blue	£5000	£1750 ☐ ☐
O87	89	1s green and red	£50000	☐

6 Royal Household

Overprinted with Type O 9

1902 *King Edward VII*

O91	79	$\frac{1}{2}$d blue-green	£190	£130 ☐ ☐
O92		1d red	£160	£110 ☐ ☐

7 Admiralty

Overprinted with Type O 10

1903 *King Edward Vii*

O107	79	$\frac{1}{2}$d blue-green	15·00	9·00 ☐ ☐
O102		1d red	7·00	4·00 ☐ ☐
O103	80	1$\frac{1}{2}$d purple and green . . .	90·00	55·00 ☐ ☐
O104	81	2d green and red	£150	70·00 ☐ ☐
O105	82	2$\frac{1}{2}$d blue	£160	55·00 ☐ ☐
O106	83	3d purple on yellow . . .	£150	55·00 ☐ ☐

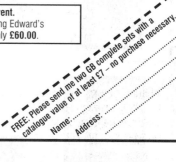

STANLEY GIBBONS

Mail Order

Quality Stamps
Direct to your Door

Irresistibly simple, exceptionally quick and reassuringly reliable, Stanley Gibbons Mail Order service enables you to economically build your collection from the comfort of your own home.

We Provide:

- Large stocks of guaranteed quality material
- An efficient despatch service
- Regular well-produced, illustrated brochures and lists
- Exclusive special offers mailed regularly
- Specialist 'wants list' service available
- Over 140 years philatelic experience

Order Straight From This Catalogue

As the world's oldest established stamp dealer, we hold comprehensive stocks. The majority of items in this catalogue are usually available, but if we are unable to supply, we will record your requirements and notify you, without obligation, as soon as they come into stock.

To order, complete your details and the SG numbers you require on the reverse and return to: Stanley Gibbons Limited, Mail Order Department, 399 Strand, London WC2R 0LX, United Kingdom.

CUSTOMER DETAILS

Account number (if valid)

☐ Please send me the items I have listed on the reverse

Name _____

Address _____

_____

Country _____ Email _____

Postcode _____ Telephone _____

☐ I enclose cheque/postal order made payable to Stanley Gibbons Ltd for £ _____

☐ I authorise you to charge my   EUROCARD MasterCard ☐   AMERICAN EXPRESS ☐   ◑ ☐   VISA ☐   🅹 ☐

Card No ☐☐☐☐ ☐☐☐☐ ☐☐☐☐ ☐☐☐☐   Expiry Date ☐☐/☐☐

Signature _____   Switch Issue No. ☐☐☐☐   or Start Date ☐☐☐☐

Order Form

Please list the items you would like supplied in the spaces below:

S.G. Cat No	Description	Mint or Used	S.G. Cat Price	Office Use Only
	Please continue on a separate page			
	Allow £3.60 for postage and handling		£3.60	
	Total Payable			

CBS2004

BY APPOINTMENT TO
HER MAJESTY THE QUEEN
STANLEY GIBBONS LTD.
LONDON
PHILATELISTS

Stanley Gibbons Limited
Mail Order Department
399 Strand, London WC2R 0Lx
United Kingdom
Tel: 020 7836 8444 Fax: 020 7836 7342
Email: mailorder@stanleygibbons.co.uk
Internet: www.stanleygibbons.com

STANLEY
GIBBONS
Mail Order

● OUR NAME IS YOUR GUARANTEE OF QUALITY ●